JADE VISIONS

The Life and Music of Scott LaFaro

To Kurt,

Enjoy!

Helene LaFaro-Fernández

11/11/09

JADE VISIONS

The Life and Music of Scott LaFaro

Helene LaFaro-Fernández

with
Chuck Ralston,
Jeff Campbell and Phil Palombi

Foreword by Don Thompson

Introduction by Gene Lees

Number 4 in the North Texas
Lives of Musicians Series

University of North Texas Press
Denton, Texas

10 9 8 7 6 5 4 3 2 1

Permissions:
University of North Texas Press
1155 Union Circle #311336
Denton, TX 76203-5017

Library of Congress Cataloging-in-Publication Data

LaFaro-Fernandez, Helene, 1938–
    Jade visions : the life and music of Scott LaFaro / by Helene LaFaro-Fernandez ;
introduction by Gene Lees. — 1st ed.
        p. cm. — (North Texas lives of musicians series ; no. 4)
    Includes discography.
    Includes bibliographical references and index.
    ISBN 978-1-57441-273-4 (cloth : alk. paper)
    1. LaFaro, Scott. 2. Double bassists—United States—Biography. 3. Jazz musicians—
United States—Biography. I. Title. II. Series: North Texas lives of musicians series ;
no.4.
    ML418.L34L34   2009
    787.5'165092—dc22
    [B]

                                                              2009016468

Jade Visions: The Life and Music of Scott LaFaro is Number 4 in the North Texas Lives of
Musicians Series

Interior design by Joseph Parenteau

The sound, pure and prolonged, which it gives forth when struck represents music.
It is the symbolic link between man and the spiritual world.

… Confucius on jade

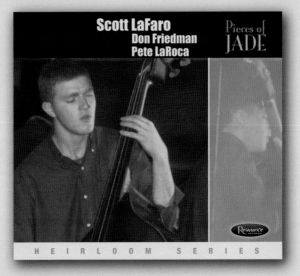

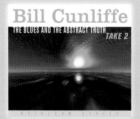

• CONTENTS •

• ILLUSTRATIONS •

Photos following Chapter 3:

1. First photo
2. At nine months
3. Christmas 1943. Scott with aviator cap.
4. Scotty and Sister 1946
5. Junior High School photo

Photos following Chapter 4:

1. Family Christmas, 1953
2. At home piano, 1954
3. As Student Band Director
4. 1954 Senior Prom
5. Senior Picture, 1954

Photos following Chapter 5:

1. On tenor at Ithaca College
2. Belhurst Orchestra, Summer 1955
3. Scotty's postcards to sister Linda
4. Buddy Morrow Orchestra, 1956
5. Scotty and Suzanne Stewart, 1956

Photos following Chapter 8:

1. At the Gellers', July 1957
2. Bass in his bedroom at the Gellers'
3. Home for Christmas 1957 with youngest sister, Leslie

FOREWORD

by

Don Thompson

In the movie *It's A Wonderful Life* Jimmy Stewart gets to see the world as it might have been if he had never been born. This is something everyone probably thinks about now and then. We all like to think we will have made a difference in the world but nobody ever knows for sure if that will turn out to be the case.

In music there are people who are so important that it is impossible to imagine the world without them. Think about music without Bach, Mozart, or Beethoven. Think about jazz without Duke Ellington, Charlie Parker, or John Coltrane. It's impossible to imagine. In the history of jazz there have been only a handful of real innovators on each instrument. These people have shaped the way their instrument has come to be played. On piano the list would include Art Tatum, Bud Powell, McCoy Tyner, Keith Jarrett, and Bill Evans. On saxophone there would be Lester Young, Coleman Hawkins, Charlie Parker, and John Coltrane. On bass there would be Jimmy Blanton, Oscar Pettiford, Ray Brown, Red Mitchell, and Scott LaFaro. Of that group of bass players, Ray Brown and Scott LaFaro stand out from the rest. Ray Brown personifies the bassist's role in a rhythm section. With his beautiful sound, amazing groove, and Bach-like lines, Ray was the man everyone wanted to sound like. That is until Scott LaFaro came along.

The first time I heard Scotty play was on *Portrait in Jazz* with Bill Evans. I had been playing the bass for three or four years but was not really that interested in it. I was playing a lot of piano and vibes at the time so playing the bass didn't really matter to me that much but when I heard that track of "Autumn Leaves" all that changed. There was a spirit of adventure and freedom I had never heard before and all of a sudden it became very important to me to really learn how to play the bass. Hearing Scotty play with Bill Evans had opened up a whole new world of music to me and I wanted to be a part of it.

Everything about Scotty's playing killed me. His sound, his solos (which actually reminded me a bit of Red Mitchell) and his time feel, which was amazing. But what really got to me was the interplay between him and Bill Evans. The idea of a musical conversation was not really that new but the combination of Bill Evans and Scott LaFaro proved to be a magical one and together they took that concept to a whole new place. Bill had provided the setting that gave Scotty the freedom to play the music however he happened to feel it.

Being free is one thing but along with that freedom comes a great responsibility and it takes a great musician to work in that setting and really succeed on all levels. Scotty had everything he needed to make it work. He had great time, extraordinary ears, a fantastic sense of form and so much chops he could play pretty well anything that came into his head. He was also blessed with the gift of melody and counter-melody but most important of all he had a beautiful musicality and sensitivity that enabled him to respond and interact with the other players without playing all over them. He knew exactly what the music needed and no matter what he played, or how much he seemed to be playing, the music was always his first concern and he never let the music down.

What Scotty played was amazing then and is amazing still today. His solos were technically overwhelming but melodically breathtaking. The solo on "My Romance" is one of my favorites and the last eight bars, in particular, is pure melodic perfection.

Scott LaFaro is one of a small group of musicians who really changed the course of jazz. It's not hard to imagine where he might have gone with music had he not been taken so early in his life. For me, and probably most of today's bass players, it's even harder to imagine the world of the bass without Scotty in it. He brought a brand new concept to the bass and in doing so he changed the way people would play it forever. Forty-five years later he is still probably the most powerful influence there is on the bass.

I regret never having known him but he will always be a part of my world and I will always be thankful for everything he contributed to it.

Don Thompson

PREFACE

I HOPE THIS BOOK WILL BRING a glimpse into the development and the life of Scott LaFaro, and an understanding of the man and his music. In my approach to writing this book, I've tried to be a modern-day Jack Webb—perhaps my own snopes.com—looking to separate the facts from the legend. It is not the story of an artist's angst, a life of hardship, emotional deprivation or shattered family relationships. It is a story of Scotty's obsession with music. Scotty was an intensely private person. He was well aware at an early age that he was set down on this planet to do something special with music. His head was full of it. He was dedicated and driven. Many thought him aloof, even haughty. He was intense, centered, and serious. He rather enjoyed being regarded as an enigma. It is also a book with chapters unwritten and ending in an abrupt and tragic plot twist. Scotty, himself, felt he didn't have a lot of time. He did what he set out to do, and we are all the richer for it.

It also has long been my desire that, when all is said and done, to have "all things Scotty" referenced in one place, thus my inclusion of the reprints of some of the more difficult to find articles, and the detailed bibliography and discography.

Are we all the sum of how we are perceived by others? I was the person who was constantly closest to Scotty during his too few years, and while I can relate many aspects of his life—and many have come to ask me about his life over the years—this book also relies heavily on my research and interviewing many musicians who knew Scotty or his work, or both, and are far more qualified to speak to his abilities, career, the technical aspects of his output, and his contributions to music than I. I thank them immensely.

ACKNOWLEDGMENTS

I'LL START WITH SHOULD, COULD, WOULD.

At least a decade ago, Chuck Ralston began a website dedicated to Scotty. Chuck is from Geneva, but I did not know him then. His dad at one time was the president of Geneva's local musicians' union and knew both Scotty and our dad. Ralston senior acquainted Chuck with jazz and with Scotty. His work took him and his family to France and it was there that they received the news of Scotty's death. Not too many years later, Chuck's interest in and appreciation of Scotty's jazz legacy led him to begin his self-assigned task of archiving, via the internet, whatever he could uncover. Eventually, Chuck, now headquartered in the Atlanta, Georgia, area, got in touch with me and over the years I have worked with him on the accuracy and dates of things posted on the website. Through all this time, Chuck has constantly been a voice in my ear saying I should do a book about Scotty. There is much to be told that only I could tell. "These are things people want to know," he'd tell me when I'd relate incidents to him. But Chuck's contribution goes far beyond urging. He helped set the outline for this book and did the total work on the detailed discography and bibliography, drawing on his past labor of love and his vast knowledge and ability as an administrative librarian.

In the mid 1990s I came to know Madeleine Crouch, general manager of the International Society of Bassists, and, echoing Chuck, in July of 1998 she wrote me: "PS: I hope you will seriously consider writing a biography of your brother. I'll buy

xviii 𝄢:   *Jade Visions: The Life and Music of Scott LaFaro*

the first copy!" This to someone who to that date had published only a couple of short stories and human interest articles in local newspapers and a couple of short pieces about Scott prefacing partial discographies of his work. Madeleine has been my constant cheerleader—telling me I could indeed do this. Every time I wavered she was there telling me I could do it and, more importantly, ready and willing to help. I needed a lot of help and help she did. She put me in contact with many folks who would make vital contributions to this book. She has been there every step of the way, helping in any and every way she could: the midwife, as it were, on this project.

Gene Lees. Madeleine had given me a phone introduction to Gene. And it is Gene who would give me the confidence to give it a shot. Gene Lees needs no introduction to anyone reading these pages. With his talent, background, and skill as a foremost author and chronicler of musicians, lyricist, composer, and journalist—highly esteemed in all his endeavors—he is a quintessential erudite, and to me, simply awesome. That he would treat me with such dignity and respect and encourage me at every turn is what would, in the end, make me urge myself to go forward. For all of this—to share his great knowledge about the craft of writing, to offer and be willing to do line editing, and checking, and to contribute to the book his Introduction—how could anyone not feel blessed. As important, however, is that over these past two years Gene and his wife, Janet, have become true friends to my husband, Manny, and me.

I am indeed fortunate to have Don Thompson write the wonderful piece that became the Foreword for this book. A great many thanks as well to Jeff Campbell and Phil Palombi, who gave of their time and talent to write the two indispensable chapters that discuss aspects of Scotty's music in detail. Over the past few years another contributor and I have also become friends: Barrie

Kolstein. Barrie's dad, Sam, had a special relationship with Scotty and it is Barrie who lovingly restored the Prescott bass. I am so grateful that Barrie has for this book, shared his personal story about Sam and Scotty, and his chronicling of his restoration efforts. Appreciation and thanks go as well to an old friend from Geneva, Bob Wooley, who has kindly allowed the reprint of his article recalling his school-days memories of Scotty.

Helping me all along the way also has been Dave Berzinsky. Dave is a font of knowledge about almost everything to do with the history of jazz in Los Angeles during Scotty's time there. Stan Levey at one time described him as "a walking encyclopedia of jazz." He has given me much of his time—always willing to go through archives with me, help in identifying any album or player, or find a way to find the answer. Ken Poston was immensely helpful in opening his archives to me and personally looking through old magazines, cover to cover. Thanks to Joe Urso for his generous help. At the Geneva Historical Society, Karen Osburn and John Marks have given me great assistance. Special thanks to my editor, Karen DeVinney. who has graciously guided me through this entire process.

Of course this book became a reality not only because of all of those mentioned above, but because to a person, everyone I contacted, or who contacted me, everyone I met and spoke to over these past three years with regard to the book, has been most willing and open in discussing Scotty and most gracious in sharing their experiences and feelings which I have tried to accurately set forth in these pages.

And then there is "La Famiglia"—as is the LaFaro "thing." From top to bottom, I have family to thank. First, thanks must be given to our parents for opening the floodgates of our minds way back in our early years, by encouraging Scotty and me to explore the worlds within ourselves as well as the one into which we were born. Applauding our little shows, appreciating the make-believe worlds Scotty and I created, teaching us by quiet example not to follow rhetorical dogma, but to be open to all people, ideas, and faiths, always delighting in having our imaginations running in high gear. Perhaps this is why within Scotty there arose an artesian spring that bubbled forth with the phenomenal energy and creative ideas mentioned by so many. He was trying to express the world and the music he was experiencing in his head.

My entire family has just been, with deference to Ornette, "Something Else." My sisters, Linda, Lisa, and Leslie, my granddaughters Jesslyn and Kristen and their mom, Haiden, and the lovely lady Trina, all giving me their ongoing, enthusiastic support. My husband and two sons, such creative and capable fellows all, inspire me and assist me always in all ways.

Thank you, thank you, thank you.

Introduction

Young Mr. LaFaro

by

Gene Lees

Scott LaFaro was something of a mystery to me. I never knew him well, and not for long. There was too little time. He played the bass for only seven years, from the summer of his eighteenth year until just after his twenty-fifth birthday, when he was killed in an automobile accident, but in that short period he became the most influential bassist of the last half of the twentieth century, and his echo continues in the work of Dave Holland, Neal Swainson, Eddie Gomez, Christian McBride, and many more. In this he was like Jimmy Blanton, who influenced the bass in terms of its harmonic role, and was dead at twenty-four, in his case of tuberculosis. One thinks, too, of Charlie Christian, who died at twenty-six but influenced probably every guitarist who came after him. He, too, succumbed to tuberculosis.

It was not only LaFaro's extraordinary technique that set him apart. He had a lyrical sensibility which reached its pinnacle in his work in the Bill Evans Trio of the early 1960s, a distinguished melodic gift that made his solos and contrapuntal conversations with Evans unique.

Bill's drummer during that period was Paul Motian. Later, Jack DeJohnette played the drums with Bill. Jack told me:

> I guess the concept of the bass the way Scott played it was not so much unusual—people like Mingus were playing with the fingers before Scotty. You had Blanton. I think had Danny Richmond been a different kind of drummer, he might have had the kind of interplay with Mingus that you got with Scott LaFaro and Paul Motian. That combination of Bill, Paul, and Scotty shifted the emphasis of time from two and four. The way Paul played sort of colored time rather than stated time. As opposed to what Miles would do. So that they made it in such a way that when they did go into four-four, it was kind of a welcome change. Then they'd go back into broken time.
>
> I remember the effect it had on rhythm sections in Chicago, because I was at the time a pianist, playing with a bassist who also played cello. We would sit up nights late, listening to the trio records. I noticed the rhythm sections in Chicago started playing that way.
>
> I had a drummer with me named Art McKinney, who was doing things like Paul Motian and Tony Williams were doing. This whole concept of broken time freed up the rhythm sections. It created a dialogue in rhythm sections as opposed to just the solid rhythm section like Wynton Kelly and Paul Chambers and Jimmy Cobb. After that everybody followed that concept.

Bill Crow, himself one of the finest bassists, said: "The big influences were Blanton, Oscar Pettiford, Ray Brown Red Mitchell, and LaFaro, for my money. Charles Mingus was impressive, but I don't think too many bassists tried to emulate his playing. Israel Crosby knocked me out when I heard his first records, and later with Ahmad Jamal he was impressive. But the five I listed probably changed the way people played more than any others.

"I was at the Village Vanguard when the Bill Evans Trio with Scotty first played there, and I remember how delighted Ray Brown was, sitting at the table next to mine. He kept saying, 'This kid has his own thing! Man, he really has his own thing!'"

Ray's widow, Cecelia, told pianist Mike Wofford that when Ray was teaching clinics, he put Scott LaFaro in his list of the top five bassists and innovators on the instrument with Jimmy Blanton, Oscar Pettiford, Milt Hinton, and Paul Chambers.

Bill Crow continues: "The Bill Evans Trio found a new game to play: all three musicians agreed on the time center so completely that no one of them felt the need to be explicit about it. They could all dance around it, play with it, decorate it, ignore it, and the time was still solid among them. Scott opened up a whole new way of thinking about the role of the bass in the rhythm section."

A magnificent illustration of Bill's—and Jack DeJohnette's—point is found in the trio's recording of Johnny Carisi's "Israel," in the 1961 Riverside album *Explorations*. After a chorus of the melody, they play a chorus of collective improvisation. No one is playing the time, not Motian (who plays brushes) not LaFaro, and not Bill. Yet you can feel the pulse at all times, so perfectly are they agreed on where it is. In the third chorus, Paul starts playing with sticks, and LaFaro goes into straight four. It is more than relief. Such is the swing that it will lift you off your chair. It is one of the most thrilling recordings in all of jazz. A footnote to this thought: after you have listened to this track, start it again immediately. You will find that the tempo has not changed by even a micro-beat. That was characteristic of Bill's playing, but obviously of Scott's and Paul's as well. A friend from Scott's high school band days in Geneva, New York, said, "Scotty was a stickler with perfect pitch. He was also a stickler on rhythm—I accused him of having a metronome in his head. Whenever I listen to Scott's recordings, I'm certain of it."

LaFaro's use of a two-fingered right-hand technique to pluck the strings came not from Charles Mingus but from Red Mitchell. Earlier bass players plucked the strings with just the forefinger or, sometimes, the forefinger and middle finger held together for strength, and often just a four-fingered grip in the left hand. Modern jazz bassists all use the classical left-hand configuration, with the index and pinky fingers outstretched and the middle fingers close together, but Red Mitchell was the primary influence in establishing the use of two fingers in the right hand, which tremendously increases facility.

Scott, according to his sister, always gave Red Mitchell credit for this development in his playing. Red told me a few years ago:

> It is the left brain that controls articulation. The right hand. That's what the right hand does—articulate. The right brain controls special visualization, fantasy, forms, abstraction. That's what the left hand has to do.
>
> Gary Peacock and Scott LaFaro were both protégés of mine. I remember one session in East L.A. when I showed them both this two-finger technique, which I had worked out in 1948 in Milwaukee, on a job there with Jackie Paris.
>
> It's a little harder than patting your head and rubbing your stomach. But it's the same kind of problem. You have a tendency, if you go one-two one-two with your fingers, and you want to go two-one two-one on the other hand, to hang up. You have to develop the independence. So that you can go one-two one-two one-two, or, even better rhythmically sometimes, two-one two-one two-one with the right hand and then random—you have to practice—fingering with your left hand so you can keep the right hand consistent and the left hand can go anywhere and not be hung

up. When you get it down, the one hand doesn't know what the other hand is doing.

And then you use your weaknesses. As Miles and Dizzy both used their pauses between phrases. You use the unevenness of it later so that the accents are where you want them. The loud notes are where you want the accents.

Bill Crow told me: "The funny thing is, Red developed that two-fingered system of plucking the bass before there was good amplification for the instrument. As a result, in the early years of using it, you often couldn't hear him very well in nightclubs. On records and in concert halls you could hear the wonderful music he was playing. But he played very softly. You can't pull the string as hard when you're just plucking with the fingers. Most players up until then got strength from pressing the right thumb against the side of the fingerboard and pulling against that leverage with the forefinger. The two-finger system raises the hand above the fingerboard where, even with the thumb as a fulcrum, the pull isn't as strong. But as soon as good amplification systems were invented for the bass, it became possible to change the setup putting the strings closer to the fingerboard, and to pluck without pulling the strings so hard. That opened up a new technique that now has bass players playing with a velocity that was impossible in Blanton's day. You win some and you lose some. Not pulling the string hard changes the tone of the instrument, and amplification won't completely replace the tone quality of a richly vibrating instrument. I think George Mraz strikes the best balance I've heard: rich tone, wonderful technique."

Charlie Haden, another brilliant bassist who was one of Scott's friends, said: "Scotty never liked pickups—he wanted a real wood sound. Sometimes he would use a microphone wrapped in a towel wedged between the tailpiece and belly of the instrument, not in the bridge."

Don Thompson, who is not only a fine pianist and vibes player, but a superb bassist, said:

> Because they've got the amplifier, guys lower the strings, lower the action, and then they can play real fast. And they get all that stuff going for them. But, unfortunately, what you lose in a lot of cases is that actual sound. Because when you hear guys play live now, you're not hearing the bass, you're hearing the amplifier. A bass doesn't sound like a bass any more. You're hearing pre-amps and speakers and effects and every other darn thing.
>
> Scott LaFaro had a beautiful sound. It was a real bass sound. Charlie Haden's sound on those old Ornette Coleman records, that's a real bass sound. Ray Brown on the Oscar Peterson record, you were hearing the bass. Now you hardly ever do. It's turned into something different. I don't like it as much.
>
> A lot of bass players are missing the message of Scott LaFaro. Scotty had some chops. He figured out the top end of the bass. He could play fast arpeggios. He could play amazingly fast. Too many bass players, I think, just play fast. But they don't hear the beauty of his melodies. They also don't hear how supportive he was when he played behind Bill Evans. He played pretty busy sometimes, but I don't think he ever seemed to get in the way or take the music away from Bill. Some other people, when you listen, you wonder: Who's playing here, is it bass or piano or what? With some guys the bass is actually distracting from the music. You can't really tell what's going on in the music because the bass is either too loud or too busy or playing too hard. The guy's not playing what the music needs, he's just playing what *he* wants to play. The music needs something from the bass, and if you don't play that, it doesn't matter what else you play, you've screwed it all up.

Scotty managed to play the foundation and play a
bunch of other stuff too and he never got in Bill Evans'
way at all.

Chuck Israels, who replaced LaFaro with Bill Evans and was
yet another friend of Scotty's, is in complete accord: "People have
misused Scotty by saying 'Oh my God, it's possible to play fast.'
And then they play fast but the content is missing."

One magazine writer called Scott the most influential bassist of the last fifty years, and I think that's true. Incredibly, his
reputation rests almost completely on only four albums. Although
he recorded with other groups, his importance emanates from
the three sessions with Bill for Riverside Records and the four
albums that came out of them, all produced by the company's
president, Orrin Keepnews.

Bill recalled the beginning of that trio: "When I left Miles
Davis to form a trio in the fall of '59, Miles tried to help me get
off the ground. He called some agents, and I asked (bassist) Jimmy
Garrison and (drummer) Kenny Dennis. They said they'd like to
try, so we had a few rehearsals and I got a booking at Basin Street
East, which was a pretty heavy club." He continued:

> We were opposite Benny Goodman, who was return-
> ing to the scene after a long absence. It was a trium-
> phant return—the place was jammed the whole time
> and they were paying him a tremendous price, chauf-
> feured limousine, the whole thing. But they treated us
> as the intermission group, really rotten—a big dress-
> ing room and steak dinners for Benny's band, but we
> couldn't even get a Coke without paying a buck and
> a quarter.
>
> Kenny and Jimmy couldn't put up with this scene.
> It really got bad. In a two-week engagement I think
> I went through six bass players and four drummers.

Philly Joe Jones was on the job a few nights and began
to get pretty heavy applause. So the boss said, 'Don't
let your drummer take solos any more' and turned the
mikes off on us."

Goodman was notorious for this. Whereas Woody Herman
reveled in the applause his sidemen got, Goodman would not
tolerate it, and would remove those solos by others that generated
excitement. This is recounted in the extended article about the
Goodman band's Russian tour, written by Bill Crow, who was on
that tour, and published in my *Jazzletter* in 1985.

Bill Evans continued: "Well, I was quite friendly with Paul
Motian. We had been making sessions together. And Scott LaFaro
was working around the corner with a singer—I forget who—
and dropped into Basin Street a couple of times. Anyway, it ended
up where Scott and Paul were the final guys.

"All I had to offer was some kind of reputation and prestige
that enabled me to have a record contract, which didn't pay much,
but we could made records—not enough to live on, but enough
to get a trio experienced and moving. I found these two musicians
were not only compatible, but would be willing to dedicate themselves to a musical goal, a trio goal. To make an agreement to put
down other work for anything that might come up for the trio."

The first engagement he obtained for this trio was at the
Village Vanguard, owned by Max Gordon who, I always sensed,
adored Bill. The club itself, on lower Seventh Avenue, was in a
basement reached by a steep flight of stairs. It was shaped like a
slice of pie, with the bandstand by the south wall. My memory
is that it was mostly in red. It had very good acoustics, and I can
think of no club in jazz history that, over the years, presented so
distinguished a roster of great musicians. It was Bill's New York
home, and I spent numberless evenings there with him, sitting

back at the bar when I was alone, or at a front table when I was with his manager (and later, record producer) Helen Keane, to whom I introduced him. Soon after that Orrin Keepnews produced the first of the albums with that group, *Portrait in Jazz,* which reached the market in March 1960.

Orrin told me, "There were two studio sessions that produced *Portrait in Jazz* and *Explorations,* and an all-day session at the Village Vanguard that produced two albums, *Waltz for Debby* and *Sunday at the Village Vanguard."*

I asked Orrin, "During the session, did you have any feeling of their historical importance?"

"Of course not," he answered. "I do remember what went on during the *Explorations* session. Bill and Scott were fighting constantly. Scott was asking for more money, because he didn't want to run the risk of going on the road with a junky and getting stranded somewhere." Orrin laughed. "So you could say there was a lot of creative tension on that session. Years later, Bill surprised me by telling me how happy he was with that album."

Scott was always angry with Bill over his heroin addiction. So was I.

Explorations was released in March 1961. Four months later Scott LaFaro was dead. Bill refused to play in public for nearly a year. He was shattered by the death, and guilty over the thought of all they might have accomplished during their brief time together had he not been strung out. He told me so. He worked with some superb bassists in the ensuing years, among them Eddie Gomez and Marc Johnson, but there was something he had with Scott LaFaro for which he yearned ever after.

Gene Lees

PROLOGUE

I often wondered if Scotty's obsession began in the front seat of Dad's 1936 Chevrolet with a fizzled car radio that emitted a single, sustained bass tone that reverberated right into our souls.

When Scotty was only six and I was four, we played almost every day in the car just so he could turn the radio's knob to the On position and listen as that low sound filled the car. I got it into my head that perhaps the Bogeyman was somehow in there. As soon as Scotty turned the volume way up on the dial, I'd run from the car and flop down flat on my belly on the front porch to peer at the haunted car from a safe distance. After a time, Scotty would join me and together we'd lie there, staring at the car, him assuring me many times over that there was nothing to be frightened about. The radio scared me, but I never knew what he was thinking. Could that deep-pitched sound have resonated with something inside a six-year-old boy, awakening the passion that led him to become a major figure in the history of jazz?

CHAPTER 1

LA FAMIGLIA

"Ovington, New Joisey. On toidy, toid and toid."
(Family joke whenever someone asked
where Scotty and I were born)

SCOTTY WAS BORN ROCCO SCOTT LaFaro in Irvington, a suburb of Newark, New Jersey. Our heritage is what America is all about—a bit of this, a bit of that. The family stock of our Mom, Helen Lucille Scott, was Scottish, Irish, and English. Her grandparents immigrated as children with their families late in the nineteenth century. Motherless at an early age, she was raised by a father who was surprisingly supportive, for the times, of his daughters' activities and independence.

Dad, Rocco Joseph LaFaro, was the first generation of his family born in America. His parents were from the province of Calabria in the extreme south of the Italian boot. Grandfather LaFaro was a stonemason by trade, an ice cream maker, and later a bootlegger to supplement the family income.

Both of our parents' families ended up settling in the small town of Geneva in upstate New York in the middle of a lovely farming area of the Finger Lakes Region. However, their families were never acquainted during the years prior to my parents' marriage.

Dad's parents, like many Italians, loved music and opera. They realized early on that their son, Joe, had an unusual talent. At age

3

three he was playing the mandolin in groups with adult musicians and began violin lessons at age five. He was performing with his teacher and other local professionals soon after. Our cousin Karmy Crupi-Henke recalls her mom, Dad's sister Mamie, telling her that practically the only memory she had of Dad as a young boy was hearing him practicing his violin in another room all the time, "even when the rest of the family was at dinner." His belief in the value of disciplined practice became deeply ingrained and he would pass this belief on to Scotty in the years to come.

At age twelve he was sent to Ithaca Conservatory (now College) of Music to study violin, where he was a student of Otakar Sevcik,[1] the renowned violin teacher from Prague. When Dad was eighteen and finishing up his last year at the conservatory, he and his friends decided to put aside their classical training and set their sights on the exciting big band and big money scene in New York City they were hearing so much about. Shortly after graduation he hit the road with the big name bands and stars of the twenties: Ed Kirkeby, the Dorsey Brothers, Smith Ballew, the California Ramblers, Paul Whiteman, Bea Lillie, and Rudy Vallee. Kirkeby and the Dorseys were playing what was called New York Jazz in its earliest days. Paul Whiteman was presenting Gershwin's "Rhapsody in Blue" at his concert titled "An Experiment in Modern Music."

Though formally trained in the classics and forever the lover of the symphony and opera, Dad also loved jazz from the start. Over the years he kept up with all the major jazz players, took Scotty (and sometimes me) to concerts nearby, and shared a lot of discussions about jazz with him.

It was a stint with an orchestra from CBS Radio that brought Dad back to Geneva to play at a debutante ball in 1934. Mom was most certainly not a deb, but her father wanted his three daughters to hear this orchestra from New York, so they dropped by the dance to catch a bit of music. That was when Dad met Helen Lucille Scott, the middle daughter of a widower and twelve years his junior. She was still in high school but this short meeting between sets was the beginning of a relationship that continued by correspondence and the occasional visit for the next year. Scotty and I used to tease Mom that she was the original groupie. On March 30, 1935, Helen turned eighteen, and on April twelfth, less than two weeks later and with the blessing of both families, they were married at the parsonage of the local Methodist minister. The young couple left immediately for New York City. They eventually rented a house across the river in Irvington, New Jersey, where Scotty was born on April 3, 1936. I followed on January 28, 1938.

"Sister," Scotty, nearly two, uttered as he pointed to the baby tightly wrapped in a receiving blanket that February morning. And so Sister it was. The beginning was the future writ large. The appellation given to me by Scotty when I was brought home from the hospital was how I was known and what everyone called me—parents, all relatives, friends and acquaintances. We became "Scotty and Sister," almost always spoken to and about as one during our early years. As I grew, "Sister" became "Sis." Only the occasional authority figure in our lives ever used my given name, Helene.

In those early years we were surrounded by Dad's many friends and fellow musicians: college cronies he came down to the city with and newer friends met on gigs. They'd gather at our home for dinner and backyard suppers or at the beach in summer. And family? There was always family. Relatives from both sides. At first, Dad's sisters came to help young Helen with the work of motherhood. Later, Mom's two sisters, Aunts Ginny and Elsie, also chose to live in Jersey in nearby East Orange while they made their careers in New York City. Granddad Scott would be there often to spend time with his three daughters. The pattern was set early—an interdependent, close, supportive family. Scotty and I bonded with all these family members and shared special relationships with all of them throughout our lives.

WWII slowed the music scene in New York. The mood of the nation was changing, growing somber. It wasn't a time for parties and hot jazz and soirees with society orchestras. Folks had to tighten their belts, and there was talk of shortages and rationing.

After the attack on Pearl Harbor when the United States entered the war, Dad tried to enlist with his many friends in the hope of being assigned to one of the services' entertainment units. He was thirty-six and deemed too old. He also had flat feet, which at that time was considered undesirable for the military. Reluctantly, he decided to take his young family back to their hometown and into the bosom of the extended family. So Mom and Dad returned to Geneva in 1942, at least for the duration of the war.

• CHAPTER 2 •

GENEVA: THE EARLY YEARS

ARRIVING BACK IN GENEVA DID not solve all the problems Dad faced. Geneva now had a population of about 18,000, having grown with the wartime installation of an arms depot and Sampson Naval Base some twelve miles away on the other side of Seneca Lake. Dad had done nothing but play music since he was three. The only work he could qualify for right away was as a night watchman at the arms depot. At least the hours were something he was used to, leaving him free to be with his family for many hours of the day, as well as time to continue his daily practice. His situation afforded Scotty and me a childhood that was at once both ordinary and extraordinary. From this earliest of ages we felt secure, loved, and trusted. We were allowed the freedom to move around in our little world—free to absorb our surroundings and personally interpret them. Free to be ourselves.

Scotty and I were also, in these early years, completely oblivious to the troubles of the world and played out the idyllic small-town childhood. Geneva, agriculturally based, had no heavy industry, then or now. It also had a broad ethnic mix for a city of its size: "WASPs" Roman Catholics, Irish, Italians, and blacks. We were set down in the middle of it, Dad choosing specifically not to live in his original ethnic neighborhood. He had left that and most of the Italian language behind him when he went off to the conservatory. The family spent a couple of months in a small apartment until a rental house became available. Mom and Dad were more accustomed to being city sophisticates. Their friends were well-read, talented folk who came from a wide economic and ethnic spectrum, with an appreciation of all the arts. But now life was different, which gave them even more time to devote to Scotty and me.

Mom and Dad wanted to create for us the idealized childhood they never truly had. They encouraged us in all of our endeavors. Imagination was applauded, creativity encouraged. In fact, throughout our family life, there was no dogmatic input imposed; our feelings and questions were always respected. And we felt always that our parents truly enjoyed our company. What more could one ask for?

Pretending and play-acting were important in our earliest years. At ages six and four we had a theater in our yard, with a blanket hanging from the clothesline serving as the curtain. We loved the exuberant applause of our parents, Granddad Scott, who lived with us, and neighbors who were invited to our performances.

We were allowed to wander about the immediate neighborhood and into the small forest behind our back yard. We were considered old enough to go together every now and then to the neighborhood market to get the few things on Mom's grocery list.

As a result, Scotty and I developed a great closeness and interdependency. Mom's evening ritual, now that Dad worked all night, was to put us to bed, then spend some time with Granddad listening to the radio for news of the war, or maybe the *Jack Benny Show*, *Fibber McGee and Molly* or another of their favorites. Often she'd visit with her lady friend across the street in the early evening, then read and nap before rising early enough to prepare a large, hot breakfast upon Dad's return. They went to bed in the early hours of the morning, leaving Scotty in charge until they rose in the afternoon. I was his charge. Throughout his life he watched out for me, paved the way, and never seemed to mind.

At six he had the burden of family handed to him, the responsibility to look after me and, by extension, "la famiglia," something often mentioned by our Dad and not unheard of in the Italian culture. This was something that Scotty never let go of, taking it in stride and seriously. He was always in charge of his own life as well, and he lived by no one's standards but his own. Our relationship was such that when Scotty started first grade in the fall I was beside myself with grief. Mom talked the principal into allowing me to enter kindergarten a year early so I could go off to school with Scotty each day.

"Does that frutin' dumb bunny (A local term. To this day I have no idea what it means.) always have to be with us?" It was 1943, and one of Scotty's friends asked the question while we were hiking in our forest with two other boys. They were all seven and I was five. Scotty became my hero for life when, quietly, he not only assured the fellow that I did, but added in my defense that I wasn't any such thing. Even as Scotty's circle of friends grew it always included me, apparently whether they liked it or not.

Though we later learned how financially lean those years were, Scotty and I never knew or felt any strain. We seemed to have whatever we needed and wanted, and did what the other kids did. We weren't aware that we were renters, and when we moved from one house to another at the end of each year's lease, we found it pretty neat. Each neighborhood had intriguing areas for Scotty and me to explore. Even though moving necessitated a change in schools as well, that didn't bother us since Scotty and I were still, in these grade school years, closer to one another than to any schoolmates.

Our third home in Geneva was actually the upper floor of a large older house that had been converted into two apartments in the center of town. Since there was no room for Granddad Scott, he moved in with our Aunt Elsie, who had a similar converted apartment around the corner from us. She was now alone because her husband, Burt, was overseas fighting the war. That was about all we knew about the war, and that it somehow meant that we took small books with rationing stamps to the market with us. Also, because of the wartime food shortages, Aunt Elsie specialized in putting neat rows of whole cloves and brown sugar on a square of strange-looking meat called Spam that Scotty and I found quite tasty.

Scotty and I found this new place pretty nifty. There was a city park on the corner between our place and our aunt's, and we had a rooftop terrace on the side of the house with access from our kitchen and stairs that led down to the yard. There was also a front balcony with a view of the houses across the street through the trees. Lovely as the balcony was, Scotty and I long remembered it as the site of one of our less enjoyable experiences. We had gotten head lice from a visiting Canadian cousin and had to sit up straight in hard chairs for what seemed like an eternity as Mom carefully parted our hair, inch by inch with a sharp metal comb and dabbed on some strong chemical that burned our scalps and brought tears to our eyes. For quite a while after that Scotty and I were wary not only of visitors, but of Canadians in general!

The most wonderful thing about this house was our secret place. This old home had a wraparound porch that was set quite high, perhaps six steps up from the entry sidewalk.

The area under the porch was closed off with latticework but we found a loose piece we could pull out a bit. We crawled in and whiled away our time in the semi-darkness on the cold, damp earth. We'd tell each other stories, talk about our great plans, make curious noises at passersby to spook them, and once even invited in a friend from the neighborhood after swearing him to secrecy. When Mom called us for lunch or dinner or came looking for us, we always waited quietly until she had returned indoors, so no one would be the wiser about where we were. We never really knew if this place was off-limits: we never asked. Scotty and I just loved the idea of it being our place and nobody knowing about it.

It was at this time that books became special to Scotty and me. Our mom's other sister, Aunt Ginny, was still working in New York City for a publishing company and now had a horse that she boarded in Geneva. She would fly upstate to visit us and ride her horse. We thought her very brave since she was the only person we knew who had actually been on an airplane. We'd see them zoom overhead and, like most folks in those days, found that thrilling. This was not the age of huge airliners but of yellow Piper Cubs with seating for two and commercial planes like the Douglas DC-3 that seated only about twenty.

Upon her arrival, Scotty and I would beg to be allowed to open her suitcase because she always had books for us, sometimes autographed by the author. Scotty also began to collect some metal airplanes and got a leather aviator's cap that Christmas.

Although our mom did not technically finish high school, she was an avid reader and read an average of three books a week throughout her life. She let Scotty and me read books that some thought unsuitable for our ages: Fitzgerald, Williams, Steinbeck, Faulkner, and Hemingway early on in high school. Later when Scotty was out on the road playing with various groups, he'd write me to recommend something I should read, or send me a book. He sent me James Joyce's *Portrait of the Artist as a Young Man* in the summer of 1956 when he was with Buddy Morrow's orchestra. He was twenty and I was eighteen, and I confess I had a difficult time with it. At first I was embarrassed to admit it to Scotty, not wanting him to think I had become a "frutin' dumb bunny."

In 1960, after I had married and Scotty often stayed with the family whenever he was back in Los Angeles, he continued to give me copies of the books he was reading. One of his favorites was Rainer Maria Rilke's *Notebooks of Malte Larids Brigge*. Looking back, it doesn't surprise me that Scotty liked Rilke's impressionistic style and Joyce's stream of consciousness. Maybe some parallels to be drawn to jazz here?

In 1944, Dad finally got work as a musician once again. Belhurst Castle, an exclusive club in town with a reputation for great food, was doing a growing business with well-heeled folks from the surrounding area and the brass from the naval base and decided to hire a small musical group to entertain. Through friends he had made since returning to Geneva, Dad got a steady gig at the Belhurst and kept it until the end of his life. This job meant a move back to what Dad considered a better part of town. We found ourselves on the same street where we began, once again in a single-family home.

This is the time that Scotty and I first became aware of music on a more serious level. Dad began practicing more and it became mandatory that we be quiet and out from underfoot during those hours. Often the two of us would sit in the upstairs hall outside of the bedroom where Dad was practicing with the door ajar. When he was finished, he finally noticed us and we'd beg to have him play Rimsky-Korsakov's "Flight of the Bumble Bee" day after day, and he'd always comply.

Now, too, there was a third child expected. A sister, Linda, arrived May, 12, 1945. When Mom was hospitalized for the delivery and post partum care, which at that time was an astonishing ten days, it was the first time Scotty and I had experienced such a separation from her and we were not too happy. We were fortunate that her hospital room overlooked the main street below. Since children were not allowed in hospitals unless they were patients, Dad took us daily to the street outside so we could wave to Mom at the third floor window, which we found reassuring. When she finally brought Linda home, Scotty and I knew immediately that things would never be the same. I once was sassy enough to suggest that our parents "Take her back where they got her."

With the growing family came money problems once again. Mom took a newly created position at the Belhurst club running the coat checkroom. She enjoyed getting out of the house and being around the diverse group of people where Dad worked. "Mom Robbins," our Aunt Elsie's mother-in-law, was recruited to baby-sit the three of us. A new routine began. Evenings brought the sitter, and Scotty and I found her formidable, a little lady so strange that we even suspected the mincemeat pies she brought to family Thanksgiving dinners.

During the mornings while our parents slept in, Scotty was once again my caretaker. We had the run of the neighborhood. Our elementary school was just two blocks away and we began to find friends and interests of our own. Now in the fourth grade, Scotty was playing softball and taking his new hobbies, collecting comic books and making airplane models out of balsa wood, tissue paper, and banana oil very seriously. I would be off playing games with Nancy, next door, or having tea parties in Mary Jane's play house across the street as Scotty became more involved in other activities. Dr. Cordell Bahn, a childhood neighbor and one of Scotty's classmates from grades three through twelve, recounts the times they spent together:

> I remember sitting at your kitchen table, waiting for Scotty to be able to play, but first he had to make you eat your breakfast. Scotty was the de facto boss during the early hours since your parents slept in late. Scotty and I would play softball behind the school until it was pitch dark. He was a much better shortstop than I was at any position. We both feared the angry man who lived over the fence on the first base side. I'm sure Scotty and others used to risk life and limb sneaking into his garden to rescue fly balls since he kept them when he found them. But the high point of our childhood relationship was the school newspaper drive we

had during the last year of the war. Scotty and I were each team captains and our respective garages were the repositories of mountains of papers, tons actually. At the final weighing in, Scotty's garage had about 100 more pounds of paper and he won!

Soon there was a lot of excitement that we were going to move once again, but this time to our very own home where we would stay permanently. This was made possible through Dad's contacts at Belhurst. He had been able to get a private loan from one of the city's elderly society matrons who appreciated his violin artistry. The house was only a few blocks away and we would still attend the same school. Shortly after we moved into our new home, Dad got a Waterloo pump organ and an upright piano. Dad played them both before or after his usual daily violin practice. We also got a Victrola and he started collecting records, classical music of course, but also the popular crooners like Sinatra and Nat King Cole, as well as some other favorites like Art Tatum, Lionel Hampton, and George Shearing. Scotty and I were still putting on little musicales at home, singing and dancing along with various records. We both got into full-blown productions at school. Scotty was in *Hansel and Gretel*.

Life for Scotty and me remained pretty much the same. Scotty was still in charge in the mornings, taking care of our breakfast and seeing that the two of us got off to school on time. Some mornings we'd be happily surprised to find the breakfast table already set for us, cereal at the ready, by Mom and Dad the night before. Part of almost every weekday was spent at our local playground on Brook Street. In the summer, Scotty was playing softball, so of course I joined the girl's league.

During fourth grade Scotty decided he had a girlfriend. He was quite taken with a classmate, Maxine, who not only had the most beautiful long, dark ringlets, but was easily the smartest girl in the class. Conveniently, her house was on Brook Street between the school and the park, and Scotty spent more than a little time there, often devouring dozens of her mom's chocolate chip cookies at a sitting. Maxine Baroody-Giacobbe says she still has many special memories of Scotty. Her favorite is when Dad took her and Scotty to the Belhurst to hear him play the violin. They ate spaghetti with white linen napkins tucked under their chins. Maxine became a friend of mine as well, and I considered her a sterling example and my personal mentor when I began high school.

Suddenly, or so it seemed to Scotty and me, when I was in fifth grade and Scotty in sixth, dissension arose in our family. We often awoke to angry voices in the night. My first instinct was to go to Scotty's room. Both of us were baffled and scared. We'd venture a closer listen or a peek, and what we learned was not pretty: our parents were having fights that began as escalating verbal matches. We noticed that many times they had bizarre, slurred speech and seemed unsteady on their feet. Since television did not yet exist in our home to show us what being drunk was, we were entirely unfamiliar with this kind of behavior.

There had always been some beer in our house to drink with meals in warm weather and on picnics, and wine on the table during special dinners and with Italian food, but we didn't know what hard liquor was at that time since we never had any in our home. Then came times when these arguments deteriorated into some pushing, shoving, and slapping. We seemed not to know these people at all, and what was worse, they didn't seem to recognize us or acknowledge our presence, or if they did once or twice, it was with anger in their eyes and admonitions to get back to our rooms. Several times it looked like there would be a physical altercation, and Scotty put himself between our battling parents and we pleaded with them to just go to bed. We wouldn't dare go back to sleep, nor could we have slept, until we felt that the nasty business was over for the night. Afterwards our parents never offered any explanation of these incidents and we dared not bring them up. Scotty and I just clung to one another a bit more and never spoke to anyone about it. After a year of tension, luckily for us all, whatever seemed to be the cause of all the trouble must have been settled. The incidents stopped as suddenly as they had begun. In later years when Scotty and I looked back on this time, we put it down to Dad having a mid-life crisis. We did catch snippets of their arguments and heard accusations about other women. Perhaps Dad felt stuck in Geneva with a family, when he could have been better utilizing his talent in a larger arena.

This ugly intrusion into what were otherwise wonderful early years became the basis for our later aversion to substance abuse. Not that Scotty didn't try stuff. He smoked weed with buddies and a girlfriend or two over the years after he left home for the musician's life. While on the road with Buddy Morrow he wrote me about all the different names for marijuana, educating me as always. He grew a bit of his own when we lived in the Silver Lake district in Los Angeles, but it was only for occasional use and was never a habit. Social drinking was okay with us. When it came to harder drugs or hard drinking, however, we just couldn't understand either and had difficulty tolerating them.

Scotty would specifically not allow my romantic interest in any of his musician buddies who were involved with drugs, warning me who was and wasn't suitable in his eyes. We both felt that people should be masters of their own destinies and not let destructive elements get in the way of leading a purposeful life. Scotty had a particularly hard time tolerating things that got in the way of what he thought could and should be accomplished, hence his absolute frustration and anger with many that he worked with, most especially with Bill Evans, whom he thought was a beautiful human being as well as a musical genius.

• CHAPTER 3 •

EARLY INFLUENCES

"Too bad Dad didn't make me play strings when I was
a kid. Think of how much farther along I could be."

Scotty
Philadelphia, 1957

OUR MUSIC EDUCATION BEGAN AS it did for many, with the
tambourines, drums, and triangles of our early childhood. Regardless of the fact that music was Dad's life, when Scotty and
I were older we learned why Dad hesitated to give us any early
musical education himself. He was trying hard to create for us the
"normal" childhood he had sacrificed to his prodigy, a gift that he
felt took him out of the family fold.

In conversations with percussionist Victor Feldman in the late
sixties, I found this same notion. Vic's career began in England at
age seven and not long after, "Kid Krupa," as he was known, was
touring the Continent. But Vic was determined. He tried and
succeeded in establishing a wonderful, settled family life in the
Los Angeles area, doing studio work along with his jazz. He and
his wife, Marilyn, had three sons and he never forced music study
on them. Like Scotty and me, they were casually introduced to it.
When interest flagged, they were allowed to set music aside and
go on to other things.

Our formal music training began when Scotty was in the
sixth grade and, since most of our other friends were taking pi-

ano lessons, it was agreed that he and I could as well. Mrs. Anna Sampson's house on Lyceum Street was just a short walk from home. The parlor where she gave her lessons had glass-paneled doors covered with curtains. Scotty and I would take turns sitting in the front hall while the other had their private lesson. While she seemed a frightening figure to me, Scotty never commented about this, so I remained silent. We were encouraged to practice, but we were not threatened with punishment if we slacked off.

I can remember only three times in my life that Scotty was less than kind to me, and two had to do with the piano. We practiced our lessons on the piano in our family living room, an upright with a heavy, hinged keyboard cover. During one of my practice times, Scotty came over and said, "Stop—it's terrible," then slammed the cover down quite forcefully before I could remove my hands. Mom came running to my cries of pain. The second incident came not many weeks later when, as I practiced, he appeared wielding a table knife. With a hint of mischief, a new approach since he had gotten a stern talking-to about the previous incident, Scotty said, "If you don't stop that darn noise, I may be forced to make you." This remark made me bolt from the piano and race through the house to escape my fate, Scotty in pursuit. Although he apologized immediately upon being caught, I got the message. I never played that piano, or any other, again.

Later in life it was agreed that this incident was probably precipitated by Scotty's extraordinary ear—he had perfect pitch. Once he approached music, it seemed to come easily to him and early on he seemed to have little patience for anything he felt was sub-standard. This intolerance stayed with him into adulthood. There were things he found unacceptable and inexcusable, in music as well as in other facets of life.

Scotty's piano lessons continued for a time, until summer and playground activities interrupted and junior high school was on the horizon.

The Geneva school system required music to be taught in the seventh grade. They offered a general class where learning to read music was the main goal, and it was mixed with classroom singing to reinforce proficiency. There was also a recruiting tool, a class to prepare students to join the high school band. This was a good alternative for an active, willful kid like Scotty. He had no preference for a particular instrument, which was good since that choice was determined by current and anticipated vacancies in the band. My close friend Gail, whose dad, Godfrey Brown,[1] was the high school music director, said he was quite good at convincing students to take up just the instruments needed to flesh out his group, with the promise of letting them switch to another instrument at a later date. And so Scotty began on the bass clarinet. This opened the door to a world that would soon envelop him to the exclusion of almost everything else.

Scotty took to everything about being in the band. He loved going to "Brownie's" for his private lessons, it being such an adult thing, and then coming home and practicing like Dad. His development was rapid and he was one of few who made the high school band while still in eighth grade. At thirteen, playing the bass clarinet, he was in the New York All-State Music Festival.

During this same time there was great excitement at home. Dad was ecstatic over a new organist at the First Presbyterian Church, Charlotte Bullock. So began the first active association Scotty and I had with formal, organized religion. Dad really wanted us both to be in the choir at this church under her tutelage and so we started attending as a family to listen to the music offerings, not necessarily to share in the religious aspects of the service, but for the inspiring influence of the classical compositions. Charlotte ripped with gusto or treaded with solemnity into Bach, Beethoven, Mendelssohn, Mozart, Haydn, and Handel. Dad was right. It was awesome. This was, in fact, the history of religion in our family. When I'm asked about our family's religious background, I always answer, "We went wherever the music was best." That was Dad's criterion, be it a mass at a Roman Catholic Church or Friday evening Shabbat dinner at the cantor's home.

Looking back, Scotty and I agreed that our religious experiences, or maybe our lack of them, enriched our lives. Although Dad and Mom were from traditional religious families—his Roman Catholic, hers Methodist—they did not bring either into their marriage or child rearing. Having left his family for the conservatory at such an early age, Dad was exposed to students and teachers from a wide variety of backgrounds and faiths, which he found stimulating. Mom, who was enthralled with this older man and his musical artistry, followed his lead. There were discussions at home with friends who were theists, deists, atheists, and agnostics, and Scotty and I listened in. We were allowed to go to our Baptist neighbor's home when she held her Bible school and we loved the flannel boards and Bible stories. Dad was a student of mind healing most of his life after learning something about Mary Baker Eddy's[2] "Mind is All" theory. We celebrated Christmas as "Peace on Earth, Good Will to Man" and the birth of hope. Santa Claus brought us plenty of toys over the years. Easter marked rebirth and renewal with eggs and the Easter Bunny. We never ate meat on Friday, a hangover from Dad's early youth. There were no dogmatic lines drawn in the sand and, as children, we were unaware of what our parents' personal beliefs were. Respect for all mankind was the lesson and the rest followed naturally.

But now there was all this exciting music happening at the Presbyterian Church and we wanted to be a part of it. After professing interest in the faith and signing up for religion classes to head toward baptism and confirmation, we were allowed to join the choir. It was a wonderful experience. I was a second soprano, Scotty a tenor, and best of all we got excused early from Sunday School to get into our choir robes and march into the glorious sanctuary to sing. The holidays became even more special thanks to Charlotte's musical selections and her natural exuberance.

We were not only enriched musically, but we found that this church and those associated with it also provided us wonderful life lessons and activities that became important in our young lives. There were social exchanges with those of other faiths and surrounding communities, and an away-from-home summer camp that we attended for two years, which left us both with some sweet memories. We both did finally get baptized and confirmed and were Presbyterians for a time.

This was not Scotty's last profession of faith. Another came some three years later when he was again baptized and confirmed in the Roman Catholic faith—a strategic move by a smitten teenager during a serious relationship in high school. Mom and Dad were always cool with whatever we did. Religion was our decision, not something imposed upon children for the sake of tradition. Perhaps one reason Scotty wasn't afraid to break the boundaries of music and the bass was that he learned from an early age to explore many paths.

SCOTT'S FIRST PHOTO

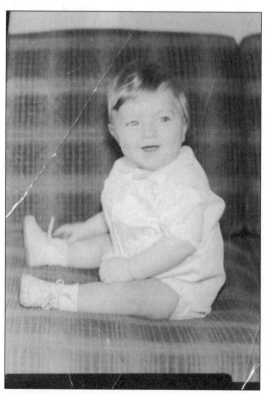

SCOTT AT NINE MONTHS

CHRISTMAS 1943. SCOTT WITH AVIATOR CAP.

SCOTTY AND SISTER 1946

SCOTT AT 13, HIS JUNIOR HIGH SCHOOL PHOTO

CHAPTER 4

HIGH SCHOOL DAYS

EARLY IN SCOTTY'S FRESHMAN YEAR of high school he started listening to some of the newer jazz music on the radio and spending more time with Dad's recordings: Art Tatum, George Shearing, Marian McPartland, and Dizzy Gillespie. This music excited him, ignited something inside him and from that time on, he seemed to know this was the music he was going to play. Shortly thereafter, he decided on and began playing the tenor sax.

Scotty participated in almost every musical activity and class the school offered, and there were plenty: theory, advanced theory, orchestra, marching band, concert band, jazz band, boys' chorus, varsity chorus, and All-State band and orchestra competitions.

"Scotty and I were close friends through high school," recalls Bob Umiker, a high school classmate who became the principal clarinetist with the North Arkansas Symphony as well as a professor of music at the University of Arkansas. "As freshmen we had exactly the same class schedule. Scott was still playing bass clarinet in band, but in jazz band he was playing tenor sax, and I played alto. In music theory class one day, I looked over at Scott and shot him with my finger. He accommodated by falling out of his chair, at which time we were kicked out of class for the rest of the year. Having to take the course over the next year gave us a thorough grounding in theory."

Scotty took private music lessons during high school with Godfrey Brown. They developed an ever-growing mutual respect and friendship. "Brownie," as he was affectionately known, gave Scotty some of the discipline that our father could not bring himself to impose. Later, Scotty's drive and passion for music overpowered nearly everything else, and he became very demanding of himself. In the meantime, though, Scotty carried on with the usual activities he shared with his friends. He'd drop by the YMCA and play basketball. He spent a good part of two summers playing golf, and sharing family time at the beach, which was nearly every sunny day. He was a regular guy, popular enough to be elected vice president of his sophomore class and involved enough to be on the committees for his junior prom and senior ball. The consensus was he had probably volunteered so he could help pick the band that would play for those events.

In Geneva, Dad earned more respect than money, but he and Mom did not want us to be wanting. If something came up that they really couldn't afford, they still found a way to provide. Instruments were purchased on the installment plan, and Mom took a second job at a lovely women's clothing shop so that, with her discount, she and I could stay stylish. They had their pride, not just in appearances, but in a good work ethic. Any work was respectable and one should do a good job. Dad constantly told us, "If you can't do something really well, do the world a favor and don't do it." I think this affected both of us. Scotty and I had many of the usual teenage jobs: paper routes, baby-sitting, picking fruit, and raking leaves. In high school Scotty did some caddying at one of the golf clubs and was a cook at the church camp. Even in these part-time pursuits we wanted to be the best, the fastest, and the most creative, no matter what the job was.

Since Mom was still working weekend nights at the Belhurst Club, Scotty continued to look after us, his two younger sisters, on a regular basis. Around one a.m. on a drizzly Saturday autumn night during Scotty's junior year I awoke to his tugging at my pajama shoulder, declaring in a calm, serious tone, "We'd better go outside, the house is on fire." Together we awoke Linda and spent the next few hours huddled in the street, being ministered hot coffee by well-meaning neighbors and receiving hugs offered by an increasing group of onlookers. A Keystone Kops corps of volunteer firemen arrived on the scene fresh from their Saturday night partying and began to assault the blaze. Since the fire had, in fact, begun in the wall next to Scotty's bed (from old, faulty wiring, it was later pronounced), he at one point offered his somber opinion that the crew might consider going around to the back of the house, where indeed the house was engulfed in flames, rather than taking their hatchets to the front exterior.

This family crisis further cemented Scotty's and my relationship with the Brown family, since Brownie invited the two of us to stay with them while Dad and Mom and Linda encamped with our next-door neighbors to oversee the rebuilding project. Besides losing almost the entire contents of our home, the family was separated for the first time for the better part of four months.

After all the expenses of remodeling and repair, we began to take in boarders. These were generally folks from Boston or New York City who came to Geneva to teach at Hobart, the local college, or to work at nearby Sampson, now an Air Force rather than a Naval base. It added to the mix of interesting people we met. Scotty got a new bedroom, far away from the old one and its memories, and there he installed a special counter in an alcove for two turntables and his sound system. He was good at putting gadgets together and as the years passed, he maintained an interest in all things electronic. Once while visiting home a year before his death, he expressed to me his frustration over the general public's lack of appreciation for jazz: "I don't know if people will ever get it. Maybe I should just forget the whole thing, go back to school and get into the electronics field."

During high school Scotty focused increasingly on his music studies. His closest pals were his fellow band mates, devoted buddies who adored him and were at our home often, hanging about while he practiced and chatting with him late into the night. Just recently, when revealing some of the unhappy aspects of his own childhood, one of Scotty's friends confided to me that he always found the environment in the LaFaro home to be open, vital, encouraging, and accepting.

"Joe, Scotty's dad, often sat in front of his newest prized possession, their Chickering baby grand piano, playing chord after chord in answer to questions tossed at him by Scotty," says Bob Bennett, a neighbor and high school friend.

> His clarinet or sax in hand, Scotty would mimic the sounds Joe played, always eager to learn more and ever more. I remember one time when Joe explained something very clearly about how the key in which the music was written immensely affected the impact of a musical presentation, and then proceeded to play a piece in several different keys until one sounded so special that even I got the point. Timing, intonation, musicality and emotional content were the things of life between Scotty and his dad. There were sometimes little tensions that cropped up, but the music itself overrode everything in that shared dance of father and son. It was this embracing of the music that always seemed to lead the rhythm of life in the LaFaro home. It was exciting as a friend to be there and share the joy of his accomplishments. He was like a big brother. He was a driven individual, but rarely unable to take time for a friend.

Bob Bennett also recalls a time when Scotty and his friend, Bob Umiker, an alto sax player, were playing for an assembly in school. He said they had no sooner started a concert piece when one of the pads fell off Scotty's horn. "Without skipping a beat, Scotty stepped to the microphone and announced that due to technical difficulties they would be unable to continue. I somehow sensed then that Scotty would forever be a capable and resourceful person."

Scotty's junior year found him branching out in many directions musically. He was one of ten chosen to participate in the New York Music School All State Concert in Buffalo on February 28, 1953. During this year as well, a school band mate, trumpet player senior Tom Kirk, got the idea of starting a dance band. He rounded up some funds to buy a few sheets of music and with a donated piano installed in his family's basement rumpus room, the Rhythm Aires was born. The group grew to seven players, and they were serious. They had formal band dress and eventually music stands with lights and the band's name in glittery letters, as well as a theme song: "My Happiness" by Borney Bergantine. They were playing the popular dance numbers of the day: "Blue Moon," "Harbor Lights," "La Vie En Rose," and "Mona Lisa," made popular by Nat King Cole. It meant more practice, but it paid off with performances at high school dances in the area as well as other civic venues. They were paid with donations that they used to buy more music and sometimes with tickets to the movies. "These years were very special for me and, I believe, the rest of the group," Tom remembers. "We got along so well for a group of teenagers and were very serious about what we were doing. Scotty and I were in charge. Together we let it be known that if anyone in the band stepped out of line, they would be history. We never had a problem. I'm very proud to say I was a part of this group and can say I was in a dance band with Scotty

LaFaro. I still tear up whenever his name comes up. He made me the trumpet player I was. Scotty, for his age, was very advanced in music and he was so special to me. He would stay after practice just to help me learn a part. He had a wonderful personality for a teenager and was so easy to get along with. He had the patience of a saint with me."

The high school marching band was very active, playing at all the football and basketball games at home as well as in surrounding communities. They would also travel to larger cities for All-State music competitions. In Scotty's junior year, at Brownie's urging, Scotty took up the baritone bugle and joined the Appleknockers, Geneva's highly regarded American Legion Drum and Bugle Corps. Scotty's world became larger. He got his first taste of the road life of musicians, traveling as far away as Washington, D.C., St. Louis, Missouri, and Florida for national competitions. Since he and the few other high school students Brownie had brought in to play with the Appleknockers weren't veterans, they were unable to be in the competitions themselves. But they still found the travel and being a part of the opening and closing parades at these events exciting. During his two years with the group it won many statewide and national regional competitions. Scotty liked the seriousness and dedication of the groups' members and enjoyed the camaraderie among the musicians. A fellow band mate, Al Davids, recalls, "My only contact with Scotty was in band, orchestra and the corps. The thing I remember most was his drive for perfection. He would never be satisfied with half way."

During Scotty's junior year new elements came into his life as he began to regard girls as something more than fellow musicians. Beginning in elementary school, girls had always given him a lot of attention. I could never be certain how many of my girlfriends were really my friends or sought me out because they had hopes of becoming Scotty's girlfriend. But now his interest was definitely picking up. He and his buddies stopped their guilty snickering whenever I was within earshot, and he started coming home later after playing at sporting events.

We developed a tacit arrangement in our adolescence. Scotty always had to okay the guys and girls I hung out with. I valued his approval, but at times he gave me his opinion before it was needed. If he saw me in the hall at school with someone he disapproved of, I'd hear about it by dinnertime. His protection extended to his female interests whom he wanted me to know, and those he did not. The former he wanted me to befriend, the latter I'd hear about through school gossip. He encouraged me to become friends with the four women he was serious about during his life, and today, some fifty years later, I'm still in touch and friendly with all of them. It goes without saying that any relationship I had over the years absolutely had to pass muster with my brother. Of the man I married fifty years ago, Scotty advised, "Don't let this one go!"

By the last half of his junior year, the spring of 1953, Scotty had a steady romance going with a popular, petite cheerleader, Anna Marie Pacuilli. The relationship had its rocky moments, but he was so besotted that he decided to prove his devotion by adopting her Roman Catholic religion. The intensity of this relationship endured through graduation but ended, as many do, when he went off to college. They saw each other once again around 1959 in Los Angeles. He suggested resuming the relationship but she had fallen in love with someone else and was engaged to be married. Scotty seemed dismayed that she had not waited for him.

"I had never met anyone quite like Scotty, whose complete dedication to one thing set him apart from others from the very beginning," says Anna, now Ann Golding. "His whole life was music and his family. For my birthday between our junior and senior year Scotty gave me a record player and a bunch of albums to go with it, including Dave Brubeck, Chet Baker, and Stan Getz. Our favorite song was "My Funny Valentine" by Chet Baker and to this day I am partial to that song. For all of his musical ability he was just an adequate dancer, mainly swaying and moving his feet as little as possible."

Because Scotty paid attention to little other than music, some classmates thought he'd become aloof, noting that he now seldom spoke to anyone but his girlfriend and me if it was not about music. Over the coming years other people also found him distant. I believe there were just times when the music in his head prevented him from being engaged with others.

By this time, it was settled that Scotty was a musician, and that he would go to Ithaca College, Dad's alma mater. He and his buddy Bob were taking sax lessons together from a Mr. Tamburino. They'd duet a lot, playing Bach's two-part inventions on alto and tenor. Now that they were both planning for college, they began more serious study of the clarinet, since it wasn't possible to major in saxophone. They'd drive together to nearby Shortsville for weekly lessons from Valentine Anzalone.[1] Val recalls that they never missed their lessons and were always well prepared. He vividly recalls that "Scott could play his pages of *SCALES IN 3rds*, rapidly (Vivace) and rhythmically even. Amazingly, he did this with his fingers coming at least 1.5 inches above the clarinet finger holes (a pedagogical 'No-No'), but it worked for him." Both Bob and Scott worked on their New York State Grade 6 Solos and received the highest grades possible. Both received "A" ratings at statewide competition. Scott played the first movement of a Mozart concerto and Bob played the third.

In December of 1953, during his senior year, Scotty shared First Place honors for the Seneca Symphony Society's Orchestral Performance Competition. He played *Concertino for Clarinet and Orchestra* (Opus 26, Jaehns # 109 in 1811) and *Concertina* by

German composer Carl Maria von Weber (1786–1826) on the B-flat clarinet. Scotty won the opportunity to appear with the symphony at its spring concert and twenty-five dollars, which was big money for a kid in those days.

Scotty became student band director his senior year as well. Nancy Fordon Johnston, a retired professional music instructor and former classmate, recalls, "It was fun to play for assemblies with him conducting. I remember his smiles mostly. He never lorded it over anyone in music groups, even though he had the most talent. He was patient, just biding his time until he could get into the field where he belonged."

Scotty began to go out to the Belhurst Club and sit in a bit with Dad and his group. Sometimes after they'd finished they'd go off to some of the local after-hours clubs either to listen or sit in, coming home in the wee hours of the morning. Scotty was often absent or tardy for school, or he'd fall asleep during a class. More than once during roll call on the first day of a new school year, teachers told me, "I hope you get a little more sleep than your brother and know how to pay attention." A couple of his teachers were miffed when Scotty aced the State Regents Exams at the end of the year and was still able to pass their courses, despite his classroom participation, or lack of it. When the powers-that-be called Dad to complain, he expressed sympathy for their position and apologized, but also explained that these late-night forays were also an important part of Scotty's education.

Scotty also became the youngest member of a sextet, the Chess Men. This was a group of adult professionals who played events at local venues. He loved playing with them as well as the Rhythm Aires and gigging around town with Dad and began to wonder, "Why college? I just want to play." But Dad stood firm on this. He believed that everyone is not fortunate enough to be able to make a steady living as a performing musician, and that

Scotty should get a teaching credential in college as a back up, something he himself had not done and regretted. World War II had interrupted Dad's career. Not qualifying for the Army with most of his musical contemporaries, where he could have continued his vocation and maintained his contacts, changed the course of his life irrevocably. Without a more rounded education, there was nothing he had to fall back on, making some times very financially tenuous. Scotty accepted Dad's advice reluctantly, lamenting, "Dad got to make his mistakes, I need to learn from my own as well. After all, one sometimes needs to read the book themselves, rather than accept someone else's opinion."

Early in his senior year at high school, Scotty had an accident while playing basketball at the YMCA. He smashed into somebody and cut his upper lip, requiring six stitches. Being away from the horn for a couple of weeks wasn't the worst of it. He was so dissatisfied with his playing once he got back to it that he practiced even more, if that was possible, trying to find a way around the problem. He became convinced that the injury, which caused a visible droop on one side of his lip, had irreparably altered his embouchure and affected his playing.

During Scotty's junior and senior years Dad started taking us out to hear some of the famous musicians who were playing in Geneva or nearby cities, such as Tony Bennett, the Mills Brothers, Nat King Cole, Stan Kenton, and Duke Ellington. Leroy Vinnegar was with Dizzy Gillespie when he played Geneva, and Dad, Scotty and I talked about how the bassist hummed all the while he was playing, a habit Scotty later developed as well. At the Zoot Sims concert in Rochester, Scotty was so blown away he was impatient for the intermission to end. I wasn't invited to see Ellington or Kenton, who also appeared out of town, since Scotty had invited his buddies along. He talked about the Ellington experience for weeks, shaking his head in disbelief of how wonderful what he heard was … how they could "fool with the melody" and make it so much more.

Gordon Hoffman, a friend and classmate, relates his special memory of Scotty. "In April of '53 he invited me to go with him and his dad to see Stan Kenton's Orchestra at Sampson Air Force Base. It was an incredible experience for me. Maynard Ferguson, Lee Konitz, Frank Rossolino, and so many more great jazz performers. It was wonderful." Another high school band mate and the Rhythm Aires drummer, Bob Wooley[2] wrote in a 1996 article in *Bass World* magazine, "As a high school senior, Scotty and I attended a Stan Kenton concert at the Syracuse (NY) War Memorial. We sat there in awe listening to Maynard Ferguson, Stan Getz, and Shelly Manne with his incredible cymbal work. Probably the greatest collection of jazz musicians in the world. On the way back to the car after the concert Scott said to me, 'I'm going to play with those guys someday.' I replied 'Yeah, and I'm going to cut Shelly Manne.' Scotty didn't say anything else but I could tell he was serious. He was always serious when it came to his music."

With college in the offing and since string study was required of music majors at Ithaca, he and Dad began discussing what instrument he should play. Dad suggested the double bass since it would be a nice addition to his group at Belhurst, and he could play with him on weekends and over school holidays. My friend Gail, Brownie's daughter, was the school orchestra's bassist and Scotty began taking a real interest in what she was doing. Gail relates, "During orchestra Scotty kept saying, 'Gail, come over here by me to play.' He wanted to hear what I was playing on bass. I used to die fourteen deaths because I never thought I was worthy of his attention to me."

In the spring of their senior year, 1954, Bob Umiker and Scotty headed to Ithaca to audition for college. Bob was driving his family's 1949 Cadillac. Approaching the first intersection as they arrived in town, Bob braked for a stop but the pedal went all the way to the floor. They crashed into the car ahead of them waiting for the light. Scotty and Bob didn't make it to their auditions that day, but after they were rescheduled, both were accepted.

Scotty's immediate future as a college freshman at Ithaca majoring in music was now foremost on the agenda. Brownie helped Scotty get a small scholarship at the high school and through wealthy and influential contacts he made at Belhurst, Dad was able to secure a second loan on our home to provide the other needed funds. In the fall of 1954, Scott LaFaro headed off to Ithaca College.

Scott wrote in his girlfriend's high school yearbook, "I'm going to really study this time; it won't be like high school because now I realize what I've waited to do since I started taking clarinet lessons. I'm going to practice until I've become as good as Konitz, Desmond, Getz and Sims rolled altogether and then I'll still practice some more. For the rest of (our lives) we'll live, eat and sleep modern jazz. There is something about music that I could never explain to you. I just go crazy when I hear it and I get the wildest feelings when I, myself, play it. I know that I can become a top-flite [sic] performer and I will realize that ambition."

FAMILY CHRISTMAS, 1953. DAD, SCOTT, SIS, LINDA, MOM.

SCOTT AT HOME PIANO, 1954

SCOTT (ON RIGHT) AS STUDENT BAND DIRECTOR, WITH MUSIC DEPARTMENT
DIRECTOR, GODFREY "BROWNIE" BROWN, AL DAVIDS, AND GAIL BROWN

1954 SENIOR PROM: SCOTT WITH ANNA MARIE

SCOTT SENIOR PICTURE, 1954

• CHAPTER 5 •

BEGINNING BASS TO BUDDY AND BAKER

IN THE FALL OF 1954, when Scotty was preparing to leave for college, Dad bought him his first bass, a light-colored Kaye, at Levi's, a shop across the street from the Eastman Theater in Rochester, and arranged for him to take a few bass lessons from Nick D'Angelo.[1] Nick was in the Air Force and leading the jazz ensemble at nearby Sampson Air Base. He was also gigging around the area, which is how he and Dad met. One night at Belhurst, shortly after Scotty had played a clarinet concerto with the Finger Lakes Symphony, Dad told Nick that Scotty was feeling frustrated because he couldn't find his niche improvising on the clarinet. Dad also mentioned to Nick that Scotty liked the sound of the bass, and since he had to study a stringed instrument as part of his college curriculum, he should begin private study with Nick.

From that point on Scotty made the trip back home almost every week to study with Nick. Nick used the Franz Simandl books 1 and 2, *Etudes for Double Bass and Piano*, which Nick called the "Bible of Bass Study" at that time.

"Scotty and I were only two years different in age—we had a lot of laughs," Nick remembers. "Scotty had a great smile. He was serious about the bass as opposed to students who wanted to be able to join a group and simply get by. He was determined he was going to be a master player—there was no questioning, albeit he didn't articulate that, but there was no question in my mind. I wasn't surprised when he was voted by *Down Beat* and everybody as the best upcoming bass player and I wasn't surprised when I got the Bill Evans recordings. He sent me a tape of him with Victor Feldman too. None of it surprised me. I just knew it. An absolute phenomenon."

He continues: "Scotty just couldn't get enough—he just practiced and practiced. Constantly. With Scotty it wasn't the general developmental things that we see—I mean like 'whoa'—he made quantum leaps—I'm talking about quantum! He just picked up everything so fast! Scotty had long fingers, big hands. I was using two fingers like a guitar. He got to doing three fingers. I remember we'd do the bowing exercise and then do it pizzicato—that's what he was interested in. Scotty just absorbed—like a sponge."

Scotty arrived at Ithaca College with determination and full of enthusiasm because at last he would be focusing on the music courses that interested him. Only European History and English Composition were outside this realm. He studied the clarinet and was in chorus, band, and marching band. He continued double bass lessons in a class with Forrest Sanders, a cellist at Ithaca who taught bass to Scotty verbally, since he did not play that instrument himself. In a matter of weeks Scotty became consumed with the bass.

Since 1968 Ithaca College's beautiful South Hill campus has overlooked the city below. But in the fifties, the college was in downtown Ithaca. Practice rooms used by the students in those days were converted army Quonset huts, with walls so thin that not only could you hear the student practicing next door, but one former classmate of Scotty's recalls the slide of a trombone breaking right through the wall. Decosta Dawson, then a sophomore pianist at Ithaca, said he and Scotty would regularly practice in the barracks past midnight. Former college classmate and friend, Tony Mele, now a retired professor of music at University of Massachusetts in Lowell, remembers that Scotty began practicing six to twelve hours a day, a habit he maintained for the rest of his life. Tony last saw Scotty in early 1961 at Trudy Heller's Versailles club in New York. Scotty was in town for a gig with Stan Getz and popped in to hear Morgana King. Tony suggested they get together for dinner, but Scotty said he only came into the city to work. He was living out on Long Island and needed his time for practice.

Many of Scotty's former classmates at Ithaca went on to important careers in music as performers, conductors, composers, musical directors, and educators: Paul Jeffrey, Richard (Dick) deBenedictis, Decosta Dawson, Elwood "Woody" Peters, Dick Ford. Tony Mele, and Phil Klein.[1]

Paul Jeffrey, who played with Dizzy, Mingus, and Monk and is now emeritus professor of jazz studies at Duke University, became friends with Scotty at Ithaca. He relates that at one point he and Scotty decided to try painting. "We bought some oils, etc. and set out to paint pictures of Gerry Mulligan, among others. After about three months and not liking the results, we bagged it," Paul recalls. He also relates an incident that strained their relationship. "I was mad at Scotty for quite a time. We had been playing in the college concert band, Scotty on clarinet, me on sax. The school was forming a new big band. There were two sax chairs but one was already given to someone. Both Scotty and I wanted the other. Scotty happened to own the music that was going to be used, so he pulled rank, as it were, and took the chair. I was really steamed. I thought, as did a lot of others by this time, that Scotty should have played the bass." Conversations with other friends from Scotty's days at Ithaca confirm Paul's opinion. Dick deBenedictis recalls Scotty's sax playing as average, but "he was a phenom on the bass."

The more Scotty lost himself in the bass the spottier his attendance became in his other classes. Academics were definitely on the back burner, with twenty-six recorded absences. He even got an "F" in clarinet, his major instrument. Scotty earned average grades in harmony and other music classes. The only "A" he managed was in ear training.

By the end of his first semester in college, the only time he spent playing clarinet or saxophone was in the classroom. This benefited his roommate, Gerry Zampino, another clarinet major. He and Scotty shared a rented one-room apartment at the Basinelli family home on Lake Street. Gerry never forgot Scotty's generosity. "I really connected with the clarinet at a young age. I had a Selmer. Scotty had a Buffet, considered the Cadillac of clarinets. He said to me one day 'Now look, I'm not going to be a clarinet player—take mine—I'll use yours.' So we switched for the remainder of the year." Gerry, now retired, went on to a career as principal clarinetist with the Syracuse Symphony for thirty-six years.

Scotty somehow found time for the usual college activities, joining Phi Mu Alpha, the music fraternity. Another friend, Reese Markewich, then a student at Cornell, recalls how his father carried a drunken Scotty home on his back after a night of partying. Former classmate Dick Ford remembers his classmate: "Scotty would spend hours at Lentz' record store with a headset on in a listening booth, playing jazz—Shorty Rogers, Bud Shank, Zoot Sims, Art Pepper. Commit stuff to memory. Scotty heard stuff others didn't hear."

An attractive blonde sales clerk at Lentz' sold Scotty his first Miles Davis record and must have made nearly as big an impression on him as Miles did. Scotty began spending time in the park across the street from the record shop and eventually managed to meet Suzanne Stewart on a more personal basis. She was a senior at the local high school and a very talented vocalist. They began dating and worked at some of the local clubs together. Suzanne recalls Scotty's obsession with the calluses on his fingers, an element of his bass playing. He was careful not to let his hands get too wet, and always dried them quickly. She also remembers fondly when he purchased his first tux. Dating soon developed into a very serious relationship, and by Christmas that year, Scotty brought Suzanne home to meet the family. She shared my bedroom during the visit and the seeds of our friendship were sown.

To earn money to help with expenses, Scotty began to get gigs around Ithaca. He played the sax with a group at the Chanticleer, a club still operating at the corner of State and Cayuga streets, and also played at Joe's Restaurant on West Buffalo Street in a group led by Charlie Delgado. When talking to Suzanne in the summer of 2005, she told me that during some of these gigs, arguments often ensued: "Scotty was playing sax and some bass. The original bass player, Bill Schott, was a fine player actually, but Scott was always telling him how to play. Ultimately, Scott quit. Scott was light years ahead. He heard notes in chords no one else was hearing, at least not in Ithaca. Scott related what you played with who you were. He was very intolerant of bad players, both musically and personally. He had a very sophisticated repertoire of standards and new music: 'You Don't Know What Love Is,' 'Don't Explain,' 'Detour,' 'Spring Can Really Hang You Up the Most,' 'Lush Life,' and 'Let's Get Lost.'"

Phil Klein, professor emeritus at Onondaga Community College in Syracuse, was twenty-five and in Ithaca College's master's program when he met Scotty. Phil remembers:

Scotty had a great harmonic ear. When he'd hear beautiful new harmonic sounds, he would get very excited and exclaim, "Wow! Show me what that is!" I'd play the progressions and he would watch my hands intently. Then he'd sit at the piano and try to play them with my help. We'd discuss what was happening harmonically and why it worked. In addition, he had what is called a "great bass ear," sensing which of the notes of the chord are meant to create forward movement, forming a bass line. Relatively few people can do this. They may hear inner harmony notes, but think vertically instead of horizontally. This type of bass player simply runs up and down the chord notes, instead of moving linearly. Since Scotty had a perfect bass ear and a marvelous harmonic sense he was able to improvise with Bill Evans melodically and rhythmically, thereby creating a new concept of bass playing, where the bass part interacted with all of the elements of music: rhythm, melody and harmony. The drummer contributed rhythmically and a marvelous and innovative contrapuntal jazz came to be. These guys [Evans, LaFaro and Paul Motian] were the right players in the right place and time.

Phil also tells of a gig with Scotty at Joe's Italian Restaurant. "Scotty wasn't playing what I expected—regular bass lines … either two-beat or four-beat." Phil said he took Scotty to task for playing so many extra notes instead of sticking to playing in 2 or 4. "I didn't know what the heck he was doing. What I was chewing him out about was an early manifestation of a style that would change all jazz bass playing!"

Throughout the rest of the year Scotty and Suzanne spent as much time as possible checking out the music scene in Ithaca, Geneva, and nearby Syracuse. In the Ward district of Syracuse he lined up some gigs at the Embassy Club. The Ward was an African-American neighborhood in the southeastern area of the city, and home to many jazz clubs that brought in a lot of the touring jazz performers in the 1940s and 1950s.

Scotty's rapid development on the bass soon became apparent to everyone. Former high school classmate and friend Gordon Hoffman recalls: "Scotty called one day when he was on break from Ithaca and asked me to come over to his house. He put on some music. I don't recall what the music was. I wish that I did. He began to play the bass along with it. I was in awe. It was as though he had been playing the bass for years."

As the end of his first year at Ithaca neared, jazz was definitely on Scotty's mind. He and Paul Jeffrey would argue about where jazz was happening, New York or the West Coast. Scotty was also thinking about leaving school and heading to Los Angeles, and he was getting varying advice regarding this from his friends and classmates. Tony Mele told me he probably gave Scotty bad advice. He sided with our dad's view that Scotty should stay in college so he'd have something to fall back on. Phil Klein also tried to convince Scotty to get his education behind him before embarking on adventures in the jazz world. This angered Scotty and he and Phil did not speak for a long while. Another friend, trumpet player Woody Peters, encouraged Scotty to head west.

Scotty was earning money playing now so it was decided that a new, better bass should be bought. Another trip to Rochester and he and Dad settled on a Mittenwald made by a respected violin maker established centuries ago in the southern German city of the same name. Scotty fell in love with his new instrument and it soon became an extension of himself.

When Scotty came home for the summer, resigned to returning to college in the fall, he joined the family on our usual daily beach outings and reconnected with old friends. "The summer of 1955 when Scotty came home from Ithaca, we played tennis," remembers old friend Bob Bennett. "He was no technician on the court, but he was agile and persistent, eventually winning. When he shook my hand, I felt the strength in his hand. I was surprised, but he simply attributed it to his practicing the bass a lot. It was, no doubt, true."

Scotty was also playing any gigs he could in the area as well as playing with Dad at Belhurst. Sundays often found Scott and Suzanne jamming at Club 86 in Geneva. Along with other local musicians, Ray DeSio played trombone and on the piano was Joe Kloess, an airman stationed at Sampson. By early 1956, Scotty, Suzanne, Ray, and Joe would all be with the Buddy Morrow Orchestra. Scotty and Joe became good friends during this time.

Scotty's bass teacher, Nick D'Angelo, relates how Scotty got his first big-time job:

> In the early fall of 1955 I got a call from an old pal who was now playing with the Buddy Morrow Orchestra. The group needed a bass player and he asked me, "How about comin' on the road?" Since I had just started teaching at Hobart and also was doing another year at Eastman, I said I couldn't do it, but I knew somebody. I discussed it with Scotty and his reaction was "Do you think I could do it?" I said, "Are you kidding? It's a piece of cake, big band stuff." So I called back right away and said I've got a kid who is interested, and was told to send him up. They were on tour and currently in Toronto. That's how Scotty got that job. I remember telling Scotty, "Look, you go on the gig—the first couple of nights you take the book with you back to the hotel and you go through it—practice a little—you're not going to have any problems with it—big band stuff is a piece of cake. You're at the bottom of the group trying to propel it, that's all." It's not like how he morphed into a marvelous dialogue player with the trio [Bill Evans].

Nick continues: "I remember the other advice I gave him. When he got out to the west coast he called me and said 'I'm going to stay on the west coast.' I said, 'Get yourself a good teacher—someone with the L.A. Phil.' Scotty was phenomenal. He had the capacity. It's motivation. He was highly motivated. God, he just wanted it. Hate using a trite adage but he took to it like a fish to water. He just sucked it up."

The Morrow group was known as a big band with a big beat, heavy blues. "Night Train" was their most popular hit. They did a lot of brassy tunes. Buddy had a lot of good jazz players with him, according to his clarinetist and saxophone player, Dick Johnson. Crossing the country with Buddy Morrow on his first big band tour was just a wow to Scotty. Scotty would call home every time he got to a new city to tell the family where he was and what he was doing, seeing, and learning. He said he'd look for LaFaros and LoFaros in the phone books of every city he visited, but never came across any. Besides his letters to me, he'd take the time to send special postcards to sister Linda, now ten.

There is a note in the book *Jumptown: The Golden Years of Portland Jazz, 1942–1957* by Robert Dietsche: "The Buddy Morrow Orchestra was playing at Jantzen Beach.[2] Buddy Morrow, top heavy with jazz talent, wanted to play the jazz-flavored arrangements of Walt Stewart. Leroy Anderson, who became music department head at Clakamas Community College was in the trombone section. The saxophone solos were by the great Dick Johnson. Danny Stiles did most of the trumpet work and on bass was the man who would revolutionize the instrument in the next decade, Scott LaFaro. After Jantzen they headed to Frat Hall. Evidently LaFaro put on a display that had other bass players there wondering if they were playing the same instrument."

Dietsche continues: "When Morrow was in Portland in 1982 for a dance date at the Hilton Hotel, he told an interviewer that he had no idea LaFaro would be the rage of the sixties. 'That's Scott LaFaro on Walt Stewart's arrangement of "You'd Be So Nice to Come Home To" from the *Golden Trombone* album we made with Mercury in the mid-fifties.'"

At Christmas the band took a break and he was back home with the family for the holiday.

In a conversation I had in the fall of 2006 with Buddy Morrow, he fondly recalled: "Scott fit into my group beautifully. His bass playing was impeccable, a wonderful musician always trying to work with the drummer and the pianist—the foundation for the band. We were a band which was dedicated at the time to mainly rhythm and blues. We were the kind that played a fraction, a millimeter behind. We had to have a strong rhythm section and he was definitely of that caliber … he could do it … he could keep good time." Buddy said, "We played tricks on him, of course. He was the youngest and extremely vulnerable. And I saw a lot of development, definitely. He was a dedicated person. He was intolerant of anyone who wasn't giving his best. Most important, I saw that he wanted to improve and he did. He was always practicing, developing. I might have been annoyed at the time but I never would stop anyone because I went through those growing periods myself. When we got to the west coast in the fall of 1956 about seven or eight men stayed in Los Angeles. That Scotty wanted to go on to greener pastures, I don't blame him. He was a tremendous talent."

To Suzanne in a letter dated February 7, 1956, and written on stationery from the Hotel Wolverine in Detroit, Michigan, Scotty wrote: "I'm pretty happy tonight, because of the compliments some of the members of the Ellington band gave my bass work." His letters to Suzanne indicated that he missed her a lot and later that February, he had Suzanne send Buddy an audition tape. She joined them on the road in March.

Occasionally Morrow would let his band members do a jazz set during intermissions, but he often had to remind Scott to play what was written for the band. That spring the Morrow group was traveling the same circuit as the Modern Jazz Quartet. Back again in Detroit, Suzanne recounts an incident. "While Scotty was practicing in his room at the Wolverine Hotel, MJQ bassist Percy Heath heard him as he passed in the hall and knocked on Scott's door. He said to Scotty, 'If you're going to go to all that trouble, man, why not play guitar?' To which Scotty replied, 'Because bass is my instrument.'"

As Suzanne tells it, Scotty's bass playing was always first and foremost in his mind. In Memphis, where they were playing the Hotel Peabody for a couple of weeks in June, the group was spending their down time poolside. Hot as it was, Suzanne couldn't get Scotty into the pool. He begged off, saying: "I can't, I've got some good callus going." Suzanne continues: "One thing I know for sure is that Scott had a profound influence on who I am musically and personally. In fact, when I started singing again some 15 or 20 years after being with Scott the influence started popping up—in the dedication and concentration it takes to get one's music off the ground, so to speak."

Scotty's first professional recordings were with the Buddy Morrow Orchestra: *Golden Trombone* was followed by *Let's Have a Dance Party* and *Shorty Tunes*, done in New York and Chicago. Even though he was becoming anxious about playing jazz, Scotty was pleased to be recorded and proudly sent off the albums to the family in Geneva, where in June, our new sister Lisa was born.

While on the road, Scotty had gotten formally engaged to Suzanne, and they began planning a wedding when the group got to California. But before it could happen, Suzanne changed her mind, quit the group, and flew home. She described her change of heart as a classic case of cold feet as she contemplated the distance from home and her family and Scotty's intensity, which she admits she found "a little—no, a *lot*—scary."

Two of the alumni of Buddy's orchestra, baritone sax player John Barbe and trombonist Gil Falco, remember Scotty as being quiet and warm, and always practicing. He forged deeper relationships with the fellows who rode in the same car during the tour.

Dick Johnson, who now leads the re-formed Artie Shaw Orchestra, was with the Morrow Orchestra when Scotty came on board. They became friendly and he has many fond memories of those days:

> Scotty was looking all the time to play. He would have played twenty-four hours a day if he could. He chose me to be his partner in crime, every time he found sessions ... "let's go here, let's go there." We used to stay at the Wolverine in Detroit, so did other musicians. Percy Heath was there about three of the times ... Scotty called me in my room, and asked me if I'd like to play with two bass players. Percy couldn't have been nicer. Scott was learning a mile a minute. Scott lived for the bass.
>
> If he didn't find a place to play, he'd be practicing all his waking hours in his room. Scott would get up and grab the bass and start playing, way ahead of everyone. At the President Hotel in New York, we weren't allowed to play in the rooms, so we got permission to practice in the cellar. We'd practice three or four hours down in the musty old cellar.
>
> We had a drummer, Jimmy McConnell, he had diabetes. Once also at the Wolverine Scotty saved his life. Scott passed by Jimmy's hotel room and the door was partially open and Jimmy was lying on the bed in a diabetic coma. Scott called down to the desk and got someone up there to help. It seems that Jimmy had been calling down, but the operator thought he probably was just juiced or something and didn't get him

any help. Scotty yelled at everyone, blasted the place out. (Funny, 'cause they—Scotty and Jimmy—really couldn't stand each other.)

After the orchestra got to Los Angeles and playing the Palladium, I had the time of my life with Scotty. Scotty found jam sessions all over the place. He rented a car so we could get around to them. Scott insisted I go. He'd call me with what our sitting-in schedule was. The guys accepted us pretty good. We'd go to this club to hear Red Mitchell. He was playing his butt off. Scott was completely knocked out with Red's virtuosity. One night I spoke to Red to give him regards from pianist Dave McKenna and he came over to our table. That's when Scotty first got introduced to Red. After that gig, Scotty decided to stay on the coast.

I saw him a time or two after that. I met him by chance one afternoon in New York City. He had a few days off from Chet Baker and was at The Loft, a place near the village. He said, "Dick, come to The Loft. I want you to hear me." Scott was excited, said, "I can play medium tempos now." He had had some difficulty with them. I went. He sounded unbelievable. He asked me "How am I doing?" The last time I saw him was in a jazz cub—Storyville—across from some the stables in Boston. He was there with Monk. Scotty seemed terribly depressed. He was drugged about something that was going on with Monk, but he gave me a hug. That was 1960.

One of the best stories I heard about him was from some of my musician friends in Cincinnati. Scott had come through town on tour, came into a club there after hours. Scott was on the bandstand playing all the tunes they wanted him to. They said Scott played so ridiculously, no one ever heard a bass player play like that. Then they were going to play a tune, "Wouldn't You," Scott started it really fast. There was a great alto and great trumpet player, it was a little too much for them and guys started getting off the stand left and right.

Scott was playing alone on the stand, playing fours with himself, the Scott LaFaro show. He did twenty choruses. He was the only one left on the stand, ended it up, put his bass away, walked out. Unbelievable, no one could keep up with what he was doing. They let him do it, and he certainly did it.

Scotty was always surging forward, changing the function of the bass—to the nth degree. I look back and realize my debt to him. For insisting I hang out musically with him. He took me along for the ride, picking me to hang out with. He knew that I would go. I tagged along with him and became a better player for it. I loved him for it. It was an enjoyable ride. I'm very flattered that I knew him, proud all of my life that I had that time with Scott. We did have a ball."

In September, Scotty decided it was time to leave Buddy Morrow. His heart was really with jazz. His last gig with Buddy was at the Hollywood Palladium from September 5 to the twenty-third. When he wasn't practicing or playing, he was getting around town to hear anyone who was there and looking for what he might do next.

After Scott sat in with Chet Baker after hours one night in October, at the urging of his tenor player Phil Urso, Chet asked Scotty to join his group for their next tour. Also playing with Chet at that time was Bobby Timmons on piano and Larance Marable on drums. Scotty was finally realizing what he had been working and hoping for—a gig with the real jazz guys. He was thrilled out of his mind at this development and called home to tell Dad and the family his great news. This wonderful prospect also probably helped get him through the rather abrupt end of his relationship with Suzanne. In an interview with Martin Williams for *Jazz Review* (August 1960), Scotty had praise for Marable: "I found out so much from Larance, a lot of it just from playing with him." But before the club dates set to start in November, Chet Baker was busted for drugs.

Walter Norris recalls first meeting Scotty at a jam session around this time. "I couldn't believe my ears; his thinking was a few years ahead of most bassists and he definitely was a virtuoso. He was twenty, I was five years older and married. He had just recently arrived, so Mandy and I invited him over for Thanksgiving dinner. His conversation pertained to music and little else. He was completely focused, to the point of obsession, on improving constantly; at all hours. I recognized a quality in Scotty's character that is rarely found: he was in awe of no one and although a few at the top were acknowledged, he was determined to be himself. I realized that his was a mission, only to improve. Let me add that he was a very fast learner and had a great sense of humor."

When Chet cleared up his problems in Los Angeles, the group finally hit the road. They played at Frazier Hall at Idaho State College on November 27. A reviewer noted that the tunes they played included "Slightly Above Moderate," "Tommyhawk," and "Ray's Idea." In late December Scotty came home for the holidays and then headed off to a gig with Chet in Florida.

Drummer Larance Marable remembers the time Scotty spent working for the troubled trumpet player and vocalist: "Scotty was a hell of a bassist. His bass playing was out of this world. He was before his time. But Chet and Scotty were from different worlds, traveled in different circles." Suzanne also recalls that "Scotty phoned often during his time with Chet, complaining of Baker's irresponsibility and waste of his wonderful talent." Scotty would always be sad about this situation.

SCOTT ON TENOR AT ITHACA COLLEGE

DAD'S BELHURST ORCHESTRA, SUMMER 1955. SCOTT IS THIRD FROM LEFT IN BACK. DAD IS AT FAR RIGHT.

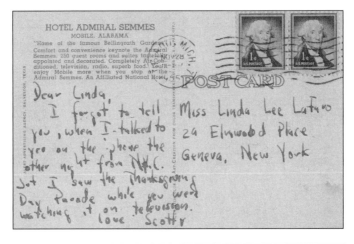

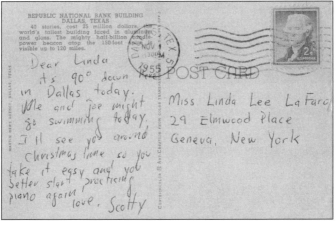

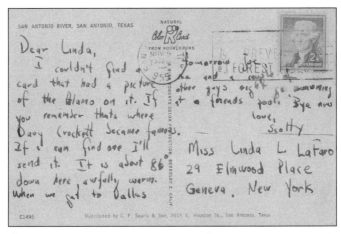

Scotty's postcards to ten-year-old sister Linda, while on the road with the Morrow Orchestra, 1955.

1956. BUDDY MORROW ORCHESTRA. SCOTT IS ON BASS, AND HIS FIANCÉE, SUZANNE STEWART, IS VOCALIST.

SCOTTY AND SUZANNE STEWART, 1956

CHAPTER 6

TRANSPOSITION

1957

AFTER THE BAKER QUINTET'S BOOKING at the Ball & Chain in Miami ended in January 1957, they headed for a date in St. Louis. Chet's father acted as chauffeur, driving their big Cadillac while the guys generally slept or listened to music on the radio. During this tour Scotty called home quite upset, remarking that driving through one of the Southern states, some folks that he called "ridiculously stupid people" derided them and threw rocks at the car for the simple fact that folks of different color were riding in the same vehicle. He could not tolerate intolerance. We had grown up in an area that had a long history of concern about human rights issues. There were the underground railroad and safe houses during the days of slavery. The women's rights movement had its start here. An African-American girl was queen of his high school class prom. And while he certainly was aware that many were not so enlightened, this was his first brush with the realities of the situation.

Phil Urso shared hotel rooms with Scotty for a while on this tour, but then begged out of this arrangement since "Scotty was up and practicing by nine in the morning in the room and I couldn't sleep." Phil continues: "He was one of the greatest bassists I've ever played with. He was an out front bass player. He started the single string soloing. A lot of bassists started copying him."

While playing with the Baker group in St. Louis at Peacock Alley, Scotty met pianist Pat Moran who recalls they "hit it off right away and became good friends." Baker booked January 25 through February 2, following Pat who was booked January 11 through the nineteenth. Pat recalls, "I met Scotty when he was playing with Chet Baker. Chet was pretty funny. He had just made an album where he sang and after the gig that night, he sat on the bandstand and sang 'Look for the Silver Lining' to some girl. We were all cracking up. He didn't have a tooth in front, but was very handsome."

Chet had signed onto the annual Birdland tour, the Bird-land Stars of '57 or Birdland All-Stars Revue. The tour, which opened at Carnegie Hall in New York City Friday, February 15, was to run through most of March. The all-star tour included Sarah Vaughn, Billy Eckstein, the Count Basie Band with Joe Williams, Bud Powell, Phineas Newborn, Lester Young, Zoot Sims, and the Terry Gibbs Quartet. To promote the tour, on February 14, Scotty made his first television appearance with the quintet on the *Tonight Show* with Steve Allen. A recording from this appearance is included on the CD *The 2 Trumpet Geniuses of the Fifties: Brownie and Chet* (Philology Records).

Chet's group did not appear on the tour's stop in Rochester, New York, since they had a prior booking at a jazz club in Philadelphia just before the tour was to play there at the Academy of Music. The family was disappointed that we wouldn't have the opportunity to see Scotty in Rochester, which is just forty-eight miles from our home in Geneva. To assuage my great dismay, I was able to arrange a short trip by train to Philadelphia to meet Scotty. My first night in Philadelphia was spent at the club hearing the group, meeting the personnel, and sharing the time between sets chatting with Scotty. He was a bit down, expressing his dismay at Chet's drug use. Scotty, as he often did, shook his head in disbelief at how guys chose to "screw up" so badly. Many did this mistakenly, he said. "A lot of guys think that Charlie Parker was great because of his drug use—that it somehow added to his genius—and maybe it'll do the same for them. Yardbird was great in spite of his drug use." He said that of all the musicians he had met, he was most unable to understand Gerry Mulligan's drug use. He thought Mulligan was really quite an intellectual and it made no sense to Scotty that he allowed himself to get caught in the drug habit.

The next day we had a late breakfast. Scotty wanted to introduce me to Scrapple (a Pennsylvania Dutch concoction of pork trimmings in cornmeal, boiled, molded, sliced, then fried). Then he was going to rehearse for the tour concert at the club they had played the night before. Though the weather was nippy, the club was not too far away so we decided to walk rather than hail a cab. Just as we rounded the corner, two police cars pulled up and four officers entered the club. Scotty tugged at my sleeve and said, "Just keep walking past." Which we did.

Later, when Scotty learned Chet would not be playing that night, he decided we should take the train over to New York and, while waiting to see what was next, have some fun there. We hit some tourist sights, visited with some old pals and went around to Birdland to hear whoever was on the bill.

The Birdland Tour dropped the Chet Baker Quintet because of the arrest on narcotics charges in Philadelphia. Scotty said that as soon as he could, he'd probably leave the group and head back to California. He loved it there and by April Scotty was back in Los Angeles. He phoned home to let us know he got there but didn't as yet know where he'd be staying and would phone again in a few days when he was settled.

On Monday of this week the world lost its greatest asset.
It wasn't the head of a state, an eminent physician, or a
leading industrialist—it was a guy named Joe! A warm,
sensitive, generous, thoroughly likeable man who was an
accomplished artist and an outstanding father. Knowing Joe was an aesthetic experience and an inspiration
toward brotherhood. He lived with an ease, attitude and
graciousness that the average would call naïve. Yet he
lived, he was a gentleman, he was Joe.

Anonymous Eulogy
Geneva Daily Times
May 24, 1957

"That does it—now I know I'll be dead when I'm
25."

Scotty
May 24, 1957

I got a phone call at work from Mom mid-morning May 20,
1957. She told me Dad wasn't feeling well and was coming by to
see Dr. Erich. I had been working for about six months for Drs.
Erich and Hildegard Hirsch, an internist and an ob-gyn. They
had their offices in their home in Geneva, as do many physicians
in smaller towns. My heart started racing and I broke out in a
nervous sweat because Dad was not one to consider a visit to a
doctor, as he was more a disciple of holistic medicine. Just a week
earlier we had had an exchange at the breakfast table. I suggested
that he cut down on eating eggs in light of the latest findings
about the correlation between eggs, cholesterol, and heart disease.
When Dad arrived, he looked grey and explained that he was
having some mid-chest pain but was pretty certain that it was
indigestion—he had eaten quite heartily the prior evening. Dr.
Erich had me assist him with an EKG, but shortly after the start
of the procedure, he stopped, told me to take Dad directly to
the hospital, and said he'd make the call and follow us there. He

gave Dad some nitroglycerine to dissolve under his tongue as we settled him into the car, our old 1947 standard-shift Buick.

I don't think the hospital is quite a mile from the doctor's office, but it was an eternity to me. I was shaking and nervous, trying to maneuver the gearshift while paying attention to Dad. The car was bucking under my tentative attempts at shifting gears. Dad started to take some really noisy breaths, then slumped. When I reached the emergency entrance, I frantically bolted into the hospital. Dad had died in the car.

When Dr. Erich and I had at last left the hospital and went home to give Mom, who was in her seventh month of another pregnancy, the news, she crumpled to the floor. My next and only thought was how to reach Scotty. The idea struck me to call information in Los Angeles and ask for the numbers of whatever radio stations they could give me. I asked the very first one I dialed for the name of the jazz station. I immediately phoned them, explaining my dilemma, pleading for them to announce on the air that if Scott LaFaro, or any one who knew him, was listening, please have him call home. Not two hours later, Scotty called and I gave him the news. He headed home. Scotty hadn't heard the radio plea himself and I forgot to ask him who did. I still wonder who it was, so if you're reading this, thank you.

After the funeral services and before all the mourners arrived back at our home for the wake, Scotty and I wandered forlornly from room to room. Displayed on one of the walls were a bridge from Dad's violin and one from Scotty's bass. Scotty remarked about the irony that the smaller bridge represented the much larger talent. After a while when the house got crowded, Scotty and I went outside. His mood, already morose, really darkened, and as he thoughtfully, gently toed at some of the stones in the driveway where we stood, he voiced his premonition that he would die young. I tried lightheartedly to cajole him out of this, but he said that he had always felt this way and now he was certain.

Before he returned to Los Angeles, he convinced Mom and me that perhaps the future of the family should be made in California. It was decided that once things settled down after the impending birth of our next brother or sister, I would join him in Los Angeles and together we would ready things for the rest of the family to relocate.

Scotty was living in the spare bedroom of a house owned by Herb and Lorraine Geller. Scotty had met alto saxophonist Herb Geller through Lorraine, who was the house pianist at the Lighthouse in Hermosa Beach, where Scotty occasionally sat in. Herb and Lorraine had recently bought a house nestled in the Hollywood Hills. They invited Scotty to move into their spare bedroom, solving his housing problem until I arrived in early October. He loved the solitude of the place and being surrounded by the scrub, natural state of the vegetation. He sent home photos with comments and started setting out the advantages of the family's impending move. In the pictures he looked happy.

Herb had a great record collection of jazz recordings. Scotty said he heard a lot of people for the first time listening to Herb's records. And he practiced, practiced, practiced. Scotty, in an interview with Nat Hentoff for liner notes for the 1958 *Victor Feldman Arrives* album, said about this period, "I couldn't find enough work and besides, I definitely needed the practice." In Los Angeles it took six months to get a union card. Until you had it, you couldn't take studio work or a steady job. Pretty much all you could do was casuals and sit in whenever possible.

Not only was the house in a peaceful and beautiful location, but there were jam sessions at the Gellers' as well. Jack Sheldon, Don Friedman, Terry Trotter, Clare Fischer, and Joe Maini were some of those who would drop in. Scotty would make the rounds with Herb, Don, and other friends to the many clubs that were featuring jazz. He did some fill-in work with the band for singer Marigold Hill at the Stardust Room in Long Beach. Another casual gig Scotty had was a garden wedding with Joanne Grauer, jazz pianist and teacher, who was then just seventeen. She told me she was thrilled to play with such an outstanding player. She had also been working with Gary Peacock and, looking back, she remarks she felt really blessed. She said she believed then that all bass players played that well, but soon thereafter had a rude awakening.

Drummer Freddie Gruber also met Scotty and played with him on casuals—first in a couple of clubs in the El Monte area then later at the Hillcrest with Paul Bley and Dave Pike. Although Scotty worked in Paul Bley's group for just a limited period of time, Paul remembers that when he hired Scotty, he put him in the front. When asked why he was putting the bass player blocking the view of the vibraphone player Paul replied, "because he was the best player in the band. He was a star … he 'paid the rent' because he was a virtuoso player. The only other person who played across all areas like that was Charlie Mingus. Scotty took bass playing to another level. He went to the top of the heap career wise. Nobody could move their fingers around the bass as fast as he could."

Charles Lloyd, composer and saxophonist, has had an incredible personal journey as well as an accomplished career spanning many years in jazz with excursions into many other genres of music. There is a depth to his voice over the phone that is a reflection of the richness of his soul. I was fortunate to be able to talk to Charles about his close friendship with Scotty.

Originally from Memphis, Tennessee, Charles had come to Los Angeles in 1956 to attend the University of Southern California. Scotty met Charles at some jam sessions with Don Cherry late that year and they made an immediate, deep connection. Now that Scotty had returned to Los Angeles, they began to play together, gigging around town with Don, Harold Land, Billy Higgins, Elmo Hope, and Terry Trotter. Charles said he was "still high from those days … we just got together and played. We just loved to play. It was like the holy grail with us. We had our mission. We were just growing, learning. There was such a rich group of people."

Their youthful exuberance—to share the joy they found in their music—brought to mind one particular gig: "We played this wedding in Glendale (a Los Angeles suburb) . It was like a community center or something. The bandstand was behind a white picket fence. There was Billy Higgins, Don Cherry and Scott LaFaro. The pianist was Terry Trotter. Imagine Higgins alone … and Scotty playing together, and Terry … punching out those Bud Powell, Tommy Flanigan chords and stuff. We were so excited to play. We were just making this music … it was very un-picket fence. We were sound Brahmans, we had gone beyond the Concord and the space barriers. We knew we were going to send this couple into infinity with the richness of this indigenous art form … off in bliss in hope—the whole thing. That was our impetus. We didn't get that far. The father ran up, waving his hands. 'Please, please stop. Stop … Please, no more … please just leave. I'll pay you now, just leave.' That union would have been cemented by that music. I'm convinced of it to this day."

Scotty and Charles became very close friends, best friends—sharing stories, dreams and aspirations as well as food and fun. As for music, Charles said, "Scotty had it … he had the magic. He had wonderful integrity, an excellent musician. He had this awesome, adventurous technique. An innovator. He and Ornette were like astronauts. Scotty liked freshness, he was always pushing himself. He was and is enormously important to music."

I was most touched by Charles' deep felt feelings about Scotty: "I really admired and loved Scotty. Scotty was close to my heart, very dear to me. Full of grace and humanity. A beautiful soul. A blessing to the universe." I think that besides their deep friendship, Charles and Scotty shared a purity of heart. As I mentioned previously, in a conversation I had with Scotty during his last visit home in his final year, he talked about "perhaps giving up music and going into electronics because he didn't know if anyone was 'getting him'." Charles got him. He got what Scotty was all about—a search for one's soul through music.

Scotty made other lasting friends during this time. Pianist Don Friedman recalls: "I first heard Scott when he was playing with Buddy Morrow at the Palladium late in '56. Then I was on the road with Buddy DeFranco from November, '56 till July of '57. Buddy asked me to drive a new car he had bought in St. Louis back to LA while he flew, which I did, taking Vic Feldman along. Not long after that I met Scott up at Herb's place and we became good friends. A little later Scotty and I worked a gig with Chet Baker at Peacock Lane on the corner of Hollywood and Western. The gig was for a week. Larance Marable was the drummer and Richie Kamuca the saxophonist. As I recall, Chet didn't finish the week. The cops were looking for him and he literally escaped from the club and never came back. I don't remember if we finished the week without him."

Scotty also met pianist, composer, and arranger Clare Fischer. Clare relates, "Scotty and I became good friends. We had an immediate musical rapport that was sensational. We did a lot of listening and talking. Besides technique, he had governing, control. I think he was the first bass player who was fleet footed in the musical sense." Clare remembers he was in San Jose traveling with Cal Tjader when he heard about Scotty's accident. "What a trauma, it struck me right down—that someone I was developing such a relationship with would suddenly not be there."

Besides jamming at the Gellers', pianist Terry Trotter recalls he and Scotty played pool, went to the movies, and smoked a bit of weed together. "Scotty and I connected in music and as people. He was humorous, funny. With his work he could be difficult and temperamental. He had a wonderful musical gift."

This was the time when a lot of talented musicians were in Los Angeles and would become part of what was known as the West Coast Jazz scene. It was in Los Angeles that Scotty first heard Ray Brown. The swing and perfection in his style really impressed Scotty. Cecelia Brown, Ray's widow, recently recalled that when Ray was teaching clinics he said that Scotty was one of the top five bassists and innovators, putting him in the company of Jimmy Blanton, Oscar Pettiford, Milt Hinton, and Paul Chambers. Scott would love knowing that!

Scotty became friends with other bass players who were in Los Angeles during this time as well. Don Payne, who grew up in nearby Santa Ana, and had just returned from a stint in the U.S. Army. Don was renting a furnished guest house on Glen Green just off Beechwood Drive in the Hollywood Hills. Johnny Mandel lived next door in an identical pad. Scotty would take his bass up and the two of them would practice for hours. Don said that he had been getting help from Percy Heath and wanted to share that with Scott. He added that "Scott was working on the high register—16th note scale partials that became part of his soloing later with Bill Evans. I really like the way he played on recordings with Hampton Hawes and Victor Feldman made there in LA." Neighbors on the same street were Red Mitchell and Leroy Vinnegar. The older two bass players took Don, twenty-five, and Scotty, twenty-two, under their wing, as it were. Scotty came to consider Red Mitchell one of his mentors.

Hal Gaylor, a Canadian who has since worked with performers as disparate as Tony Bennett and Ornette Coleman, was another bass player who was in Los Angeles at the time. He recalls that he and Scotty talked of the coincidence that they both played the clarinet before starting on the bass and that both of their fathers were violinists. They would rehearse together, spend a couple of hours playing, exchanging stuff. Hal said, "No matter what you had, someone else had something else. We'd play for each other. The music was just so exciting, there was just so much going on then. Scotty was a bit isolated, but if you knew him, he had a warm side. He had drive, not a lot of patience. Often he'd be a little cool, but when he got inspired, he got very excited and it showed. Scotty was one of the greatest exponents of jazz of that era. He is important like Jimmy Blanton, Oscar Pettiford and Charlie Mingus." Later in 1958, Don Payne and Hal would drive across the country to New York and when Scotty later returned to New York, he would renew these friendships. Scotty and Don remained friends throughout the rest of Scott's life.

Gary Peacock, who later also played bass with Bill Evans, first met Scotty and heard him play at the Lighthouse. He said,

> I think it was with Stan Levey, Vic Feldman and Richie
> Kamuca. It was scary ... I mean he ... whew ... I
> was listening to him and I thought JC, he was ... A
> wonderful thing that he gave me at that time, without
> giving me anything, was that he showed me what was
> possible ... there was the potential ... there was po-
> tential technically, potential musically ... that hadn't
> even been tapped yet. In that sense he was so far ahead
> of everybody else at that time. It was just scary. But
> also encouraging and enlightening. Inspirational, like
> ... Wow! And he had only been playing for a year and
> a half or two years! That was the other part that was
> scary. In two years he did this? What did he do? Play

twenty-four hours a day? But apparently before that he had some training with the clarinet or something. Scotty kicked everybody's ass.

Also when we met, we talked briefly about always striving, moving forward constantly ... we kinda put the kibosh on that. Brings you more in the moment. What we were doing ... had a tendency to be crowded with all this thinking that's going on, kinda has a tendency to stop to think of what the possibilities are of the moment. But in spite of all that, there was very little of that in his playing.

There was a lot happening in jazz in Los Angeles. Many clubs booked groups a week or a month at a time. Miles Davis and John Coltrane played at Jazz City in Hollywood. Charlie Haden was playing regularly with Paul Bley at the Hillcrest on Washington Boulevard. The IT Club was down the street. The Haig on Wilshire booked Gerry Mulligan. The Slate Brothers on La Cienega. The Renaissance, Crescendo, and Interlude all along Sunset. Cosmo's Alley on Yucca. The guys who weren't working would drop by and sit in during the sets and after hours. The strip clubs, The Pink Pussycat and Largo Strip Club on Sunset Boulevard, booked some cool talent like Herb Geller as well. Duffy's Gaiety at Cahuenga and Franklin, a club run for a time by Sally Marr, Lenny Bruce's mother, booked Joe Maini and Don Payne when Lenny was also on the bill.

Howard Rumsey's Lighthouse in Hermosa Beach was ground zero. There was jazz nightly and, on Sunday, twelve-hour jam sessions. Shorty Rogers, Victor Feldman, Lorraine Geller, Herb Geller, Maynard Ferguson, Bud Shank, Hampton Hawes, Marty Paich, Shelly Manne, Stan Levey, as well as bigger luminaries of the time—Miles Davis and Chet Baker—all played there.

When I spoke with Howard Rumsey in the fall of 2005, he said that "few show progress like Scotty did. I was amazed at the progress I saw in his playing. I saw him for at least four years total. I was so happy every time he came to the Lighthouse because I knew the musicians wanted to play with him and I wanted to hear him. What was evident about Scotty … he had his life organized … he always knew what he was going to do next. He was just outstanding. He had a falsetto sound that was unique and a walking sound that was big, different. I think that coming from a string family he knew what a string bass should sound like. What he accomplished in seven years no other bass player has done. Scotty was very intelligent. In my mind the history of the development of bass playing went from Blanton to Scotty. He and Blanton were bright stars—shooting stars that fell from the skies. His work with Bill was an even greater achievement than that as a soloist. No bass player with Bill has the same empathy as he and Scott had. With all the musicians I've met few have made the impact that Scotty did on me. He had an unlimited capacity."

Summer brought Scotty an opportunity to work with Pat Moran in Lake Tahoe. She recalls: "When we were working, Gene Gammage (the drummer) and I would get frustrated with Scotty—he didn't want to come out and have some fun. It was so beautiful in Tahoe in those days, but he would stay in the cabin and practice two or three hours every day with a metronome, playing exercises from a clarinet exercise book, then go to work and play all night."

Scotty's routine was pretty much the same after I arrived at the beginning of October and we settled into the upper floor apartment of a lovely old hillside house on High Tower Drive in Hollywood, quite close to the Hollywood Bowl. When I arrived with Sandra (Sandy) Upson, a friend and high school sorority sister, we were met by Scotty and Vic Feldman. Victor had first heard Scotty during the Birdland tour in the east. A few months later, they were both in California, sat in at clubs, worked together, respected one another's talent and established a friendship. They were on the same wavelength. Victor had a droll sense of humor and Scotty played to it. They developed a true affection for one another and so not only did Scott want me to meet Victor, but Victor had a car. The drive from the airport is still etched in my memory. It was like "Mr. Toad's Wild Ride" on the Los Angeles Freeway, and colors continued to spin my head during my first fitful night in sunny Southern California, which isn't always so sunny, as I discovered the next morning. The place Scotty chose was lovely and we had a great view from the balcony that ran across the entire front of the house, but everything was seen through the infamous smog. I had just come from the clear, blue-skied farmland of upstate New York and now it actually hurt to breathe! Scotty had failed to alert me to this and when I called him on it, he assured me Los Angeles was worth putting up with this small discomfort. He found it the land of opportunity for him musically and was sure it would prove to be the land of opportunity for our now fatherless family.

My first days were full of the fun of seeing our neighborhood and outfitting our place with whatever dishes, pots and pans, and linens we could with our meager budget at the Five & Dime Store on Hollywood Boulevard. Since Sandy was staying with us only until another friend was to arrive in early December, these outings were often just Scotty and me. He pointed out the twenty-four-hour market, Hughes, at the corner of Highland and Franklin, where he had sighted Paul Newman and Joanne Woodard more than once. We'd have laughs after convincing waiters that we were twins so I could also have a glass of wine with dinner. Scotty turned twenty-one that year but he looked young so they'd card him and then we'd plead that I forgot to bring any ID. We looked not at all alike—fraternal, we'd explain, confounding them. It always worked.

Sandy and I eventually found work and Scotty spent the days practicing. Sandy and I spent nights hanging out at clubs with

Scotty whenever possible if he wasn't playing, or listening when he was. He'd get real excited to take us to something he thought was great. He insisted we come along for the entire night when he was on the bill with Lenny Bruce at Cosmo's Alley. He wanted me to catch Don Rickles at the Slate Brothers with him and made sure I went with him to see Mort Sahl. One night Scotty ushered me into the Crescendo and after approaching some guy from the back, he tapped him on the shoulder. As Steve McQueen turned to face us, Scotty said "So, Sis, what do you think? Do we look alike?" Many of his friends had remarked about their physical similarity.

Victor was often with us. He was such a dear, sweet guy with a droll, British sense of humor. He was living in Manhattan Beach in a small place, just one step from the sidewalk on a steep street not far from the Lighthouse. Sandy and I would take the bus there from Hollywood after work if the guys were playing, pop into Vic's to meet him and Scotty, then we'd all climb the hill to Poncho's on the corner for some good Mexican food before going the few blocks to the club. Often we'd stay out at the various clubs till closing time when Victor would drive us back to Hollywood. Every now and then Vic would stay while I'd cook up something simple for us all to eat and we'd just sit around laughing our heads off about one thing or another until I'd discover it was seven in the morning, which meant it was time for me to shower and catch the bus for work.

The four of us celebrated an unforgettable first California Thanksgiving together. Sandy and I promised Scotty and Victor a real traditional, multi-course home-like meal. Never mind that neither of us had ever cooked this meal at our own homes, or that we had only two stove-top pots and one oven-friendly pan. And who ever heard of a meat thermometer? We needed the available money for the food. However, we never thought about the expense of calling our moms for their sage advice as the day wore on and it became apparent that none of the four present had any idea about how to actually prepare the food we'd purchased. The Three Stooges had nothing on us. Vic was just slightly more adept at cooking than he was at driving and besides, they don't celebrate Thanksgiving in England, so he had the most valid excuse. Most dishes were served a la carte, after having had their turn in the available pans. Thanksgiving day turned into Thanksgiving evening and then Thanksgiving night and at the end of the day our insides ached as much from laughing as from overeating the over-done and under-done foods.

December brought this all to an early end. Our other girl-friend, Peggy, had arrived and she and Sandy found an apartment just a few blocks away. Actually our landlady was quite relieved. She was a very dramatic woman who assured us she was once an important starlet. She shared her home on the lower floor with her grown son. While he was best described as a mama's boy and quite flamboyant, he was also quite taken with Sandy, she being a tall, gorgeous blonde. His job was taking care of the place as well as of his mother. During our two months there she would often take Scotty aside and tell him that Sandra was spending too much time flirting with and distracting her son. Sandy disclosed to me just recently that during this same time, she had tried to seduce Scotty when I was at work, but he didn't go for it due to the circumstances and that several months later, when the living situation changed, he mentioned it, but by that time, she was about to get married.

Not long after, Scotty got a call to go to Chicago to work with Pat Moran. Since he wasn't certain if the gig with Pat would be extended, we decided to let our lovely place on the hill go and for me to share Sandy's new place until his return, when we'd look for a place suitable for the whole family since they were scheduled to arrive in the upcoming summer of 1958.

Pat Moran has vivid memories of this time:

> Scotty and I became very dear friends. I learned so much from him—I was also totally intimidated by him. At that time I wasn't too confident about my playing, but Scotty always encouraged me, at the same time giving me a hard time when I didn't measure up. I had studied to be a concert pianist, but had always played by ear, so I leaped into jazz not really understanding it, just going by sheer guts. Scotty was a wonderful person and funny. He was never a drug addict—he was a very moral young man. Scotty and I talked about a lot of things—some spiritual. We had good times together, great musical moments. I'm sure if he were around today he'd be amazed at all the awe and wonderment he's receiving from around the world. He deserves it, but he'd probably not believe it—although he was very aware of his genius and used to love to go into clubs and intimidate bass players. A lot of bass players were scared to death of him. He was in the course of changing the whole style of bass playing. He actually was quite a character, lots of fun.
>
> At the Cloister Inn when Scotty and Gene Gammage joined me, we played opposite Ramsey Lewis. Ramsey had a bass player, Eldee Young, who played like Ray Brown and the competition between Scotty and Eldee was lots of fun! Scotty loved Eldee because he could get such an incredible big sound and groove. Eldee was awe-stricken with not only Scotty's amazing technique, but his new concept of bass playing. Scotty believed the bass was capable of doing more than just providing the basic pulse for the rhythm section. He did all that, of course, but he also added beauty and color to the music as no bassist had ever done before.

With fondness of this time in his voice, Eldee, too, recalled the gig when I spoke with him on the phone in early 2006: "I was playing in Chicago with Ramsey Lewis and Red Holt on drums opposite Pat Moran's trio. Scotty and I would go in the back room between sets and have two bass sessions, alternating doing rhythm and melody. There was a camaraderie among musicians then, especially between bass players. George Duvivier, Percy Heath and Oscar Pettiford were heroes to Scotty and me. Scotty had a lovely style. He could play his butt off and he was a nice guy."

Paul Berliner in his book *Thinking in Jazz: The Infinite Art of Improvisation,* speaks of how bass players learn from each other: "At the recording session where they first met, George Duvivier and Scott LaFaro, who was 'more or less the pioneer of facility on the bass' expressed surprise at each other's playing technique. LaFaro had thought that Duvivier played with two fingers, as did LaFaro himself. In fact, Duvivier was using only one finger like Ray Brown, who managed 'a lot of speed with it'. Never having observed two-finger playing before, Duvivier was equally fascinated by LaFaro."

The Pat Moran Trio played Wednesday through Sunday nights at the Cloister Inn through the rest of the year. Scotty also did some work with Ira Sullivan, a world-class multi-instrumentalist on reeds and brass, during his weeks in Chicago. He said, "Scotty was just a wonderful, memorable player—brilliant—a blazing technique. I remember I told him 'your technique is great, but you need to get grit'."

To Mom's surprise and delight, Scotty found a way to get home to Geneva for the Christmas holiday with her and the three younger sisters, including the little one born in July after Dad's passing. It meant a lot to have Scotty there for her first Christmas without him.

The year had been full of great upheaval for Scotty musically and emotionally but that only stoked his drive to get to all the things he felt were inside him. It was a year he devoted to learning, practicing, exploring, practicing, growing, and more practicing.

CHAPTER 7

WORKING THE WEST COAST
1958

As I was now living with my girl friends in Hollywood, when Scotty returned to Los Angeles he shared Victor's digs in Manhattan Beach. The big scene was still at the Lighthouse in Hermosa. Scotty would sit in regularly and met a lot more musicians who were doing the same. Drummer Eddie Rubin, who later worked with Neil Diamond, remembers that Scotty always had a bag of sunflower seeds in his pocket and nibbled them constantly. He did one casual gig with Scott and said that over the years all the bass players he met were envious that he got to meet and play with Scott, that he was an idol to all of them. Eddie said, "Scotty was a virtuoso, he just had it. Came out of nowhere and was way ahead of his time. His approach, concept, chops. He was a prodigy, had something special. You thought he was playing a violin or a guitar. No one played the bass like he did, what he got out of it. There has never been a trio like that Evans trio. If Bird was alive then, Scott would have been playing with him. And Scott was bright, intelligent. A nice person, warm, friendly."

The Arrival of Victor Feldman was recorded in late January. Drummer Stan Levey's wife Angela helped with the photos for the album cover after Stan, also well known for his great photography, set up the shots. She said it was freezing cold that day and their kids were running all over the beach. They were all laughing and someone said, "doesn't somebody have a rope?" Angela recalled that Scotty had dinner with them quite a lot. "He was funny and cute as he could be. Stan just adored Scotty. Never had anything but great things to say about him." Stan's oldest son, Robert, said that "all I ever heard from Dad was that he loved Scotty. He said that Scott stayed at their house in Hermosa and his dad helped him quite a bit in the beginning of his career. He said that Victor's (Feldman) and Scotty's playing was 'out of this world' and that 'he was glad they let him hang around them.' Dad was quite modest in that respect." His son Chris recalled that in the last year or so before his dad passed away he told him that "Scotty was the finest player he ever worked with. I believe the description was 'a monster.'"

In the liner notes for the *Arrival* album, well known jazz critic and author Nat Hentoff wrote, "Bassist Scott LaFaro, who makes his first full-scale recording debut on this album, is in the estimation of this fearer of hyperbole, the most important 'new' bassist since Paul Chambers and Wilbur Ware. Rather than rearrange the customary adjectives of acclamation, I expect his power, sound and invention in these performances will invade your attention more effectively than verbal gymnastics. It may be necessary to add for those hearing LaFaro for the first time that his bass is not electrically amplified. That huge sound and strength of attack is finger-sprung alone." Ralph J. Gleason in the September 1958 issue of *HiFi and Music Review* wrote: "this LP is very pleasant, full of nicely played and interestingly conceived solo passages by Feldman and carried along on excellent rhythm provided by La-Faro and Levey. It is, however, as vehicle for bassist LaFaro that the LP really impresses. His solos and his section playing are both of the new, hard swinging school, with great rhythmic strength and imaginative solo flights aided by a thorough command of the instrument and surprisingly masterful execution."

Right after completing this recording session and before Scotty was to leave for San Francisco to replace Leroy Vinnegar, who had been injured in an auto accident, he and Victor took me out for dinner to celebrate my twentieth birthday at Frescotti's on Sunset Boulevard. It was a fun evening etched in my memory by all the laughs we had at one another's expense. Then, just a day or two before he was to leave, Scotty called me excitedly and said he was coming by to get me as he wanted me to sit in a rehearsal recording session he was doing with Frank Sinatra. Scotty was asked by his friend Red Mitchell to sub for him and since Sinatra was always an icon to everyone in our family, it was a pretty big thrill for us.

Scotty played with Stan Getz and his Quintet at Guido Cac- cianti's Black Hawk in San Francisco from January 31 through Sunday, February 9. Walter Norris was on piano, Billy Higgins, drums, and Scott on bass. Walter Norris recalls, "Getz was im- pressed and remarked that he thought Scotty was the new bassist 'shooting star' in jazz. Scotty was the dedicated virtuoso, he played constantly and always with imagination."

It was at this gig that drummer Dick Berk first met and played with Scotty. When he sat in he said Scott leaned over and said, "don't play too loud (meaning that bass drum)." He thought "Scotty was amazing, worked with all five fingers, ridiculously wonderful, most inventive."

During this gig, on February 8, Scotty recorded with Stan and Cal Tjader on their *The Cal Tjader-Stan Getz Sextet* album. Also on the recording were Vince Guaraldi, piano, Eddie Duran, guitar, and Billy Higgins on drums. The *Down Beat* magazine reviewer John A. Tynan noted in the October 2, 1958, issue: "On repeated playing of these tracks one is left with a happy feeling that the rhythm duo were the 'baddest' cats on the date. Higgins is a solid time player with good technique and unshakable conception (dig his fours on 'Ginza'). LaFaro, however, is a much more potent cup of tea. He solos only once in this set, on 'Nest,' and it is a breathless experience, indeed. Clearly, a brilliant future is in store for this youthful bassist from Geneva, N.Y." In his liner notes Ralph Gleason mentions that "Getz' Black Hawk group featured two young jazz players who were totally unknown then: bassist Scotty LaFaro and drummer Billy Higgins ... Higgins is a painter as well as a musician and LaFaro says he's too busy for hobbies, adding he's catching up on Bird recordings. Both these men will make their mark in jazz history. Their technique and their ability to blow with the veterans on this date is almost frightening in light of their youth."

When Scotty returned to Los Angeles, we went car shopping and finally bought a used green and white Ford Fairlane with fins to share. He was staying at Victor's still but when he had sudden need for a tonsillectomy, the doctor I was working for had him taken care of immediately and he spent his recovery time on the couch at my apartment, all three of us women nursing him, and he enjoyed that immensely. As many will tell you, his smiles were most rewarding.

On Mondays he would play at the Lighthouse with Victor and Stan Levey. When he wasn't working he was hanging with friends at the Lighthouse, Diggers in East LA with Richie Kamuca, or the Troubadour, where he met and dated a waitress. Bassist Jack Bruce and he would chat about race cars at Cosmo's Alley. But during the day time, when not off rehearsing for some upcoming work, he'd be at home and his routine was pretty much get up, eat something, then practice all day. During this time he played with Victor and Frank Rosolino on Steve Allen's new show taped at a studio next to Hollywood Ranch Market on the northeast corner of Fountain and Vine streets.

The *Jazz at Ana* album was recorded at a Carlsbad concert February 24, 1958. Howard Rumsey writes of this:

The Army Naval Academy at Carlsbad, CA., asked us to appear (my Lighthouse All-Stars) and let them record the concert as a Firstclassmen project. The audience for this event was really an inspiration to us. The Senior Class had really worked to give us a feeling that the music we loved would be well received. Details like sound, lights, rapport were in place. We produced the music and their response made it become alive. The personnel for this concert included Bob Cooper, tenor saxophone and oboe, Frank Rosolino, trombone, Victor Feldman, piano and conga drum, Stan Levey, drums, and myself playing bass. There was added inspiration this particular evening among the musicians as well. We were presenting a guest player with the All-Stars. A bright new star, Scott LaFaro, had agreed to be on hand and he was sensational, inspiring us all with his absolutely brilliant ability. The album recorded that evening had four tracks with a full quintet, one track with a trio and one a quartet. Scott played on the trio track and one with the quintet.

On Sunday March 9, Scott appeared with Howard Rumsey's Lighthouse All-Stars in a Concert of Contemporary Jazz at the Malaga Cove School in Palos Verdes along with Victor Feldman, Larry Bunker, Stan Levey, Bob Cooper, Bud Shank, and Frank Rosolino. From *Down Beat* ("Strictly Ad Lib: Hollywood," March 6, 1958, page 49): "The Lighthouse's Howard Rumsey, raving about Scott LaFargo's [*sic*] talent, states 'Scott is the most important bass player since Jimmy Blanton.'" This was followed shortly in the March 20 *Down Beat*, by a remark by John Tynan: Bassist Scotty LaFaro is "a guy who could easily be the next really great bass player. And he's only 20!" (45).

In an interview for "Cross Section" (1958) Bud Shank offered his views on a variety of subjects. When asked about Scott LaFaro he replied: "A gas and a half. He's going to have a very big effect on bass players in the future. His uninhibited way of playing in my quartet already has had a great effect on Larry Bunker, Chuck Flores and myself."

I met Bud at Ken Poston's Jazz Festival in Los Angeles in the fall of 2005 and later he told me:

> Scotty worked with me at a club at Hollywood and Vine for about a month. The club had only a short life (I think the month we worked there!). This was not an established jazz club. It was in a hotel—maybe the Vermillion? On Hollywood Boulevard near Gower if I remember correctly. Gary Peacock, who had been working with me for most of the previous couple of years, decided he wanted to go to New York so I asked around LA. "What do I do now?" And several people said Scott LaFaro is in town. "Whoopee" says I. I don't think I had played with Scotty before he started that job with us, but I didn't have to. I already knew all about him. He was my kind of bass player. After all I had been playing with Gary for the previous two or three years. In Germany and in Los Angeles. From Gary to Scotty was a logical step. He and Gary are two of my favorite three players. The third is Bob Magnusson, but he is totally different. Musically it was a delightful month. Too bad we didn't record. Personally I remember Scotty as being very studious, very intellectual about the bass and his approach to music.

Chuck Flores was with Bud Shank at this time and recalled that they did a couple of other dates with Scott on bass, one in Long Beach at Strollers and another in Malibu at Drift In. He recalled that he didn't particularly care for what Scotty was doing and during the Long Beach gig yelled at him to just play time. "I realized after two weeks what he was doing. He was right. He was paving the way—his way—a new and best way. His solos were superb. He had boyish charm and was very bright and knowledgeable about lots of things."

Jazz was to be found all over town and Scotty played at most of the venues at one time or another: the Jazz Cellar on Las Palmas just south of Hollywood Boulevard with the Bill Holman-Mel Lewis Quintet, and with Barney Kessel's group at Jazz City on Hollywood Boulevard near Western. He was making what he thought was pretty good money and was indulging in one of his loves, nice clothes. He'd shop at Zeidler & Zeidler on Crescent Heights Boulevard at Sunset and Lou Ritter in Westwood. Once, after returning home from a gig in Chicago, he told us about getting into an elevator in his hotel with Harry Belafonte. They looked at one another and laughed. They were dressed totally alike!

Scotty met Charlie Haden in the fall of 1956 when Charlie had come to Los Angeles to study music at Westlake and was playing with Paul Bley at the Hillcrest Club, and now that Scotty was back in Los Angeles they renewed their friendship. Since I was still living with my girl friends in Hollywood, in March Scotty began rooming with Charlie Haden in his garage apartment on Gramercy Place just south of Hollywood. Scotty spent most of his hours practicing. Jack Bruce recalled that when he dropped by, "Charlie would come out, say Scotty was practicing. That's just about all Scotty did—get up, eat something, then practice all day." Charlie Haden, quoted in *Down Beat* (June 2, 1966), said, "Scotty practiced and played all the time. His rate of improvement knocked me out."

In my conversations with Charlie, he said that they didn't practice together much. He related:

> Scott would wake up, do his exercises—push ups, all that stuff, then begin practicing. I remember coming

in one time and Scott was sitting on the bed with his head in his hands. I asked him what's wrong and he said "I'll never be able to play, man." Scotty would also become disconsolate and express his frustration saying "I just can't play what I'm hearing." Scotty would copy down Sonny Rollins solos—Sonny was one of his favorites. Scotty was obsessed with practice. He'd go over to Red's [Mitchell] house and stay there all day, playing.

Scotty and Charlie would kick around town together. Reminiscing, Charlie said:

We'd go to Carolina Pines Coffee shop on La Brea for breakfast, or maybe Tiny Naylor's. After our gigs we'd go to different guys' houses and play music, some classical, and we'd talk about different composers and musicians. We'd talk about art, life, music. Discuss Satie, Sonny Rollins, books, spirituality, improvisation, creative things, technical things. I remember one time Scotty came home with an LP under his arm. He was excited. He said "Man, you've gotta hear this. This is the best piano player I've ever heard." It was Bill Evans' first record. Scotty knew and talked about lots of things—politics, art, life, philosophy. I always thought Scotty was brilliant and told him so, but he never said anything to me about my playing, so I always thought he didn't think much of it. Later, when I was working with Paul Motian, I mentioned this and Paul said, "Are you kidding, man?" then told me of a time when he was playing with Scott. Between sets and during a snowstorm in New York, Scotty said to him "Get your coat—I want you to come with me (to the 5 Spot, where I was playing) and hear this great bass player." I really loved Scotty. He was a human being of humility, graciousness, appreciative and sensitive. He was not self-destructive. I remember when I last saw him in New York in 1960. It was snowing. He was waiting for a cab. What were to be his last words to me, with tears in his eyes, were "I love you, man." When I heard about his accident, I was at the Troubadour in LA. I was devastated. I cried all night long.

Scotty began to get more calls for work. In March he recorded with Hampton Hawes on his *For Real* album and worked with Ornette Coleman at the Hillcrest Club. On April 4 he did a recording session with Buddy DeFranco. The review in the April 13, 1961, *Down Beat* noted: "LaFaro's bass helps tremendously in swinging the up-tempo pieces." After recording the *Live Date* album, Scotty appeared on Bobby Troup's *The Stars of Jazz* television show on April 7 with Richie Kamuca, then went out on tour with Buddy's group along with Victor Feldman. Buddy said, "At that time Scotty was into playing what I called butterfly bass. He was all over the instrument. He'd be cluttering up things too much for me with the group. I'd be wanting him to play more 4/4 … to the surprise of many he was one of the best at playing 4/4 as well. I thought that Scotty was a great—marvelous musician. He launched a whole new era of bass playing. He influenced ideas of technique. Fugue type. It surprised me that he practiced on the bass from his *Klose Method Clarinet* books." Frank DeVito, who was the drummer with Buddy on the *Live Date* album, said he found Scotty "likeable and enjoyed working with him. He fit in real well. He was the kind of bassist drummers like working with … makes it easy for you."

Scotty was seeing an Italian American girl from the Monterey Park area at this time and she wanted to go with her girl friends out to Palm Springs for the infamous Easter week blast that was a tradition for college kids in Southern California. Since Scotty had to work, he insisted I go to keep an eye on his girl. That romance was short-lived, although not due to anything I reported!

When he returned from the gig with Buddy late in April, and after working a gig at Jazz City with Harold Land on tenor, Charles Lloyd on alto, Hampton Hawes on piano, and Billy Higgins on drums, he stopped along Hollywood Boulevard to run into a coffee shop to pick up a quick late night snack. He had our shared car and his bass was in it. During what he said wasn't much more than ten to fifteen minutes, someone stole his Mittenwald from the car. He came up to my apartment absolutely devastated with disbelief. He suspected someone must have followed him just looking for an opportune moment. With tears in his eyes and not knowing really what to do, he decided to head back over to the club and then file a police report in the morning.

That was the night Maggie Ryan came into his life. She recalls him standing outside the club crying about the loss of his bass. She commiserated with him and that night he went home with her. Actually he had had two previous encounters with Maggie, a tall, absolutely beautiful girl with a mane of glorious red hair. Maggie was married to Saul Weiss, one of the owners of Fantasy Records, and had first met Scotty at the San Francisco recording session with Stan Getz and Cal Tjader. She said that when she walked into the studio, she was "struck by lightning when I saw him and walked right out into the rain." She later saw him at a pool parlor next door to the Black Hawk where they chatted briefly as she became "shaky." Scotty's relationship with Maggie became very deep and joyful and lasted throughout the year.

After the theft of the bass, Scotty used a loaner while searching for a new instrument. Red Mitchell was also looking for a new bass. At Stein's on Vine, Red finally settled on his famous cut-away Lowendahl bass but he also had found a Prescott that was three-quarter sized. Red felt it was too small for him, but thought Scott might like it and called him. This instrument, made by Abraham Prescott in Concord, New Hampshire, around 1825, would become part of the LaFaro legend. Bill Evans said, "It had a marvelous sustaining and resonating quality. He [Scott] would be playing in the hotel room and hit a quadruple stop that was a harmonious sound, and then set that bass down on its side and it seemed the sound just rang and rang for so long."

Guests continued to hang out at the Gellers' and Walter Norris recalls Scotty's dedication and determination were again evident on a hot sunny afternoon. "Many musicians were there, some playing while others listened. Lenny Bruce was sun bathing, a few were in the pool. However, Scotty was in the bedroom practicing for a couple of hours, like a roaring lion, with door and windows closed. No one disturbed him, then he stepped out with his bass and entered the living room to play. It was as though he was on a bandstand. He tuned, suggested a title and the music began."

Scott and I started house hunting in earnest, since the plan was for Mom and the younger sisters to arrive in late July. We finally settled on a place in the hills in Los Angeles' Silver Lake district. It had some thirty-six steps up to the front door and the living space was on four levels. We had fun hitting the used furniture stores along Western Avenue and downtown to get what was needed for the place. Maggie moved in as well, sharing Scotty's room on the lowest level. She and I were quick friends. As well as waiting tables at the jazz club the Renaissance on Sunset, Maggie was doing a lot of modeling for some of the well-known photographers, Bob Willoughby and William Claxton, as well as for John Altoon's class at the Art Center College. She arranged modeling jobs for me, Scotty, and Billy Higgins there as well.

Maggie recalls the summer of 1958 as "magical, an amazing special time." Their time together was filled with long walks—they loved the Hancock Park area of Los Angeles—and studying vocabulary—they loved finding new words and their meanings together. Maggie remarked that this wasn't surprising since "Music is a basic language and Scotty loved the sound of words as well." They studied the Chinese philosophy I Ching together. This theory expounding the dynamic balance of opposites was of real interest to Scotty. Maggie remarked how "amazingly intense he was. He was always in control of everything in his life. Music was his passion. He'd practice 'til his hands bled." The nights they weren't working would be filled with going to the clubs together to listen to jazz.

As Scotty and I were trying to put money together to help support what now was a family of four beside ourselves, he'd take almost any work that came his way. Maggie and I found some humor in him playing a school prom. Scotty also got a call to play in Las Vegas. By this time I was also seeing someone regularly. A handsome Cuban, Manny was in Los Angeles studying at the Art Center College and sharing an apartment with his brother in the same building where I had been living with my girl friends. When Manny and I were helping Scotty load up the car for the Vegas gig, Scotty casually suggested Manny and I drive to Nevada to see him. He was a bit taken aback when Manny expressed some shock that my brother would suggest his unmarried sister go out of town with a guy! That's when Scotty decided that this was the one I should marry. (And several months later, I did.)

The gig in Las Vegas came about when pianist Frank Strazzeri needed a replacement for his bass player, Marvin Shore, for his trio that included drummer Victor Kircherello ("Kirch"). They were playing in a club off the strip in Vegas, and Scotty took the job for a couple of weeks. They would start at eleven p.m. and play until seven in the morning. When word got around that Scotty was there, Frank said, "Every bass player in town came in after their shows around three to four a.m. to hear him."

Scotty returned from Las Vegas in time for the arrival of Mom and the three younger sisters. Mom, Maggie, and I shared the housekeeping chores and cooking. There was a bit of tension be-

Working the West Coast 89

tween Maggie and Mom. It was the fifties and unmarried folks living together was not yet the norm, especially in small towns like the one we came from. In later years Maggie and I spoke of this, and she understood the difficulty our mom was having making the transition of losing her husband, moving three thousand miles, and adapting to the big city mores.

In August Terry Gibbs hired Scotty for a four-week gig at the Slate Brothers, a club on La Cienega Boulevard. They played from August 22 through September 18 and Terry's records show that he paid Scotty $120 a week for the gig. Terry said that Scotty was a young guy, a dynamo; in slow songs Scotty would jump into the open spaces to fill them up, if Terry left any. He always liked the young players because they had more energy.

More folks were hearing about Scotty and calls for work were starting to come in pretty steadily. *Down Beat* (August 21, 1958) had Scotty placed second as Bass—New Star in its International Jazz Critics Poll, right after Wilbur Ware. He was working some at the Lighthouse with Victor, Richie Kamuca, and Stan Levey. Some tracks made there in September by Howard Rumsey were released on the CD *West Coast Days* in 1992.

In October Scotty was very happy to find himself playing with the Sonny Rollins Quartet from the seventh through the nineteenth at the Jazz Workshop in San Francisco. Lennie McBrowne was on drums, and Elmo Hope was at the piano. Hal Schaefer in his *The Owl Steps Out* column in the Saturday, October 11, issue of *The San Francisco Chronicle,* noted: "Tuesday night the Jazz Workshop had the biggest opening night in its history as Sonny Rollins and his quartet played to standing room only. Almost every musician in town as well as members of Dizzy Gillespie's quintet and the Modern Jazz Quartet, up from Monterey, were in attendance to hear Rollins, who many consider the successor to the all-time great Charlie Parker."

In his 1960 interview with Martin Williams, Scotty said, "I think horn players and pianists have probably influenced me the most. Miles Davis, Coltrane, Bill Evans and Sonny Rollins perhaps deepest of all. Sonny is technically good, harmonically imaginative, and really creative. He uses all he knows to make finished music when he improvises."

Harold Land followed Rollins' booking at the Jazz Workshop using the same rhythm team of Lennie McBrowne, Elmo Hope, and Scotty, so Scotty remained in San Francisco until November 2. From there this group went to Vancouver, appearing at The Cellar. A recording of the live performance was made and has been aired on WKRC in New York. In 2007, Lone Hill Jazz put this out on a CD.

Back in Los Angeles in early November, he was once again playing around town with Richie Kamuca, Victor, Stan Levey and vocalist Ruth Price. They played several gigs at the Renaissance and on the third this group did the *Stars of Jazz* show. In 1993 Ruth founded, and is now director of the Jazz Bakery in Los Angeles, one of the most prestigious jazz clubs in the country. She is petite, sparkly eyed and has a most delightful personality. Recalling the fifties she says, "We were young! Everything was so exciting! No one else was doing what Scotty was doing ... still aren't. He was a wonderful player, a blazing talent. Imagine what he'd be playing today! Or even twenty years later."

Scotty also played with Sonny Rollins, Elmo Hope, and Lennie McBrowne again, this time at the IT Club on Washington Boulevard at La Brea. I dropped him off, then returned shortly before two a.m. to hear the last set while waiting to take Scotty back home. Following this gig, Scotty then headed for New York to record with Pat Moran. His plan now was to live in New York City for a time.

Two records came from the Pat Moran sessions, which included Gene Gammage on drums. Later in 1960, when Scotty was interviewed by Martin Williams for his article "Introducing Scott LaFaro" in the August 3, *Jazz Review,* he remarked, "I don't even like any of my records except maybe the first one I did with Pat Moran on Audio Fidelity." The second record from this session was *Beverly Kelly Sings with the Pat Moran Trio.* In an email in 2005, Beverly Kelly reminisced fondly about Scotty's enthusiasm and enjoying the time they worked together on club dates and on the Moran albums.

While in New York, Scotty took the time to hit all the jazz clubs, sit in with whomever he could, and visit with his friends. Don Payne was now living at 16 W. 68th Street, near Central Park West. He recalls, "One day there was a knock at the door—'Open up, it's the police.' I looked out the peephole and could only see a raincoat, ivy shirt and tie. 'Hear you have an underage female in there. You have to open up or we'll have to break in.' When I opened the door it was Scotty, Gene Gammage and Wilfred Meadowbrooks—they then continued the charade, conducting a search of the place. It was pretty funny."

While home for Christmas, 1958 Scotty played with Paul Bley and his quartet (Bobby Hutchinson, vibes, Nick Martinis, drums) at the Masque Club on Washington Boulevard, then headed for Las Vegas for a gig on December 31. Walter Norris recalls spending the afternoon in a car with Scotty on the way to Las Vegas. "Scotty drove like he played: no inhibitions or fear. He sped with the gas pedal to the floor. Being a survivor, I asked him to reduce his speed. No chance, perhaps his nerves wouldn't permit a slower tempo. His thinking was always serious and definitely in high gear whether behind the wheel or playing music. That evening we arrived just in time to change and join Buddy DeFranco to play for a small private New Year's Eve party at the Sands Hotel."

• CHAPTER 8 •

KENTON, GOODMAN, AND MONK

1959

SCOTTY WAS READYING TO LEAVE for the East Coast in the fall of 1958. Maggie had recently taken a job at 20th Century Fox as secretary to the associate producer of the TV show *Dobie Gillis*. Scotty asked Maggie to consider coming along with him. When she questioned if there was ever going to be anything more for her than being the girlfriend of a jazz musician, he said that he felt he "wasn't going to be around that long." She said she decided she wanted to get away from the jazz scene and modeling, and thought this straight job would be a good way to change her life. This separation actually ended their relationship. Early in 1959, Scotty called from New York and asked her once again to come to New York, telling her it would probably be hard financially, but that he loved her and wanted them to be together. She told him she was looking for a different life, and soon thereafter married Bob Denver. Later Maggie said it was very, very painful for her when in 1961 her friend Miki Shapiro, one of the owners of the Renaissance Club, called and told her of Scotty's death. Maggie had seen him just that April before in Los Angeles when he was playing with Stan Getz. Afterward they had gone out to a coffee shop and then spent the rest of the night driving around and talking. She said he told her, "he felt he was going to die very soon, but would wait for me and always watch over me." She said that she has never really worked through her feelings about Scotty and still feels close to him and feels the continuing influence he had on her as a woman and human being, even though their time together was brief.

The best-laid plans often get waylaid, however. Although Scotty intended to have New York be his home base at this time, the overthrow of the Batista government in Cuba at the beginning of the New Year brought him back to Los Angeles. Cuba's change in government made my plans to marry Manny in April in Los Angeles, followed by a honeymoon in Havana, impossible so we decided to get married in a small ceremony in Los Angeles on February 20. Of course Scotty, as head of the family, flew home to do the honors: giving away the bride.

While back on the West Coast he picked up some work playing at Sherry's, a club on Sunset and Crescent Heights Boulevard in West Hollywood. He also got a call to record *The Broadway Bit* with Marty Paich at Warner Brothers and shortly after, on March 2, recorded *Latinsville* with his good friend Victor Feldman.

In March, Scotty got a gig with Stan Kenton. This was tremendously exciting for him, since to play with Kenton had been one of his dreams as a kid in Geneva. Just before leaving Los Angeles to go on tour across the country[1] Stan recorded *The Stan Kenton Orchestra in Concert*. Lenny Niehaus, who was principal soloist and writer with Kenton, remarked in the liner notes: "Scotty had a wild sound and I liked it a lot."

Steven D. Harris mentions Scotty in an interview with Archie LeCoque in his book *The Kenton Kronicles: A Biography of Modern American's Man of Music: Stan Kenton*. He quotes LeCoque: "My roommates for three years with Stan's band were Bill Trujillo, Billy Catalano and, during the spring of '59, bassist Scott LaFaro. Scott and I decided we were awfully pale and decided to buy a sun lamp. We would lay under it after work and a few times fell asleep and got burnt very badly. Stan used to harp on us all the time to get rid of that sun lamp. Scott wasn't what one would consider a big band bass player. We all knew something important was going to happen with this guy."

As it turned out, Scotty didn't stay on for the whole tour. There are a couple of versions of what exactly happened, but it came down to the same ending. Scotty had a problem with a drummer whom Stan had just hired. Scotty told Stan, "Either he [this new drummer] goes or I do." Stan said, "You're gone—Where do you want a ticket to? New York or Los Angeles?" So before the end of March Scotty found himself back home in LA.

When he phoned his friend Herb Geller who was in New York City with Benny Goodman to tell him of the turn of events, Herb said Benny didn't like the bass players he had auditioned thus far for their upcoming tour and he'd ask him about Scott coming in to audition. Scotty got the go ahead and flew to New York. Herb told Scotty, "Benny is very conservative, don't do any of those fast things you can do. Don't get fancy, no double beats, Benny won't appreciate that. Play what's written."

As Scotty was auditioning, Herb said he looked over at Benny, who gave him the thumbs up on Scotty.

That first night together in New York City, Herb recalls, he said to Scotty, "Let's go around to hear Bill Evans. Motian was on drums , Nobby Tobah on bass. Scotty sat in. There was great rapport. Bill had first heard Scotty with Chet Baker three years earlier—in 1956 when he was conducting some auditions for Chet. I think not long after we were back off the Goodman tour, there was a call waiting for Scotty … that Bill wanted him to work with him."

Herb continued: "The Benny Goodman Orchestra went out on a six week tour of one niters. Scotty played on the conservative side. He got everything fast. Red Mitchell taught him some techniques he had invented. Also on the tour were Dakota Staton and the Ahmad Jamal Trio with Israel Crosby on bass and Vernel Fournier on drums."

Bob Wilber was playing clarinet and soprano sax with Goodman. In a BBC interview May 14, 1959, he related:

> When Scotty started with Goodman he was a new name to all of us in the band. He didn't have much chance to solo with the Goodman Band. Scotty loved to jam. In those days there was always a lot of after hours action in most American cities in the black section of town. Pepper Adams, Scotty and me [*sic*] would go to the clubs and that was the first time I really got to hear Scott, what he could do. He was an amazing soloist, played more notes than anyone else. I asked "where did you get the concept of playing these very complicated lines?" Scotty said, "I started out as a clarinet player and think I'm influenced by the clarinet." Thinking about Scott always brings to mind the time we were driving through the cornfields in Iowa. The bus driver had his radio on and the announcer comes on and says that Sidney Bechet[2] had died in Paris. Way out there in Iowa! They played a recording of Bechet's. Scotty was listening and said, "I never heard this guy play. You know, he plays what Benny tries to play." That was his comment. That was a great comment from Scott about Benny.

In an interview on the BBC in July of 2004, Herb Geller said, "I really liked the music from *Gypsy* and I set up a recording date with Ahmet Ertegun. I wanted Scotty on it." After getting back to New York after the Goodman tour, on May 21, he recorded *Gypsy* with Elvin Jones on drums, Hank on piano, and Thad on cornet. In the fall of 2005, Herb talked at length with Gene Lees and me about this session.

> I needed a vocalist. Around that time I happened to bump into Barbara Long on the street, and knowing she had a nice voice, hired her for the recording gig. First day of a two day recording session, Elvin not there … finally came in—he overslept. Hank was slumped at the piano, falling asleep, couldn't play, Scotty kept yelling at him to wake up. Hank: "yea man." Scotty had no toleration for people who didn't play up to their best. Then Barbara comes to the session … she had lost her voice. She told me "this happens every time I'm in a studio." I'm thinking, thanks for telling me. But Barbara's husband, who was there, said he knows what to do, steps out, comes back with a bottle of vodka, she drinks down the whole thing, and all is well.
>
> Day two, I had to make a seven p.m. flight to LA, pick up a car, drive to Las Vegas to play with Louis Bellison opening in the lounge of the Flamingo for a two to three week gig. Elvin was late again. They did "Some People," which was hard and fast. Billy Taylor had to come in and do the piano work on "Cow Song," which I had arranged for Scotty. It got done somehow and I was able to make the flight. It was hot, I got my car and half way there blew a tire, changed to the spare … that also blew, so I hitchhiked to a station and phoned Louis. The gig was to start at eight and it was still a hundred miles to Vegas. I got stressed out, but Louis had Pearl pick me up. Not too long after, a huge Caddie pulled up and Pearl said "get in, honey child, we're on our way to Vegas." I got on stage at five to eight, and was featured in the first number.

Joseph Muranyi, respected clarinetist and the last surviving member of the Louis Armstrong All Stars, worked as a producer and sleeve note writer for major record labels in the fifties. In his notes for the *Gypsy* album, he writes: "Another youngster who contributes much more than what one would expect is string bassist Scott LaFaro. Scott's only 23, yet his playing sings with the authority of an old professional like Milt Hinton or Oscar Pettiford. He's featured on *Cow Song.* [*sic*] Scott's version of the melody and his improvisations upon it mark him as a jazz musician of considerable talent. That he has a sense of humor is apparent in the way he slips in a few "moos" between the end of the first statement of the melody and his beginning improvisations. Scott's accuracy of pitch, fine rhythmic sense and creative way with a jazz line portend great things for his future in jazz." In a note in 2007, Muranyi mentions that Scott "was very highly thought of as the new bass wonder. People were equating his advance in technique and concept to that of Jimmy Blanton. Scott has raised the bar for bass players in general."

When Scotty returned to New York after the Goodman tour he shared digs with his pal Don Friedman. Don says, "It was a real cold water flat. It was on York between 79th & 80th next to the East River. Cost $18 a month. Got it from the city, it was to be torn down. It was so cold at times we'd have to keep the hot water running in the bathtub so the rising steam would keep us warm. For a dining table we'd place a board over the bathtub. Once in the still of the night (early a.m.) we decided to take the couch which probably hadn't been cleaned in years and wasn't worth anything, and cart it out of there … we did … dumped it into the East River."

Besides re-establishing his friendship with Don Friedman, Scotty palled around a bit with pianist Hod O'Brien. They had first met in Chicago in December 1957, when Hod was playing at the Blue Note and he had gone over to the Cloisters to hear Pat Moran when Scotty was her bassist. Now they were both in New York doing pick-up work, whatever came their way. Hod recalls those days:

> Scotty got me a gig with Terry Gibbs at the Jazz Gallery, a one-nighter. Sometimes we'd have a gig out on the Island along with Al Levitt. Usually Charlie, the boss at the club there, would take us to the train for our trip back into the city. One time we went out by car and were at a stoplight and got rear-ended. Charlie told us we should all claim whiplash, get some money. I never did and Scotty later told me he never did either.
>
> Once Scotty called me to come play a session with him, Tony Scott and Paul Motian at the apartment of Richard Ney, a film actor in the forties who later became a successful investment counselor and author. Ney was married for a time to Greer Garson, whose son he played in the well known film *Mrs. Miniver.* He was giving a party for his daughter, a jazz buff, and we played with hopes it could lead to more work.
>
> Scotty had more chops and musicianship, than I did … he could read. And he just astounded everybody, including me. I just never heard anybody play the bass like that up until that time. Nobody else had either. He was such an upbeat guy. I remember having such a good time hanging with him, he was so fun loving: smiling, laughing all the time. He recommended me for a Dick Haymes gig, but I didn't get it, Don Friedman did. I have very fond memories of the little time I did play with Scott.

Don Friedman and Scotty began working with Dick Haymes. One gig was at the Living Room in Manhattan with Elvin Jones on drums, followed by some road work. Al Levitt was the drummer on those gigs. Pat Moran recalled of that time, "Even Haymes who had a big career in films as well as being a very popular singer then, was intimidated by Scotty. Scotty would tell him to send a car to pick him up for work, and he would."

Haymes, as well as traveling with his own musicians, also had a group of backup dancers and a comic on the bill. Gloria Gabriel was one of the dancers and in reverie recalls noticing Scotty noticing her during rehearsals. One day in Pittsburgh, acting on his interest, he pretended to have forgotten which was his room at the hotel and knocked on the door of the room Gloria was sharing with another dancer. He used the "mistake" to ask her out and began a serious relationship with her that endured until the time of his death.

When the tour was over and Scotty returned to New York, he and Don were still sharing digs. Don thought that Scotty was a lot of fun, they had lots of laughs. He relates:

> Once he took the book *The Idiot* and held it up in front of his face for a picture. He was full of fun, full of life. We both liked and listened to Bartok—*The Mandarin Suite* especially. And violin concertos. I recall Scotty always seemed to have the bass in his hands, practicing during the day and playing somewhere at night. I thought he was amazing.
>
> He was using three fingers. He used to play my piano, too, and was very interested in minor 7th chords with the flat 5th. In fact, the tune "Gloria's Step" was an outgrowth of his interest in those chords. I remember another time when Scotty was living down on the lower East Side with Gloria and Ornette Coleman was there and Ornette was asking us what the tonic note of our instrument was. Both Scotty and I were a bit puzzled by the question, because as far as we knew there was no tonic note of an instrument. Ornette had a very unique way of thinking about music.

> Another time when Bill Evans was playing at the Jazz Gallery and he got sick, Scotty called and asked me to sub for Bill. I played a couple of nights with Scotty and Paul Motian.

Drummer Al Levitt hung out with Scotty a bit in New York as well, and in his memoirs he reminisced about their hitting the clubs to listen or sit in and practicing together. He mentioned that Scotty listened to Bela Bartok, Charles Ives, Zoltan Kodaly (his *Suite for Violincello* recorded by Janos Starker), Miles Davis (especially his work with Gil Evans), Stan Getz, Chet Baker, Art Blakey, pianist Martial Solal, and Booker Little.

Tony Scott actually brought what would become know as "the trio" together when he recorded *Dedications* and *Sung Heroes* on October 28 and 29. The British concert pianist Peter Pettinger, in his 1998 book *Bill Evans: How My Heart Sings*[1] talks about these recordings.

> The session (*Sung Heroes*) marked the first studio collaboration of what was to become a historic threesome: Bill Evans, Paul Motian, and a twenty-three-year old bassist named Scott LaFaro. "Misery," written by Tony Scott for Billie Holliday, is a four-minute gem, a deeply poignant composition given a fabulously beautiful opening by Evans, who focuses again on his lyricism, his spiritual domain. LaFaro plays a simple line while indulging a subtle variety of attack and timing, but the melding of the line with the piano, in its placement and tone, gives the number distinction. Not much happens, but a wavelength is established. For Evans, having drifted for some months, "Misery" offered a glimpse of a relationship to come.

Scotty had been very taken with Bill's work since hearing him on the album he had excitedly brought to Charlie Haden's attention the previous year. Pat Moran relates, "One night after I got off work at the Hickory House in New York, Scotty came running in and said I just had to come with him to hear this wonderful pianist at Basin Street East, Bill Evans. When I heard him play, I sat mesmerized and even had tears. After Bill's set Scotty jumped up and said, 'Come on, let's go sit in.' You can imagine I wasn't too keen at that moment to follow Bill at the piano, but I did it. Of course this was Scotty's way of getting Bill to hear him! It wasn't too long after that that they started working together."

Scotty was playing with pianist and singer Bobby Scott around the corner from Basin Street where Bill Evans, having left Miles Davis after working with him for almost a year, was playing. Bill had formed his own trio with Jimmy Garrison on bass, and Kenny Dennis or Philly Joe Jones on drums. He was having a lot of trouble and changed rhythm sections several times. When Bill called Paul Motian on November 5 to sub for Kenny, Scotty had just replaced Garrison, who had quit because of terrible treatment from the club owners.

In his autobiographical notes, Paul says he first met Bill in the mid-fifties at the Union Hall in New York when they would go there to find out about gigs.

> We both went to an audition with clarinetist Jerry Wald. I did most of the gig—but had some previous commitments, so Philly Joe Jones did some of it. It was rough on Bill. It was an important gig because it was a major jazz club located in mid-town Manhattan.
>
> I first heard Scotty play with Chet and wasn't too impressed with his playing at that time. But when Scotty came around and sat in with Bill at Basin Street I *was* impressed. Then we played a month at the Showplace in Greenwich Village. I felt that was actually the real beginning. Magic. Everything fit. The music was beautiful. We were "one voice" … the customary pi-

ano trio with rhythm accompaniment was a thing of the past. Not for us. We were on to something new. Something different and it felt great. Scott was an incredible bassist. His playing was different from what I was used to. He didn't play the usual 4. Some people said his playing sounded more like a guitar.

Scott started a revolution for bass players. He was the first to play in a different style than was the usual and normal way of playing the bass. It didn't take long for me to adjust and for us to gel. Playing with Scott became very comfortable and natural. He was intelligent, articulate and his love of music was always first in his thoughts. When I would visit him at his apartment I would always find him practicing … he made me feel and believe as if the music we played would always be the best and … it was. There didn't seem to be any doubt in his mind about what he was doing or what he wanted to do. About the music he was involved in, about the music he wanted to play and about his own playing. He was sure … and he was confident about it all. He had a strong personality and a strong presence. In later times if I didn't play my best or if Bill wasn't in top form, Scott spoke up. "Bill, What are you doing? Are you sick? You're not playin' your best!" Scott could be relentless in his opinion. It was because he wanted the best from everyone involved in the music … and he was usually right in his criticisms.

In November on the twenty-eighth, Scotty did two shows with Thelonious Monk at Town Hall. John S. Wilson of the *New York Times* (Monday, November 30, 1959, page 26) noted Scott's contribution in just one line of his review.

Bill's trio was booked next at the Showplace, following which the group recorded *Portrait in Jazz* for the Riverside label on December 28 in a nine-hour studio session. Orrin Keepnews, who produced this album, told me:

It is difficult to determine when the concept of treating the trio as three almost-equal voices entered the picture. In retrospect, Bill talked on later occasions of having had the idea for some time, but there is good reason to believe that it really entered the picture as part of Bill's initial reactions to working with Scott. In any case, the idea was clearly still a work-in-progress at the time of the first album. There are only two numbers—"Autumn Leaves" and "Blue in Green"—that offer anything like full indication of the "simultaneous improvisation" approach that Bill and Scott were trying very hard to bring into their work together.

In his biography of Bill, Peter Pettinger gives his view of this recording:

"Peri's Scope" was the first number to be recorded, and LaFaro immediately homed in on the pianist in a special way. When Evan breathed between phrases for a bar or so, LaFaro filled in with a plunging line, the sound ample and resilient. Significantly, at such moments, the bassist had taken the initiative for propelling the performance as a whole; he was already an equal partner. His choice of notes on a walking bass was intriguingly unconventional, and an infectious swing was generated by all three players in rapport. Maintaining the medium-tempo feel, "Witchcraft" was next up. LaFaro created all manner of patterns from note one; during the first four bars alone he had climbed a ladder to dizzying heights, in sequences that sound roughly like triplets but are actually resolved in a quite independent meter. This sort of strategy bore out some remarks Evans made later: "... that he was a marvelous bass player and talented, but it was bubbling out of him almost like a gusher. Ideas were rolling out on top of each other; he could barely handle it. It was like a bucking horse."

Pettinger continues: "Never satisfied, (LaFaro) can be heard trying out chording, a procedure made easier by the way his bass was strung: by lowering the height of the bridge, he brought the strings closer to the fingerboard than was the norm, making possible a more guitar-like technique. This unfailing enthusiasm for experiment was just what Evans wanted—it was vital to his concept of interaction between the players. After the theme of "Witchcraft" both players soloed in tandem, Evans initially dropping in and out of short phrases to allow LaFaro into the dialogue. The concept was beginning to work. The pianist's invention on these two tracks, with its instant execution was staggering, the ideas direct and clear."

About six months later, *Down Beat* carried a review of this album, noting that "Autumn Leaves" is one of the finest trio tracks in recent years. "The quick thinking, anticipation, and group understanding, particularly on the part of LaFaro can carry you right off your feet." Paul Motian told me as I was working on this book that *Portrait in Jazz* is his favorite. He thinks it's "a great record."

This year Scott was named Bass New Star in *Down Beat's* 1959 Jazz Critics Poll. He was twenty-three. *Down Beat* noted: "He played in no established manner and his artistry required a thoughtful participation from the listener."

AT THE GELLERS', JULY 1957. SCOTTY'S NOTE ON THE BACK READ: "THIS WOULD
BE A LOVELY SPOT TO LIVE."

SCOTTY'S BASS IN HIS BEDROOM AT THE GELLERS'. SCOTTY'S NOTE ON BACK
READ: "SCOTTY LEANING ON HIS BED."

HOME FOR CHRISTMAS 1957 WITH YOUNGEST SISTER, LESLIE.

GIRLFRIEND MAGGIE RYAN, 1958.

Stars of Jazz TV SHOW, LOS ANGELES, NOVEMBER 1958. VICTOR FELDMAN, STAN LEVEY, AND SCOTT LAFARO. COPYRIGHT RAY AVERY/CTSIMAGES.COM, AND USED BY PERMISSION.

SCOTT AT PAT MORAN RECORDING SESSION, NEW YORK CITY, DECEMBER 1958. PHOTO BY GENE GAMMAGE.

February 2, 1959, at the Silver Lake family home after Helene and Manny's wedding.

Latinsville recording session, March 2, 1959. Walter Benton, Victor Feldman, Scott LaFaro. Photo copyright Roger Marshutz, courtesy of John Koenig. Used by permission.

New York, 1958. "The Idiot."

"Investigating" Don Payne's New York City apartment, 1959. Gene Gammage, Scotty, Wilfred Meadowbrooks. Copyright Don Payne and used by permission.

CHAPTER 9

NEW YORK:
GETZ, COLEMAN, AND EVANS

1960

CHARLIE HADEN TELLS THE STORY that when Scott went over to Thelonious Monk's place to audition for him, Monk just stared out the window for a long time before asking him to play something. Scotty did and Monk stared out the window again, then asked him to play something else. This was repeated four or five times and the last time Monk turned to Scotty and said, "Nice talking to you." Nevertheless, Scotty did play with Thelonious Monk for the Town Hall concert in November of 1959 and again the second week of January at Storyville in Boston. Scotty said that he learned a lot more about rhythm when he played with Monk and that it was a great experience, telling Martin Williams in an interview published in the August 3, 1960 *Jazz Review*: "With Monk, rhythmically, it's just there, always." Paul Motian, who was also on that one-week gig, mentioned to me that he learned to listen with Monk, and he recalled that they got paid $200.

The Bill Evans Trio played two concerts, 8:00 p.m. and 11:00 p.m. in New York on Saturday, January 30 at Town Hall, and Scotty spoke of his experiences with Bill extensively in the interview with Martin Williams in *Jazz Review*: "It's quite a wonderful thing to work with the Bill Evans Trio. We are really just beginning to find our way. Bill gives the bass harmonic freedom because of the way he voices, and he is practically the only pianist who does. It's because of his classical studies. I found out playing with Bill that I have a deep respect for harmony, melodic patterns and form … we were each contributing something and really improvising together, each playing melodic and rhythmic phrases. The harmony would be improvised; we would often begin only with something thematic and not a chord sequence. I don't like to look back, because the whole point in jazz is doing it now. There are too many things to learn and too many things you can do, to keep doing the same things over and over. My problem now is to get that instrument under my fingers so I can play more music. My ideas are so different from what is generally acceptable nowadays that I sometimes wonder if I *am* a jazz musician." Scotty went on to relate how he listened to Miles' records, Paul Chambers, Percy Heath, Stan Kenton, Lee Koeniz, of the influence of horn players like Miles, Coltrane, Rollins, and that he felt he must practice, or feels he couldn't play.

The trio left New York to tour across the country, playing in Boston, the Sutherland Lounge in Chicago, and in San Francisco February 2 through the twenty-first at the Jazz Workshop. They came back to New York late in the month, appearing in a concert package at Town Hall.

The trio was booked at Birdland March 10–23. Count Basie was the headliner for this stint. During this booking several early-hours radio broadcasts were made. Some excerpts from these came out on bootleg LPs in the early 1970s and this same material appeared in the 1990s on a CD called *The Legendary Bill Evans Trio: The 1960 Birdland Sessions*. This was recorded live at Birdland on March 12 and 19, April 30, and May 7.

The trio was booked at Birdland again from April 28 through May 11 with Dinah Washington receiving top billing, then John Handy. Recordings exist from radio broadcasts made at this time as well and were released on the same album.

Now that he was back in New York, Gloria came to stay with Scotty at his and Don's place for a short while. Then they found a small apartment for themselves in the Village. She was working in a show and sometimes Scotty would pick her up at rehearsal, but often he'd spend the day practicing. Gloria told me, "I could hear him when I came up the stairs. The people in the building just loved hearing him because it wasn't drums, it wasn't horns, it was just this beautiful bass. That's when he wrote 'Gloria's Step.'" Many folks thought that title was because Gloria was a dancer, but Scotty told me it was because when he was practicing in their apartment, he'd always listen excitedly for Gloria's step coming up the stairwell.

Between her rehearsals, and his work, Scotty and Gloria would bop around town. Gloria said,

> There'd be a lot of musicians down in the Village, we'd go to some of the places after hours. It was happening. It was wonderful. Scotty was moving, moving. We did a numerology. I was supposed to live longer than him. He told me he always felt that there was a place for me in this world, but said, "I don't fit in right now. They're not ready for me yet. I'm ahead of my time. I'll have to come back, reincarnated or something."
>
> Scotty would take me to his friends' houses, even warn me about some of them. He was very protective of me. At clubs he always sat me with friends he trusted. Also at the clubs, Scotty used to get a lot of girls coming around. I'd laugh and smile. Scotty was oblivious to it.
>
> Scotty and Bill had a wonderful relationship. Scotty didn't do drugs and they'd argue over Bill's drug use,

and also over music. But Scotty would say to Bill "If
you weren't worth it, if it wasn't that I enjoy working
with you, I wouldn't be wasting my time." They did
beautiful things.

Scotty became friendly with trumpeter Booker Little when
they played and recorded together. Scotty recorded *Booker Little,*
April 13 and 15 in New York. Booker described Scotty as "distant, but close—a paradox that resolves only for those who were
simpatico." Little said, "Despite Scotty's taciturnity, many felt close
to him, and that he felt that this was a natural reaction to Scotty's
intensity and his enormous powers of musical communication."
In the liner notes from this album, Booker writes, "Scott is technically, I feel about the greatest bassist we have and he's still developing. In addition, he does so much more than just accompany.
As I mentioned, some of this material is difficult harmonically,
but he had no problems. I just gave him the chords. While any
competent bass player can play the roots, Scotty interprets. He is
much more of a conversationalist behind you than any other bassist I know."

The Toronto Globe and Mail, in its *Jazz Scene* column review of
this Booker Little album, noted, "It is possible to hear every note
played by a bassist named Scott LaFaro, who solos continuously
no matter what—or who—else is going on at the time; this is the
same Scott LaFaro who in a recent interview told the *Jazz Review,*
'Sometimes I wonder if I'm a jazz musician.'"

Roy Haynes was also on this date and, though he said he
had most likely first heard Scotty when they were both on the
Birdland Tour in 1957, this was the first time he played and recorded with him. Roy said, "Booker must have known something
… well, he did know something." Talking between sets during
his appearance at Catalina's in Hollywood in early 2007, Roy

recalled that when he was playing with John Coltrane at Zebra Lounge in South Central Los Angeles in the late fifties, Scotty may have sat in, playing with him, McCoy Tyner on piano, and he thinks Jimmy Garrison was on bass.

Another friend Scotty made early that year was bassist George Duvivier. George took Scotty to meet luthier Samuel Kolstein who had a shop out on Long Island. Sam Kolstein's son, Barrie, also a luthier, wrote a memoir of that meeting that was published in the Spring 2004 issue of *Bass Line*, the newsletter of the International Society of Bassists and is reprinted here as Appendix II.[1] During this same period bassist Herb Mickman met Scotty. Herb, then nineteen, had read something on the back of a Red Mitchell album noting Scott as an up and coming talent. Shortly after, Herb got the *Arrival* album Scotty had done with Victor Feldman. Herb said:

> I listened to that and thought this guy is into some new stuff. On that record with Vic, the bass was right up front. I don't think anyone ever recorded the bass right up front like that before. You could hear all the notes and they had such a long sustain.
>
> Whenever I heard Scott was going to be at Birdland with Bill Evans, I'd go. It only cost $1.50 or $2.00 then. I'd sit there all night. If you got there early you could sit right next to Evans, literally one foot from him. As a young bass player, if I didn't know a song, I'd look at the piano player's left hand and could see what the bottom note was and I would play it. If he played an F, I would play an F and it would work. But Evans was into some new stuff. He wasn't playing what we call the root on the bottom, he was playing other notes. I couldn't tell what the hell key he was in. He didn't play the root until the very end. Then it finally hit me: If I watch Scott when they played the melody, I could tell the key because Scott would play the roots when he played the melody. It was a big lesson for me, like going to school

every night. Something else that was different was the kind of strings Scott was using. New strings on the G, D and A: Golden Spirals, made of nylon wound on gut. I never saw anyone with those strings before 1960. On the E he was using a string made by Tomastik Spiral Core. Nobody had ever heard of those strings then. Now they're a standard thing. Scott must have increased their sales by thousands of percent.

I finally introduced myself to Scott, told him I was a bass player. I became a Scotty groupie of sorts. He was getting used to me being there. I found out that Scott would come in early to practice and if I got down there early enough I could go into the back and watch him. I think he liked my interest and he'd be nice enough to tell me what he was doing. Eventually he consented to give me some lessons (it ended up being just two) over at the apartment he had with Gloria. He wasn't a real teacher, but had a lot of information and also played the piano a lot more than I could at the time. He showed me these books he had put together. Collections of songs he liked. He started me on that and now I have fifty-five different fake books with thousands of songs. I remember one time we talked about John Coltrane and he wrote out the chord changes in this song called "Giant Steps" that Coltrane had just recorded. It was a very interesting song at that time, all the jazz musicians were talking about it. I remember he wrote it out for me.

(From Scotty's notebook)

Scott made such an impact on me. While he was having Sam Kolstein do some work on his Prescott, he borrowed a bass from the shop to play. I ended up buying it later, since my hero had played it. It had a great, big sound, but I traded it in eventually since I realized it was wrong for me because my hands were too small. The last time I saw Scott was at the Village Gate. Scott was there to hear Vic Feldman with Cannonball Adderly. Scott had once shown me the diminished scale and I couldn't do it at first. I told Scott I had been practicing it all summer long and Scott gave me a little smile.

No matter how busy his schedule, Scotty always made regular calls home to Mom and me with a "Hi" to the younger sisters. He was very excited about who he was playing with and would tell me who was currently "blowing his mind" musically. He'd tell us proudly of what Gloria was doing and would regularly send the cheesecake we all loved from the Turf.

On Monday, May 16, the Bill Evans Trio was booked at Circle in the Square in New York for an evening devoted to Gunther Schuller's jazz compositions. Along with the Evans group were Ornette Coleman, alto saxophone; Eric Dolphy, alto saxophone, clarinet, bass clarinet, and flute; Robert Di Domenico, flute and piccolo; Barry Galbraith, electric guitars; Eddie Costa, vibes; Buell Niedlinger, bass; and the Contemporary String Quartet (Charles Libove, Roland Vamos, Harry Zaratzian,, and Joe Tekula). Well-known New York critic Dan Morganstern in his *Metronome* review ("In Person: Jazz by Schuller," August 1960) mentions that in "Variants on a Theme by John Lewis," "Scott LaFaro contributed a striking bass solo, remarkable for its technical skill as well as its musical weight." While with Ornette Coleman, Scotty would work with Schuller again at the Third Annual Monterey Jazz Festival Saturday, September 24, in California.

Gunther Schuller, a musician, composer, and scholar of contemporary classical music, is the originator of the term "Third Stream" music, a combination of classical and jazz techniques. In 1991 he was a MacArthur Foundation "genius" award recipient, and he won a Pulitzer Prize in 1994. He has received many lifetime achievement awards and Grammys as well. When I spoke with Mr. Schuller in late 2006, he discussed his work and Scotty:

> Duke Ellington was always my great hero, still is. Ellington often used two bass players.[2] Duke never fired anybody, never had the wherewithal to do that. Starting in 1935when his first bass player couldn't cut it anymore, he just simply hired another player, more advanced than the first one and then after about half a year or so the first one caught on and left. Then Duke had one bass player until he became a little behind the times, then he'd hire another.... I learned that very quickly because I was transcribing.... Point is, that when I started writing, I also started using two basses.
>
> My three bassists were Scotty, Richard Davis and George Duvivier. Because they were the ones.... Here I was into Schoenberg, Stravinsky and all of that and I needed people who could read, who could improvise. So when Scott came to town it was like manna from heaven because here was a guy who not only could read anything, and he had an unbelievable finger technique, right hand finger technique.

Mr. Schuller, continued:

> Scotty recorded *Jazz Abstractions* with me—with Ornette Coleman and Eric Dolphy. Scott was the first bass. I used George Duvivier too. George was a wonderful walker. Scott walked fabulously too, but George's tone

was a little bigger. Scott used somewhat thinner strings because he liked to play way up in the high register, like a cello. So I used George more for the walking because he had this big, fat sound and then Scotty would play on top of him, like two octaves higher. George would go along 4/4 and Scott would play 16th or 8th notes above that because he had this incredible, virtuosic technique at that time. The only one that was even close to him in that was Charlie Mingus.

On this album Scotty did some of the most marvelous playing of that time. On "Variants on a Theme of Thelonious Monk." In that there is an amazing duet with bass clarinet, played by Eric Dolphy. The way he and Scotty played off each other. Scott would play some kind of lick, then Eric would answer it, do it slow, do it upside down. They really collaborated. We played that piece a number of times and, of course, every time it was like a duet cadenza, the two of them. It would be different of course, but the one that is on the recording is really amazing because what I had done wasn't just a free jazz, go off and play anything you want. I had organized this duet cadenza in six different chords and I had indicated stay on this chord for about eleven seconds, more or less, then go on to the next B flat 7th chord, or whatever. Organized chaos. The way they both handled that, it's almost like they read each other's mind and knew exactly how they should bounce off of each other's ideas and when they would come to a kind of resting place before they would move on to the next chord....

I wrote a little interlude for a string quartet, like a transition and I moved into another key, A Major, I remember that. I gave Scott the walking this time, a solo to start things off. It started off real soft, kind of slow and blues-ish and I had each player coming in one after another and Eric finally ended up playing on the flute very, very high. But the way Scott started that A Major passage, I mean he swung like mad, but quietly and if you hear that, if you sit still during that, you're clinically dead. You're not with it anymore. I have that sound, I have that whole thing in my ears forever. That I haven't forgotten. Scotty did those kinds of things just so easily, so beautifully.

Dan Morgenstern in his July 1960 review of this concert in *Jazz Journal* noted, "The main event of 'Variations (On Django)' was a bass solo by Scott LaFaro, a young bassist who here demonstrated that his ample and beautiful instrumental technique is matched by a musical imagination of the first order. But he could have, and has, played as well in a purely jazz environment."

The Evans trio was booked at the Jazz Gallery in New York from July 26 through August 7 opposite Thelonious Monk, who received top billing. This was cut short and the Birdland booking that was to begin later in August was cancelled when Bill became seriously ill with hepatitis and went to Florida to recuperate at his parents' home. Rumors swirled among the jazz scene in New York that he had died, but they were squashed when Gene Lees placed a call to him from the jazz hang-out Jim & Andy's, as public proof that he was alive.

Having met Ornette Coleman originally in January when Ornette's group was on the bill at the Town Hall with Bill's group, and because Bill was not booking for a while, Scotty now began to work regularly with Ornette Coleman's Quartet (Don Cherry, trumpet, Ed Blackwell, drums). They were booked into Art D'Lugoff's Village Gate in Manhattan from August 19 through September 7. On August 28 there was an appearance of the quartet at the Philadelphia Music Festival, held in a baseball stadium, which was not considered very successful. *Down Beat* (October 27, 1960) noted in "The Evidence of the Damage: Philadelphia":

"Ornette Coleman, playing his first large eastern jazz festival, garnered polite applause."

By September 13, Ornette's group moved on to Detroit and played at the Minor Key until the eighteenth. They went on to California for the Monterey Jazz Festival September 24 and 25. On Saturday afternoon, the twenty-fourth, the Gunther Schuller group played two compositions: "Abstraction" and "Conversation." Scott played on the first of these, but dropped out for the second. He then returned to play a set with Ornette's group. On Sunday, Scott played with Ornette once again, with Ed Blackwell on drums. John Tynan in his review for *Down Beat* (November 10, 1960) states: "Coleman's set provoked some in the audience to leave the arena. After an original 'Diminished Night,' the altoist chose to play an unusual, for him, choice—the ballad 'You'll Never Know.' It was patently bad, disturbed and utterly unhappy, but Coleman stubbornly stuck with it, taking it at an agonizingly slow tempo and allowing for a long bass solo by LaFaro whose brilliant technique and ideas were remarked by all."

Bob Chinello, a jazz fan who was in attendance, noted many years later: "And Scott LaFaro! I will never forget a Saturday afternoon in September, 1960, watching the Ornette Coleman Quartet on the main stage of the Monterey Jazz Festival. There were seven thousand mouths hanging open in disbelief at what we were seeing and hearing, and I'm not talking about Ornette's white plastic alto. It wasn't quite like being at the Paris Opera House in 1913 for the premiere of *Le Sacre,* but we all knew we were witnessing something revolutionary."

After the festival, Ornette was booked at the Jazz Workshop in San Francisco from September 27 through October 9, followed by a booking in Los Angeles at the Sanbah in Hollywood. They began on the twelfth, but difficulties with the club management over money ensued and the group did not finish out its engagement.

Bassist Putter Smith recalls going to this "dingy little joint" and his conversation with Scott that evening. Scott had come over to sit with him and Putter said, "You've never studied classical." Scott, noticeably embarrassed, asked, "How could you tell?" Putter said that he was highly amused at the time that this greatest player of the instrument could be embarrassed even slightly by someone whose technique was looking upwards to mediocre. That evening they had quite a detailed discussion and Putter tells me that over the years since, he relates the substance of the conversation and information to his students and other bassists. Putter said:

> He wasn't using the Simandl fingering, was totally at ease to the top of the fingerboards, didn't have the raised left elbow … his technique was unique and quite refined. He wasn't grasping or grabbing. Obviously he had developed a system. I asked him what he worked on. He was working on arpeggios. He touched the tabletop with the 1st finger and 2nd fingers of his left hand. He pulled the 1st finger back leaving the 2nd extended … "I'm playing major thirds with 2 and 1." Then he lifted the 2nd finger and set the 3rd down (extended): "Minor thirds with 3 and 1":

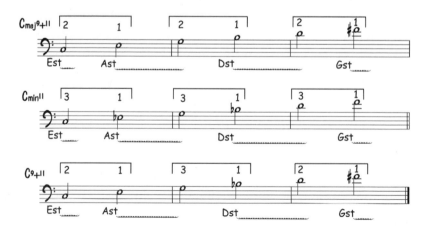

This simple concept can be carried to great lengths; longer arpeggios, starting arpeggios on the 2nd degree etc. A little work on this shows the speed possibility.

I believe that he was using George Russell's *Lydian Chromatic Method* as his harmonic basis. I was ignorant of that great work until in my forties some twenty-five years later.

… In 1958 Don Cherry told me that he and Scotty would start each night (back in the days when a local jazz band would work six nights a week for three months in the same club) with a motto: "Triplets are in"—all solos were to be entirely triplets. The next night "Sixteenths are out," etc. This is truly experimental music leading to new ideas that sound good.

Listen to Scotty playing "Israel" with Bill Evans: dotted quarters are in….

Scotty's combination of his physical gift, musical inspiration, and courage to persevere in the daily grunt work of mastering a musical instrument rarely occurs. He was also a real good guy. Warm and witty, slender in his button down shirt, grey ivy league suit and his buzz cut: the coolest of the cool.

Scotty had Gloria with him on this tour and the family got to meet her. With the spare time afforded Scotty because of the shortened Sanbah gig, they were able to have more recreational time at home with our family. We'd sit around the kitchen table after dinner, laughing at one another's irreverent humor. He and Gloria took Mom and the two youngest sisters, now ages three and four, to the beach out at Malibu for a walk along the shore. Lisa, an impetuous four-year-old, suddenly dashed into the ocean and Scotty ran in, losing in the successful rescue his wallet and their return tickets to New York. He was dapper even for the stroll, wearing a velvet-collared jacket where he kept his wallet in the inside breast pocket. It apparently fell out in his haste to grab

Lisa and was washed away in the Pacific. Getting back to New York required a short-term loan from my husband, Manny.

While in Los Angeles during this visit, he got a call from a friend and did a small part in the movie *Splendor in the Grass.* Barely noticeable, he was the bass player wearing a straw hat in the party scene.

Upon their return to New York, Scotty began a gig at the Village Vanguard with Ornette, who had been booked at the request of John Lewis, musical director for the Modern Jazz Quartet who was heading the bill from November 1 through 13.

In the November 3 *New York Times,* reviewer John S. Wilson noted: "Mr. Coleman wove a sufficiently compelling spell over his audience at the Vanguard to hold their attention steadily. An important asset in this respect was Mr. LaFaro, who played some startling solos on his string bass, using it in one instance as though he were plucking a Spanish guitar."

Immediately following his gig with Ornette, Scotty stayed on at the Vanguard and began a gig with Bill Evans and Paul Motian that ran from November 15 through 20. This time they played opposite the Miles Davis Quintet, which received top billing.

Composer and bassist Frank Proto recalled that although he had heard Scotty during this time at the Vanguard and had never met him, Scotty was the cause of a bit of trouble between him and the leader of the group he was working with at the time:

> In the early sixties I was working at a club on 52nd Street near 8th Avenue by the name of Jilly's. [Jilly's is named after the late Jilly Rizzo, who was Sinatra's best friend and bodyguard. The original Jilly's was a dark 120-seat saloon at Eighth Avenue and 52nd Street. Its glory days were between 1952 and the mid-1970s.] Usually we worked from 10:00 p.m. 'til 4:00 a.m., but one night for some reason I don't remember, we fin-

ished up quite early—around midnight. Having nothing to do, the drummer and I went down to the Village to search out some music and found ourselves at The Vanguard witnessing a set by Bill Evans, Scott LaFaro and Paul Motian. Although I had heard Bill on recordings I had never seen him live before. As to Scott, I had heard about him, but had never seen him either. The trio was wonderful. Everything had a different sound from what we were used to. The unusual approach to the time, where both the bassist and drummer floated along with the piano rather than laying down 4 beats to the bar was a revelation to both of us. There was absolutely no problem feeling the time—it was certainly there—but the amazing thing was that no one seemed to be responsible for keeping it going! We stayed until closing time and then wandered around talking excitedly about what we had just heard for a couple of hours.

The next night we went to work at Jilly's. The leader of our trio was a singer/pianist by the name of Bobby Cole.[1] He was actually quite a good musician and we played mostly good tunes—lots of great standards and many East Side tunes. The kind that never became popular, but were enjoyable to play because they usually were well written with strong melodies, decent chord progressions and fairly sophisticated lyrics. The group's overall sound and feel was jazz-based with straight-ahead time laid down by the bass and drums. If we played a moderate 4 tempo, I played four beats to the bar about 95% of the time.

Well that night, right off the bat on the first set, both the drummer and I started experimenting with the free time techniques that we had heard the night before. At first we just dabbled in it a bit, but by the third or fourth tune, we were getting more and more into it. Around half way through the set Bobby turns around and says: "What the hell are you guys doing? What's going on?" Since I stood practically on top of him, it fell on me to answer his question. I replied: "Oh, man, we went to the Vanguard last night to hear Bill Evans. He had this unbelievable bass player by the name of Scott LaFaro. You should have heard ..." As I said this to him, the drummer was leaning over with a big smile on his face, nodding and nodding away, sort of underlining everything that I said. At this point Bobby interrupted me and with a gangster-type voice that was oh, so familiar in that joint, said "I don't give a shit who you saw last night. I wanna hear four fucking beats in every fucking bar or the two of you are gonna be outta here on your fucking asses!" And so ended our little experiments in time—at least on that gig.

Even though Scotty moved back to New York, he realized that he was not a city man and often spoke of his regard for the countryside. The decision was made to move out to Long Island with Gloria and her family. He really liked being out of the city even though he didn't like the trip in on the freeway and generally only went in to work. Gloria recalls that when he wasn't in the city rehearsing for his work, or working, he was home practicing, hour after hour. He began shortly after breakfast when she left and was still at it when she returned late in the day. Since Sam Kolstein had recently introduced Scotty to Fred Zimmermann of Juilliard and Scotty had begun some bowing lessons with him, his custom was to practice most mornings with the bow, then devote the later part of the day to other work or preparing for whatever gig he had coming up.

About the trio rehearsals, in a *Jazz Journal International* article (March 1985) Bill recalled: "there was so much music in him [Scotty], he had a problem controlling it ... (his) talent—bubbling like a gusher. Ideas were rolling on top of each other—he could barely handle it—it was like a bucking horse." Bill often used this description of Scotty in print and radio interviews, which I thinks speaks to the immediacy that Scotty was feeling. Bill continued, "His was a unique and exceptional talent. Scott expressed interest in building and developing in the trio … interested in spending one or two years growing … merge talent. It was a struggle at first.…"

In this same period the friendship between Scott, Paul, and Bill grew. When asked about his experience with Scott, Bill recalled in an interview article in *Jazz Times* of February 1997: "It's been marvelous. It wasn't only a musical experience. Scott was one of the most lively persons I've ever known. He's always been a source of inspiration to me."[38]

As well as their music, the three also found a mutual interest in existentialism and Zen. Paul recalls that they would discuss Zen, but that Bill was more a student of Zen than either he or Scotty. Bill expressed to Don Nelsen in his article for *Down Beat*: "I don't pretend to understand it. I just find it comforting. And very similar to jazz. Like jazz, you can't explain it to anyone without losing the experience."

One explanation of Zen is that it is a way of seeing life without abstractions and preconceptions, that Zen represents spontaneity in living. Bill Evans in his liner notes for the Miles Davis album *Kind of Blue* notes, "There is a Japanese visual art in which the artist is forced to be spontaneous. He must paint on a thin stretched parchment with a special brush and black water paint in such a way that an unnatural or interrupted stroke will destroy the line or break through the parchment. Erasures or changes are impossible. These artists must practice a particular discipline, that of allowing the idea to express itself in communication with their hands in such a direct way that deliberation cannot interfere." Perhaps they brought these Zen ideas to their music. In talking with Gary Peacock when writing this book, I mentioned Scotty's interest in Zen. Gary remarked, "It surprises me the lack of interest by lots of musicians in Zen. My understanding is that you're revelling in a muse that has more Zen logic to it than it has any other logic. What's interesting to me is that not more musicians are attracted to it. Kinda odd."

On November 29 Scotty got together with Steve Kuhn and Pete LaRoca to do a promotional tape in New York at the studio of Peter Indo, a bass player and highly acclaimed recording engineer. Steve, at twenty-one already a noted jazz pianist, was a child prodigy who had begun classical piano study at age five. A native New Yorker and Harvard grad, Steve met Scotty originally at the Five Spot when Scotty was playing with Bill Evans sometime late in 1959. Remembering the first time they played together, Steve said, "I never experienced that in my life. It was like an instant marriage. What I did, he heard immediately and vice versa. It was incredible and it hasn't happened since, the connection. I don't know about Scotty, but for me musically it was just incredible."

Music from that November session was eventually released in October 2005, by Polystar Co. LTD in Japan. A review from the Japanese magazine *The Walkers* (2006–2007 Winter Vol. 8, pg 24–25) stated: "The focus of session was modality, compositions or improvisations based on the arrangement of modes (in tones or semitones based on the scale ((medieval church music—13 century rhythm system)) [*sic*] major or minor) rather than a series of chord progressions."

Scotty was to do two more recordings before year's end: *Jazz Abstractions* with Gunther Schuller and *Free Jazz* with Ornette Coleman, the latter of which was recorded in one uninterrupted take of 36 minutes 23 seconds as it was performed in the studio, with no splicing or editing.

I had a lengthy chat with Ornette in February 2007, and he was most gracious in relating his regard for Scotty. Ornette said that he hadn't discussed free jazz concepts with Scotty as a theory.

I was more interested in how he played. He was freer than free jazz. He brought something special to the table. He could create ideas that no other person could at that time. Scotty could change the sound of a note by just playing another note and he's the only one I ever heard that could do that with the bass. His notes actually changed the … notes … to notes that are not in the keys that the bass is in. He's the only one I ever heard do that. Usually people use the piano as a guide-line for what we call keys and melody, but the bass is freer than the piano … a different key. But you can play more than one note, it's not the same thing. But with Scotty, he'd change the keys and chord.…

When we did the record *Free Jazz*, that really opened up a lot of territory for music for me. It was unheard, where the instruments that you are using to support what you are doing became the lead. You were expecting another sound. I never used the bass player to support the notes. I've always used every musician equally to an idea. But Scotty was way ahead of the idea—totally—he was really something else … not was—is.

I don't think there's been that same quality as far as the bass since. It's not something everyone can do … that people can actually learn how to expand their own ideas. Scotty was just a natural, played so natu-rally, had a love of creation. I'm not only talking about music, but being human. I would say he was closer to a mystic. Very spiritual. I felt that way when we first played. He had that air of being … very … I never met anyone like Scotty …

Ornette's voice trailed off and he expressed to me how much talking about Scotty meant to him. I had to take the opportunity to tell him that I knew Scotty would have loved him saying he was "something else," since I could remember how excited Scotty was when he brought around to play for me the first record of Ornette's he owned: *Something Else.*

Scotty spent Christmas that year with Gloria and her family. In a letter he wrote to the family on December 29 he said he was spending the days in uninterrupted practice and study and contemplating his present situation: "I should have been this absorbed when I was sent to college. It has taken me these past couple of years to find any meaning for me. That is, what I want to put into music. But one important thing is that I realize day by day the true artist and musician is becoming more and more meaningless in terms of public comprehension. This brings about the situation of whether I should spend these hours and months developing what I seem to be able to foresee, or should I dump it and get another job as an entertainer again. My day consists of such a singular preoccupation—the physicology of music. I'm in the position of having nothing you can put your finger on for sale."

He closed with "I'm trying to remember a bit of Zen I like so well: 'If you seek the fruits of … (good action) … so shall they escape you.' I try to smile everyday with that."

• CHAPTER 10 •

REALIZATION

1961

THIS YEAR SCOTTY WAS TO be exceptionally busy, flying from coast to coast and places in between several times a month. The Bill Evans Trio did a New Year's tour of the Midwest. January 17 to 29 he was back with the Ornette Coleman Quartet, which included Don Cherry and Edward Blackwell at the Village Vanguard. They were playing opposite Nina Simone, who received top billing. A review in *Variety* ("Night Club Reviews," Wednesday, January 25, 1961, page 54) was skeptical: "This Greenwich Village cellar continues its modern jazz policy with the return of Nina Simone and Ornette Coleman, who's split the jazz buff ranks into distinct camps of dig and don't dig with his atonal [*sic*] plastic alto sax. The Ornette Coleman return precedes an eight-week assault on European jazz centers, which probably will do little to clear up the domestic controversy.[1] After several catches, it's this reviewer's considered opinion that Coleman's cacophonic protest to current jazz forms has about run its string, and the group should move ahead, or maybe backwards. However far out, (the) group seems now to be blowing it own clichés, and if they keep it up the vanguard crusade may end not with a bang, but a bat squeak. Besides Coleman, there's Don Cherry on trumpet, Eddie Blackwell, drums, and Scott LaFaro bass."[2]

At the end of the month, Scotty was in the studio again recording with Ornette, this time for the quartet recording titled simply *Ornette*. In his book *Ornette Coleman: A Harmolodic Life,* John Litweiler conjectures: "There is no way of knowing whether additional experience in the quartet would have furthered the integration of Scott LaFaro's music, or how his and Ornette's forceful musical personalities might have gone on to affect one another, for the group did not perform again that winter."

Just two days later, on February 2 Scotty recorded once again with Bill's trio. It had been thirteen months since their last album. Orrin Keepnews produced this album as well, and he described to me details of the session.

> There clearly had been a lot of progress in the interaction between them, although again most of their jobs had been on the road, so I was hearing much of this for the first time. I actually remember the record session primarily in terms of the personal tensions between the two of them. Scott was being very explicit about his problem; he was very reluctant to go back on the road unless it was for a lot more money. As he put it, being out with a leader who was a junkie put him at risk of being stranded. Bill complained that the tension was upsetting him and giving him a headache; I was trying, without much success, to calm everything down. The tensions ebbed and flowed during the afternoon, but strangely enough we were accomplishing what we had set out to do. When we reviewed the material several days later, which was standard procedure, it sounded much better than I expected. The lesson to be learned here is probably something about the value of professionalism—despite tensions and negative feelings, everyone continued with the work schedule and the results were more than acceptable.

Peter Pettinger noted in *Bill Evans: How My Heart Sings,* that "LaFaro was grappling with a replacement bass while his usual Vermont-made instrument was being repaired. As a result he was shy of the high register and indulged less than usual in his personal brand of chordal experiment. For whatever reasons, there is a feeling of restraint in the trio's playing—an exploration of an elegant sound-world dedicated to the understatement."[104]

Gloria recalls a special evening that winter in New York that they spent at someone's apartment. Bill was there, as was vocalist Morgana King. "Bill started out playing light stuff, Scotty started playing on the bass. Then they played classical stuff. Morgana started doing things with her voice, like an instrument. When it was over, I remember how quietly, carefully, Scotty put away his bass and walked out of the room. He was in tears. There are things that happen once in a lifetime. Bill didn't even move."

Gloria was working for a time with noted choreographer Jerome (Jerry) Robbins in *West Side Story* on Broadway and they became friendly.

> He would come in to hear Scotty at different clubs. He loved Scotty and what he was doing. Said he never heard anyone play the bass like that. He was completely enthralled. One time Jerry had a concert pianist come sit in and play jazz when Scotty was down in the village playing with Don Cherry and Philonius—that's what Scotty called Thelonious Monk. That really turned Scotty on. Scotty later showed Jerry a piece he had written and they talked about maybe doing a dance concert at Carnegie using four bass players—Scotty and three classical players. I think he had actually gone to rehearse with them, but can't recall who they were. Scotty was so excited about it ... it was one of the things he really wanted to do.

Stan Getz had just returned from Europe and from February 15 through the twenty-sixth was booked at the Sutherland Lounge in Chicago and Scotty took this gig. Steve Kuhn was on piano, and since Roy Haynes was unavailable, Scotty wanted Stan to bring in Pete LaRoca on drums. On the twenty-first they were set to record. In the end, Stan wasn't particularly happy with his own playing and didn't want the album done at this time released. The tracks remained in Verve's vaults for several years, when different tunes started to be included in some later releases.

By early March, Scotty was back on tour with Bill, playing at the Town Tavern in Toronto, the Minor Key in Detroit and then Chicago March 15–26 at the Sutherland Lounge. On March 15 and 16 the Evans trio was broadcast on WSBC-FM as part of the nightly radio broadcasts from the Sutherland Lounge.

On March 31, Scotty got an opportunity to come back to Los Angeles for a concert at the Shrine Auditorium on Vermont Avenue, playing once again with Stan Getz, opposite Miles Davis. Steve Kuhn was at the piano, and Roy Haynes on drums. Next the quartet followed Davis at the Renaissance, starting April 4 and continuing for two weeks.

While back in Los Angeles Scotty, of course, stayed with us at the family home in Canoga Park. His days were practice, practice, practice. He always practiced facing a corner in our living room. Even though our younger sisters, now ages four, five, and sixteen were in and out and all about, he had tremendous concentration. He was using the bow a lot. I remember his finger strumming and his humming. Almost always, his eyes were closed. He was still concerned with culturing his calluses and I'd tease him about how he couldn't very well be a soft touch, in the romantic sense. During this time, he'd get calls almost daily to work. If he wasn't already busy, the first thing he'd ask was "who's the drummer?" and turn down jobs if that presented a problem for him. He started talking to me at this time about the Eastern philosophy of Zen. He was quite introspective, wondering about the future of jazz and if anyone would ever "get" him. He told me he had considered at times chucking it all and going into electronics.

One of the things that my husband Manny will always remember about Scotty occurred at this time: "I have a 1955 Jaguar. During his last visit home, I was in the garage trying to tune the car. Scotty was there, kibitzing. I was messing around with a timing light to get the spark right. Scotty had his hand resting on the fender. He said, 'It's tuned now.' I looked at him, puzzled. He said, 'There's no vibration now. You've got it right on,' I was shocked. Just by touching the car he could tell."

During this period Scotty did a gig at Shelly's Manne Hole with Frank Rosolino's group and he played the Zebra Lounge with John Coltrane, but by April 30 he was back with the Getz group playing at the Lighthouse in Hermosa Beach.

While Scotty was home with us in the west end of the San Fernando Valley, Steve Kuhn was also staying in the valley at the home of one of his relatives a bit closer to the city in North Hollywood. Scotty, using the family car, would drop by to pick Steve up for their gigs together. Steve recalls that Scotty "liked to drive a little too friskily for my taste" through the canyons into town. Scotty's driving seems to have become a topic for discussion through the years since he died. It has been remarked by some that he did everything in high gear, including driving. Others he was on the road with told me they confidently slept when he was at the wheel. Gloria noted that Scotty felt she drove too fast. Vic Feldman's driving scared Scotty. Certainly Scotty had liked watching Formula One, Indy, and sports car racing since high school days.

The Stan Getz Quartet was booked at the Black Hawk in San Francisco May 2–21. Scotty wanted Mom to experience a city that was one of his favorites and she flew up to visit him as soon as he settled into his hotel. She stayed for the better part of a week and upon her return, Manny and I headed north to spend a week with him there as well. In the countryside just north of San Luis Obispo we were hit head-on by a driver coming around a blind turn on our side of the road, which put a damper on our trip, but we eventually left the sparsely populated area on a Greyhound Bus and got to San Francisco, where Scotty was waiting for us. He had already arranged doctors' appointments for us to check out our minor injuries. We then swung into the previously planned daytime sightseeing and nights at the club. After a short visit with Scotty's friends in the city who had recently become parents he decreed: "You guys should have a baby." As it turned out, unknowingly, I was already pregnant.

All the reviews of Scotty's work were not necessarily raves. Of his stint on this gig at the Black Hawk, Ralph J. Gleason, co-founder of the Monterey Jazz Festival and *Rolling Stone Magazine* and the first full-time jazz critic on a daily newspaper, noted in his column in the *San Francisco Chronicle*, Tuesday, May 9: "Scott Lofaro, [*sic*] is one of the most talented of modern bass players, but one whose solos sometimes seem to be triumphs of technique over communication."

Following San Francisco, Scotty returned to New York City where Stan had booked his quartet at the Village Vanguard from June 6 through 11. In a review published in the August 1961 *Metronome,* Dan Morgenstern wrote: "La Faro is unique. His prodigious technique enables him to play all over the bass, often creating patterns reminiscent of the guitar or the harp. He wisely rations his virtuosity when playing in the section, where his unerring ear and good time are constant. In addition, his pleasant demeanor and obvious joy in his work enable him to capture the attention of audiences not always receptive to good music on its own merits" ("Heard and Seen," 7).

While Scotty was busy playing and recording with Bill, another fine bassist, Chuck Israels, was in town recording with Scotty's friend, Don Friedman. Chuck recalled that Scotty had been stand-offish in the times they had met previously (as noted elsewhere, others have commented that they also found him dismissive and seemingly arrogant as well, especially upon a first meeting). This was, however, the first time Scotty had heard him play and it was the first time he felt Scotty allowed for the possibility of friendship. This time he found Scotty was open hearted and welcoming and they became fast friends. Chuck, not long after, dropped into the Vanguard during one of the recording sessions of what would be Scotty's last album, and they had an opportunity to talk about the music.

Chuck was in Spoleto, Italy, on a European tour with the Jerome Robbins Ballet Company—Ballet U.S.A—when he got a call from his friend, flautist Paula Robison about Scotty's death. Many years later, at dinner one night at Vic Feldman's, Chuck told me of his shock and sadness when he got the news, dashing the possibility of enjoying a longer relationship with Scott.

June 13 through 25 Scotty was back with Bill and the trio, playing at the Village Vanguard. Their final recording was done there on June 25.[3] On Sundays the Vanguard would schedule a matinee as well as an evening performance: two afternoon sets and three in the evening. Two albums came from the material performed that day: *Sunday at the Village Vanguard* and *Waltz for Debby*.

Orrin Keepnews told me, "We normally would not have scheduled it that closely [to the session in February], but I remained worried about how long they would remain together, and thought they had a better chance at good results under the presumably more relaxed circumstances of on-the-job recording. The Sunday when we recorded was their last day at the Vanguard, but that was less important than the fact that working the usual Sunday matinee meant we had an all-day total of five sets to record. Of course it all worked out far better than anyone could have anticipated. After a panicky beginning—there was a brief power outage during the first number (it was a tune of Scott's: 'Gloria's Step')—everything went very well and both skills and attitudes were in great shape. So it turned out that this last recording became a legendary classic and a lasting memorial. The sort of conclusion you would never accept in a work of fiction, since Scott died ten days later—which was just before we were scheduled to review all the material. Bill was being very brave and pulled-together about it, and the decision was quickly reached to think in terms of releasing two albums—with the first one designed to feature Scott by including his two compositions and all of his solos."

In his book *The View from Within: Jazz Writings, 1948–1987,* Orrin writes more extensively about Scotty's recording sessions with Bill. Orrin told me that he has continuing satisfaction at having been able to play an important role that day at the Vanguard and in retrospect, "I did want to add a specific point about the Vanguard recordings—to make it clear that, all things considered, that had to have been the luckiest day in my career. To have scheduled things so as to capture that music on what turned out to be literally the last opportunity, to have had their last day turn out to be such a remarkable consistent example of what they were capable of accomplishing, to have that early technical failure turn out to *not* be anything serious, and to have the material survive and be properly appreciated for such a long period of time."

Remarking on the work on these recordings, Ted Gioia remarks on the importance of these recordings in *The History of Jazz*:

> The twenty-one selections recorded that day achieve a
> telepathic level group interplay, one in which the line
> between soloist and accompanist—isolated and dis-

tinct in the swing and bop idiom—often blurs and at time totally disappears. The piano work, the bass line, the percussion part weave together in a marvelous, continuous conversation. Such a description might make it seem that the music is busy, filled with content. Nothing could be further from the truth. The marvel was how this music could say so much while leaving so much unsaid. One would struggle to find a jazz recording from the day with a slower tempo than "My Foolish Heart" yet the performance never lags; indeed, it could serve as textbook case in how to use space and silence to accentuate the forward momentum of jazz music. Other tracks are equally exemplary: the intimate dialogue between the bass and piano on "Some Other Time"; the shimmering percussion work on "My Man's Gone Now," supporting Evans's poignant solo; the probing across-the-bar lines phrasing on "Gloria's Step" and "All of You"; the pristine beauty of "Waltz for Debby" and "Alice in Wonderland"; the avant-garde deconstruction of "Milestones." A group could deservingly build a major reputation on the basis of such a performance, and, as it turned out, that was exactly the case.

Much has been written over the years about that day at the Vanguard and the times immediately following. Particularly interesting is Adam Gopnik's essay for *The New Yorker* magazine (August 13, 2001), discussing the session with Orrin Keepnews and Lorraine Gordon, owner of the Village Vanguard, and Paul Motian.

Jim Roberts (*Bass Player*, December 1995) noted, "While the bass playing on *Sunday Night at the Village Vanguard* is amazing for its technical facility, the emotional content is even more remarkable. On track after track, LaFaro just pours out his heart, playing with the focus and intensity of a great artist making his final statement—which, tragically, he was."[74]

Some say the trio established, with these sessions, the ultimate yardstick against which all subsequent trio-based jazz would be compared. Walter Norris last heard Scotty with Bill at the Vanguard and said, "Scotty, as always, gave everything musically of himself."

In interviews in ensuing years Bill said he was very grateful they recorded those sessions. He said they had definitely gotten to something, that every set was satisfying and that they were excited when they first heard tapes. Scotty told Bill that he finally made a record he was happy with, that he liked what he heard and thought there was "some good stuff."

In retrospect, that day at the Vanguard became a high note to many. His old home town friend, Bobby Bennett recalled: "Scotty never forgot his old friends. He called me up (I was living in Brooklyn) and told me he was at a club in Manhattan and invited me to come over. He introduced me to Bill Evans and Paul Motian. We had a small conversation, then Scotty said he might not be able to spend much time with me as they were recording some things. Little did I know that this would be the now famous *Vanguard Sessions*."

Since Bill had nothing set up immediately following the Vanguard date, Scotty took a Stan Getz gig playing at the Newport Jazz Festival. As before, it was Getz, Steve Kuhn, piano, Roy Haynes on drums, and Scott on bass. Pretty thrilled to be playing at the famous jazz festival, Scotty called home with the news. We couldn't help remarking about all the greats who were also on the bill: Louis Armstrong, George Shearing, Oscar Peterson, Duke Ellington. How much it would have pleased our Dad. What a long way Scott had come since Dad had taken him, as a kid, to hear Ellington. The festival was to run Friday, June 30, through Monday, July 3. Stan's Quartet was on the program Sunday, July 2. This turned out to be Scotty's last appearance. Some of this was recorded and released on a compilation recording of Miles Davis and Stan Getz in 1994.

Scotty's work on this last gig brought varying opinions: Graham Collier in his *Highlights of Newport* review in England's *Jazz News* (Wednesday, July 19) said, "Getz showed that his stay in Europe has not changed him—he still plays the most rhapsodic tenor in jazz—but one wishes he had brought along a European rhythm section to accompany him. The main offender in his present rhythm team, which never achieved that loose swinging beat it should have, was bassist Scott LaFaro. He is without doubt the best technician since Oscar Pettiford, but on this showing, he has no conception of the bass' function in a rhythm section. (I hope he was able to stay around long enough to catch the last group of the evening, the Oscar Peterson Trio and to appreciate the melodic swinging beat that Ray Brown and Ed Thigpen gave Peterson.)"

On the other hand, Ray Brown had this to say: "I got a chance to hear him at Newport only a few days before his accident and I was really amazed by his facility, his intonation, and his ideas. We struck up a conversation and talked for about an hour. It's a shame. It's going to set the instrument back ten years. It will be that long before anyone catches up with what he was doing."

What stood out most to Roy Haynes on their last date in Newport, however, was not the music: "… something about that last gig … my wife lived in Newport and she came with me. Scotty was dressed up … that last gig … and I was recently mentioned in *Esquire* magazine during that period. She said he said he was dressed up because of me. I got mentioned as 'Best Dressed' in 1960, I think it was … it would have been the fall of that year … the September issue I think it was. He was definitely—he was a special person."

Scotty planned to return to New York City to work with Bill again rather than continuing on tour with Stan.

GLORIA, SCOTT, AND HIS MOM, SEPTEMBER 1960

MONTEREY JAZZ FESTIVAL, SEPTEMBER 25, 1960. SCOTT LaFARO, EDDIE BLACKWELL, ORNETTE COLEMAN. COPYRIGHT RAY AVERY/CTSIMAGES.COM, AND USED BY PERMISSION.

OCTOBER 1960, NEW YORK CITY STREET. SCOTTY AND GLORIA GOING
HOUSESITTING FOR DON. COPYRIGHT DON PAYNE, AND USED BY PERMISSION.

SHRINE AUDITORIUM, LOS ANGELES, MARCH 3, 1961. SCOTT LAFARO, STAN
GETZ, ROY HAYNES. COPYRIGHT RAY AVERY/CTSIMAGES.COM, AND USED BY
PERMISSION.

CARD TO SCOTTY FROM MILES DAVIS, 1961

SCOTT AT PRACTICE, JUNE 1961

SCOTTY'S WORD STUDY LIST

• CHAPTER 11 •

LAST DAYS

IT WAS JULY 3 AND Scotty was determined to take care of business for Mom back in our hometown. We talked to him in the morning the day after he'd played at the jazz festival in Newport, Rhode Island and he mentioned he felt happy about the way things had gone. He remarked that George Shearing was on the bill that night and wouldn't that have been something to Dad, who was a great Shearing fan? He wondered if we had any news about the sale of our family home in Geneva. We hadn't. We had tenants whose lease option was expiring and Mom was getting anxious, since she needed to sell the house. There had been only a small insurance policy and since our dad's death, things were pretty difficult for Mom financially, who had our three younger sisters to care for. Scotty and I had been helping to keep the family afloat as well. Scotty thought it might be a good idea to drive there and talk to the tenants to see if he could get them to make a decision sooner rather than later. And so it was decided. He planned to hear a couple of musicians that day, then head out after the Fourth of July when things wound down at the Festival, swinging by Geneva before returning to Long Island where he was living with Gloria and her family.

Leaving Rhode Island at a very early hour on July 5, he drove for about eight hours, reaching our Aunt Elsie's home on Seneca Lake just outside Geneva, in the late morning. While Scotty was taking some of his gear out of the car, an old friend from high school, Frank Ottley, now married and living about five houses away, stopped to see him. Frank was excited to run into Scotty. They had discovered a mutual interest in Gran Prix car racing and jazz in high school while I was dating Frank, and the two had sometimes encountered each other when Frank visited a mutual buddy in Ithaca during their college days. They chatted for some time and agreed to do some serious swimming in the afternoon. After dinner with the family, Scotty excused himself to spend the evening with Frank.

Their first thought was to drop by the home of a friend, Lon Flanigan, to listen to records. Lon had long been a jazz fan and had done some playing around town with Scotty and Dad when Scotty was in high school. Frank said Lon had a great sound system. When they dropped by, Lon was deep into a bridge game and suggested they come back much later that night. They headed for Sam's Bar and Grill, which is still a little out-of-the-way place on Tilman Street in Geneva. Though the sign says "Sam's," everyone knows it as Cosie's. Cosmo Fospero, the owner, just never bothered with the expense of changing the sign when he bought it. In the fifties it became a hip hangout for college kids.

After a few drinks—Cosie said Scotty had a couple of beers—sometime around eight that evening, Scotty and Frank decided it was time to hear some good music. Frank called a friend of his, Judy Fuchs Weislow, who was in Warsaw, New York, taking care of the children of friends who were away on vacation. They decided to drive the eighty or so miles to visit since there was a good stereo there.

Gap Mangione, the pianist and brother of Chuck Mangione, recalls that night:

There was a knock at the door and when we answered, there was, to my complete disbelief, Scott and some guy that I didn't know. It seemed that the two of them had been hanging out in Geneva, had had a few and at Frank's suggestion, drove over to Warsaw to visit Judy. I had never met Scott but had heard him often on recordings and in person and we quickly took to talking about mutual friends and listening to and talking about music. The other two had gone off to another part of the large house.

We listened and talked at least a couple or three hours … Chet Baker, some Bartok: *Miraculous Mandarin—le Mandarin Merveilleux*—and Scott's first magical recording of *Autumn Leaves* with Bill Evans (December 1959), and many, many others. We smiled and laughed with elation listening to that last one. Chuck and I (as the Jazz Brothers) had recorded two of our albums on Riverside, the same record label as Bill and Scott and that came up.

In spite of his quiet way, we had no difficulty in conversation or in creating an immediate friendship," Gap continued. "We were only a couple of years apart in age, and it seemed easy to hang out and talk together. It was a good, happy and joyful time and we enjoyed each other's company, the conversation and the music. There was an excellent record collection at the house so there were many choices. We drank a lot of coffee.

I remember that we listened to Chet Baker singing, among other songs, "Grey December," a very dark and haunting song. I also remember clearly, after that track ended, Scott saying that he thought Chet Baker was "an American tragedy", having the success and recognition that he had as a young, very talented, white trumpet player with movie star good looks and all the potential for a musical career to quite equal that of Miles Davis (the most successful jazz musician in our reference at the time). Instead, he got heavily into drugs, was arrested, jailed, got his teeth knocked out and seemed destined for the junk pile of jazz life.

When the others returned, we drank more coffee and encouraged them to stay the night. The guys were a lot better off than when they'd arrived but I think Frank had to get back to his home situation. I read about the accident the next day in the Rochester newspaper. Neither of us in Warsaw knew what happened until then. Over the years, (Scott's) using the term "an American tragedy" still strikes me as incredibly ironic and portentous that night.

About 1:45 a.m., Thursday, July 6, Scotty apparently fell asleep at the wheel and the car went 188 feet on the shoulder of the eastbound lane of Route 5-20, hitting a tree and bursting into flames. Both he and Frank were killed instantly.

The afternoon mail that arrived in California that Monday, July 3, carried the papers that Scotty had gone out of his way to have signed, sealed and delivered, rendering his trip to Geneva unnecessary. But we couldn't reach him by phone that day or the next to tell him not to go.

• CHAPTER 12 •

AFTERMATH

THE PLEADING RING OF THE phone disrupted the heavy early-morning darkness. To silence the annoyance, I turned to the bedside phone. Half asleep and slow, I finally recognized Gloria's voice on the other end. But the message was not coming through … what she was saying was coming through all wrong: "Scott has lost his legs" … how could this be? I wondered. I repeated what I thought I was hearing: "Scotty has lost his legs??? How???" I asked, "could he have done that"?" "No, No … lost his life" … she was trying to say through her tears, I finally made out, but it wasn't registering with me … such a thing could not be. "He's dead!!" she hysterically cried out. Perhaps she didn't want to say that—not wanting to verbalize what she didn't want to be.

That night's dreams became nightmares, then reality. That short interruption of a lazy July morning would bring a loss whose effect would be felt in two very diverse places—a modest home in Southern California and in the esoteric world of jazz.

Gloria related: "Just a few minutes after Scotty left the house for Newport, he came back. I was upstairs, so he told my Mom, 'I just came back to tell her I love her.' My Mom is superstitious and felt it was bad news to come back when you had just left. I said don't say that, Mom. A few days later, I got a call from Scotty saying he was coming home, but then in the early morning the next day, Mom answered the door and it was a policeman asking if there is a Gloria Gabriel here, he wanted to talk to her. That was the worst morning in my life. I lost the love of my life. Mom said she knew he should have never come back."

Apparently it was the time Scotty knew would come.

"Bill was destroyed by Scotty's death and couldn't talk to me," Gloria told me. She said that a while later she got a letter from him, talking about how he felt that Scotty's passing was a price he was paying for his transgressions and told her "no matter who I get to play, I don't have Scotty." She got many letters from a lot of musicians.

Following Newport, Stan, Roy, and Steve left for Saranac Lake and upon their arrival Stan's manager called from New York and told him the news that had come over the AP wire about Scotty's accident. Stan and Steve were able to get over to Geneva for the funeral services. Many years later, Stan Getz told Gloria he was pretty destroyed as well. He said to her, "I want to tell you how I feel about everything. Bad enough I felt rejected by Scotty … he was always busy. I was so glad we got to work together. There was nobody like him … still there is nobody like him. Bill Evans and he were the dynamic duo."

In November 22, 1962, Gene Lees, a close personal friend of Bill's, in his article "Inside the New Bill Evans Trio" in *Down Beat,* quoted Paul Motian: "It's hard to describe what Scott's death last year did to us. Bill telephoned me. I was sleeping. It seemed like a dream, what he told me, and I went back to sleep. When I woke up, I was convinced it **was** a dream. I called Bill back, and he gold me it was true. When it began to sink in we … we didn't know what to do. We didn't know if we'd still have a trio. We'd reached such a peak with Scott, such freedom. It seemed that everything was becoming possible. We didn't work for six months—between the last two weeks of June (1961) until Christmas."

Paul Motian told me about this same dream years later and how it unsettled him. Paul continued,

> I loved Scott very much. He was a close friend and a beautiful musical companion. I began to hear differently. I always play from what I hear and I tried to incorporate what he and Bill were doing into my playing. They had a symbiotic connection. At first with Scotty and Bill, I started breaking up the time and playing more open stuff. What happened, just happened, we didn't talk about it. Nobody played like that before … the interplay, as equals. Before that it was piano, then drums and bass accompaniment. We didn't talk about it that much. Playing with Scott in the Bill Evans Trio resulted in some of the best music of my career. The music we made together sounds as good today on the recordings we made as it did over 40 years ago. I'm happy about the short time I knew him. The music we played together with Bill will always be with me. A lifetime worth of wonderful memories.

Gene Lees wrote again of the effect Scott's death had on Bill in his 1988 book *Meet Me at Jim & Andy's: Jazz Musicians and their World*. "The shock of LaFaro's death stayed with Bill for years, and he felt vaguely guilty about it. This is not speculation. He told me so. He felt that because of his heroin habit he had made insufficient use of the time he and Scott had had together. LaFaro was always trying to talk him into quitting. After La-Faro's death, Bill was like a man with a lost love, always looking to find its replacement."

Walter Norris said, "The news of his (Scotty's) death spread through the jazz world like the wild fire he certainly was made of. To my knowledge he never used any stimulants to enhance life; but his every moment was seriously lived to the fullest."

Pat Moran recalled, "I was with him in Los Angeles several weeks before he was killed. I was stunned. My heart was broken as was that of the many other people who knew and loved him."

The August 17, 1961, *Down Beat* eulogy "A Light Gone Out" (p 13) quoted several of his contemporaries about their reactions upon learning of Scotty's death. Ray Brown said, "It's a shame, really a shame. It's going to set the instrument back ten years. It will be that long before anyone catches up with what he was doing." Bill Evans described him as "one of the most, if not THE most outstanding talents in jazz. His development was accelerating beyond belief in the last year. And the *Vanguard Sessions* recording will demonstrate, for those not already aware of it, how much the jazz world has lost."

Metronome magazine (September, 1961, pg 1) noted: "The death of Scott LaFaro in early July gratuitously extinguished one of the brightest young talents in jazz. He was one of those rare artists who are gifted with both amazing instrumental facility and true musical sensibility. He had passed the 'promising' stage of his development and was already a great bassist. He handled his cumbersome instrument with an ease and grace which reflected the joyous spirit of his music and his gracious personality. Scott LaFaro will be well remembered and sorely missed."

• CHAPTER 13 •

HIS MUSIC I

Scott had only begun composing in his final year and left only two completed compositions: "Gloria's Step" and "Jade Visions." I have been asked about the titles of both and did mention in an earlier chapter the meaning behind "Gloria's Step." He didn't tell me, and I haven't uncovered since, his exact reasoning for the title of "Jade Visions." It could have been from its Oriental flavor musically or from his interest in Eastern religions and culture or even tied into the jade stone itself. (In the last year of his life, Scotty did wear a small jade fish on a gold chain around his neck.) Jade signifies love, virtue, fidelity, humility, and generosity. It is thought to help one live in harmony with the laws of nature and is the symbolic link between man and the spiritual world. Confucius opined on its link to music. There may have been many reasons for his choice.

Gloria told me that Scotty had been writing a lot those last months. As mentioned before, he had talked with Jerome Robbins about working together on something for bass and ballet. But if he had begun writing for that, it, along with his other work in progress, was lost in the fire of the auto accident. There are some small snippets of things he wrote that he jotted in his notebook of tunes he was playing with Bill. After Chuck Israels replaced Scott in the Evans trio, Gloria gave him this notebook. Chuck said he felt "that Gloria was making a gesture of friendship and some kind of acceptance of my work with Bill when she gave me Scotty's notebook, as well as recognizing that Scotty had some sense of common purpose with me in the short time that we knew each other. I took it as a kind and thoughtful gesture on her part." Chuck kindly made a complete copy of the notebook to give to the family, remarking that "It's nice to have it as a reminder that this was a real person who worked hard on his music and needed to make notes to himself just like the rest of us."

Scotty's notations from one of his notebooks for "I Fall in Love Too Easily" by Jule Styne and Sammy Cahn are reprinted here:

And here is a snippet of a tune of his own that Scotty was working on:

About Scotty's two completed compositions, Chuck Israels notes: "The interesting things about 'Gloria's Step' are the unusual form and phrase lengths. Both of Scotty's recorded compositions [with Bill] indicate a fine sensibility and a gift for musical invention. It is interesting that those two pieces ('Gloria's Step' and 'Jade Visions') are so personal and unusual in nature that they receive few performances by others. As far as his bass playing was concerned, Scotty had already risen far beyond the position of being 'promising.' He was so technically ambitious that he raised the bar for everyone. No one since Jimmy Blanton had set such a high standard."

Eddie Gomez said regarding "Gloria's Step": "I've played it a lot. With Bill and the trio, and on my own, and recently with Chick Corea. I always loved that composition. It's really a look into the future at that point in time because it's in asymmetrical form and harmonically it just moves in a very totally different, unique way. It's wonderful writing and it's visionary writing and it's as contemporary as it gets."

Scotty's two compositions have been mentioned by Victor Verney in his review of Peter Pettinger's book *Bill Evans: How My Heart Sings,* and Keith Shadwick in his book, *Bill Evans: Everything Happens to Me—A Musical Biography.* Verney noted: "Bill Evans' own 'Waltz For Debby' is possibly the single most likeable jazz song ever recorded. 'Gloria's Step' (a Scott LaFaro composition) is one of the most memorable. 'Jade Visions' (also a LaFaro composition) is a jumping off point for so much piano-based jazz that has followed in the past forty years."

Regarding "Gloria's Step," Shadwick writes: "The tune swings contentedly through a major-minor verse and bridge pattern." And of "Jade Visions": "Its deceptive simplicity hides considerable musical sophistication … the piece harks back harmonically and rhythmically to the Debussy of the second book of *Images,* its pensive Oriental atmosphere having few precedents in jazz. This short piece has a minimum of improvisation, the bridge completely chorded with no leading voice, and is given interest by falling into 9/8 time throughout and by LaFaro's triple stops over a low bass pedal note" (89–90).

Shadwick also remarks about the state of the art of bass playing at that time: "LaFaro lived during a time when jazz bassists were generally still using gut strings. This meant that there was less opportunity to produce natural 'sustain' for a note—a problem shared by the guitar until amplification gave it a completely new lease on life in the 1940s. His technique was therefore built upon assumptions about the physical nature of his instrument that no longer applied to bassists of (Johnson's) generation. LaFaro sustained melodic ideas often by using techniques associated with classical acoustic guitarists: rapid note repetition to sustain a melodic curve, especially in the upper registers; occasional plunges into the instrument's lowest registers for dramatic effect; and long diatonic and scalar runs interspersed with well-worked pauses and ostinato patterns, often on asymmetric rhythms. LaFaro's timbre was also much more biting, more conversational, than that produced by later bassists."

The bassists who followed Scotty in Evans' trio have talked with me at length about Scotty, his music, and his influence.

Gary Peacock and I had some extensive phone conversations in 2007 about his friendship with Scotty. He mentioned something I have experienced constantly for these past forty-eight years. "People still want to know about Scotty: what he was like, what he did, how he trained himself, how he practiced, where he put his head. That is not going to go away." Gary continued,

> The contribution he made to my life was a major one. His contribution musically as an instrumentalist is just immeasurable. Musically, Scotty was a risk-taker. He provided an example of something that was simply non-existent at the time: made a really major innovation, particularly in terms of dialogue. His ability to play in the context where while he was playing was actually intended to interact and have a dialogue with the soloist, without taking anything away from the soloist. There were some bass players who were already doing that to some extent: Red Mitchell and Paul Chambers, but what they were not doing was anchoring the time without playing it. We call this "broken time," that is, instead of playing 1–2–3–4, Scotty would actually do some kind of rhythmic phrase, the rhythmic phrase would be melodic and at the same time, it would be consistent with the harmony and would be an internal dialogue with the melody or other improviser.
>
> Scotty was aware of what he was doing, but I do not think at the time he was at all aware of the huge

contribution he was making. I don't think he ever took himself for granted. I never got that sense. At the same time, he had the beginner's mind ... when you have the beginner's mind there is a tendency to become very, very self-critical and sometimes illogical. And he was very self-critical about his playing. Some of that had to do with just the nature of the beginner. But the other side of the beginner is there is a sense of discovery and joy and celebration. It's open-ended like a little kid—you're always moving forward, but you're moving forward from a fresh start every time. And, if you're actually looking, you see how, musically speaking, there's no end to it. You'll just keep discovering and exploring. You're never, ever going to be an expert. If you become an expert, then you're dead, might as well be.

I asked him how he developed his ear, what he did about that. He said, "I'd listen to a record one thousand times." That's the key ingredient. It's so significant, so important. Listening is an art. I was so surprised when he told me he was listening to Webern. (Austrian composer Anton Webern) That he was immersing himself in it. It was particularly interesting to me because at that particular time, I was immersed in Bartok, especially the quartets. We were moving in different directions. I ended up liking Weburn when at first I didn't like him at all. I was kinda shocked when I talked to Scotty once about early Evans' recordings. He said he didn't like them. I asked 'What don't you like? My God, Bill's playing is incredible!'

But Scotty's heart at that time was really in the free music thing that was happening. He wanted to work with Ornette and did—traveled and recorded with him. That album, *Free Jazz,* was a mind blower! I could hear in that music, as well as stuff Scotty did later with Coleman on *Ornette!* certain approaches in his playing that would be musically rewarding to an extent not available to him in a traditional setting. But Scotty sure didn't have problem with traditional settings.

Scotty and I talked about music development. I happened to notice here, in America, and in Canada, there's very little stress on music development. Scotty and I agreed that if you wanted to get into music, you've got to start with hearing. Gotta start with your ears. Are you really hearing what you're hearing? You've gotta hear what you're hearing. Are you just hearing sounds or are you really, really listening to what's happening? That's all gone. I've talked to some composition students, even some with master's, who've had one semester of ear training. Who've said in the writing they do, it doesn't make it necessary for them to hear. It really blew my mind!"

I mentioned to Gary that our dad had made a point of ear training with Scotty and that it was the course of most interest to him at Ithaca. Gary continued:

Yep, that was my favorite course, too. I was only in school for six months, but the ear training course meant the whole universe to me. I knew there was so much more that I wasn't really hearing, so I really started listening. It's so significant. I mean you can go to school now, you can learn how to play John Coltrane, Charlie Parker, Keith Jarrett, Bill Evans and not really do any work, just read it off the page. The difference between that and what Scott and I did is that if you want it written down, you had to transcribe it. Sit down with a pencil and paper and take it off the record. That takes a lot of time. The time it takes is an indication of the depth of your hearing. It doesn't happen anymore. There are still some players out there that can do it … hear it. Marc Johnson … some players from Europe. Italian, French. They're hearing what they're doing.

Everyone back then was in a mode of learning. Scotty's training, how he trained himself, where he put his head is really significant. Then everyone was inspired. There was so much further to go. Times have changed radically. When Scotty and I were in New York you could work club dates six nights a week. Today there are more schools to study jazz, and not enough venues, making it a viable art form available to more people. Now everyone comes out with degrees, producing a whole population of trained seals. They graduate, maybe win a contest and think it means something. Don't recognize that it doesn't. I mean can you imagine a bass player walking up to Miles and telling him "I have a master's degree in bass playing and I'd like a job?" It doesn't work that way.

What Scotty created still reverberates. If anybody is playing jazz bass and they haven't heard of Scott La-Faro, they're not playing jazz bass. His contribution was probably the highest state of art of bass playing and I don't think his influence will ever end. I have some talent, a little bit. But his talent was beyond the pale! I think it's rare that someone has the ability to develop that quickly and be mature. I know some people who always think of Scotty as "well, yeah man, he could play so fast." That was just Scotty. He had the ability to do that and sometimes that's what he played. Of course then everyone wanted to develop speed in playing. I wanted to. Many can play fast—but nothing from the heart—nothing musically significant—just fast playing—who cares. Give me somebody who plays one note that means something.

Wanting to cover some other points regarding Scotty's development and influence, I asked Eddie Gomez if he was aware of any metamorphosing from recording to recording in Scott's work. He noted:

A little bit. More so just with the trio. I felt like the whole thing seemed to be happening. The whole thing seemed like from the beginning to the end seamlessly was a real voyage, played into uncharted territory.

As I got older, I listened to more and more different horn players myself and you can certainly hear in Scott's playing that he was at first a sax player. In his concepts. He made it work for him and for the art. Scott had a real connection to the song, and melody and the dance. Just did that whole thing with the trio—made it a real ensemble.

I spent eleven years with Bill and it took me a long, long time before I could begin to understand the process and relax. When I started playing with Bill, it haunted me that I was going into a position that really, well Scott, of course, was my greatest challenge, but the other bass players, too, that had played with Bill were terrific … and Gary Peacock was great. There was a real legacy there with the bass and a real challenge and it took me a long, long time to just not be psyched. I was really scared and wondering. Bill told me about the second month of our tour that he really wanted me to stay in the trio and I was thrilled. I didn't ask Bill a lot about Scott. Obviously Scott meant the world to Bill. He said that Scott did things intensely and in high gear. The impression I got from Bill was that Scott was on an express train on the way to wherever he was going.

About four or five years into my tenure with Bill, I knew that there was no comparison to what I was doing to what Scott was doing with that trio. And no one would. That was special. No one would ever even come close. For a lot of reasons. That was special. Bill, himself, was in a different place, a special place, a very special place and Scott and Paul—what they did together. That trio that really has a historic place in jazz. A major influence not only for bass players, but for music. The musical course that he charted as a group with Bill. And as a bass player, he just broke out of the chains of how to support. How to be an interactive, counterpunctive, melodic contributor throughout the music. So even when he was playing behind the solo, he was being part of the conversation. He was always interactive. That's the way I love to hear the bass. I'm really bored with trios. Even some of the great trios now are piano centered. Their trio wasn't like that. Theirs was interactive. Some try to play à la Bill's trio. Maybe a great pianist, a very good bass player. But still always piano centered and I find that, at the end of the day, boring. And their trio wasn't. They broke out of that. Scott was right there, he was part of that vision and so that's a huge, huge piece of history. He really changed the course of bass, the way he played the bass, the things he could do on the bass. Boils down to—his genius—always going to be there in bass playing and music. They heard it at the same time, they felt it, went together, created a way, forged a new way. With Scott it was not only about the song, the melody and the interaction, but it was also about the dance. They way they danced together, sang together, interacted, and the emotion: a complete artistic package.

In his review of Phil Palombi's book *15 Solo Transcriptions from the Bill Evans Trio Recordings Sunday at the Village Vanguard* and *Waltz for Debby,* for the ISB's magazine *Bass World* 28, no. 1, pp 54–55, Marc Johnson notes regarding Scotty: "It's a great artist who creates his own universe. For an improvising jazz musician, that boils down to three essential things: creating your own sound, your own sense of rhythmic feel, and your own linear or melodic vocabulary (harmony)."

I first met Marc Johnson at the 2001 ISB convention. The bass society had arranged for its closing concert to include a tribute to Scotty featuring bass players who followed him with the Bill Evans trio. I was touched by this tearful first meeting, when he declared: "You don't understand, I wanted to *be* Scotty." Over the years since, we have talked in more depth about Scotty's profound effect on him. Marc related how the last recording by Evans, La-Faro, and Motian, *Live from the Village Vanguard,* began a lifelong musical relationship with that trio.

> Scotty's sound, full and warm and yet clear and trans-parent; his choice of notes and rhythmic placement, his rhythmic freedom over the bar lines and through the structures, the melodic inventiveness when solo-ing, his interactive approach within the trio; all these things made me want to play the bass in that way, in a group like that. This was in the fall of 1972. In those years at college I must have listened to those recordings with Scott thousands of times. At some point when my classical technique brought my left hand to the point where I could negotiate the finger-board quickly enough, I tried to play along with the recordings. I copied what I could but mostly, it was a conception of playing that I came away with, suited to my technique and ability. To this day, I still don't see how Scott articulated his ideas with such startling clarity and velocity. I learned recently that Scott had the string action quite low to the fingerboard and that would explain some of it, yet he still had to put his fingers down, and pull the string. It's pretty amazing. But all that listening to the trio had another effect on me. Those early years at the university were thor-oughly engaging intellectually but were also a time of deep introspection. Those years of self-discovery can be challenging at times and those moments found their perfect expression for me in the music of Bill Evans. That time of my life was accompanied by the *Village Vanguard Sessions* and Bill Evans' album *Alone.* I listened to that music for so many hours that it be-came my constant "silent" companion and a beacon

of hope. I knew I wanted to play music this way for my life's calling.

I joined Bill Evans' trio in the spring of 1978 and performed and recorded with him until his death in September 1980. I was thrilled to be a part of Bill's trio. All those hours of listening and playing along with the records and in some way, visualizing playing in that trio had brought me to a strange reality where I was living the dream.

I wrote a song with the dubious title of "Samurai HeeHaw" (named by drummer Adam Nussbaum because of its pentatonic melody and country swing feel) that has as its structure two ten-bar phrases and the harmonic sequence was two perfect fifths, the first starting on the tonic and the next on the sixth tone of the scale. When I realized this, I had to laugh at the subliminal influence Scott LaFaro had on even my writing! Scott's tune, "Gloria's Step" is a twenty-bar tune built on two ten-bar phrases and the opening harmonic sequence of Scott's tune "Jade Visions" was also the harmonic basis of "Samurai." A much more deliberate nod to Scott came some years later on another ECM recording I did called *Shades of Jade*. The title track is set in 11/4 time signature and I was really trying to capture the mood of Scott's "Jade Visions" (from the Vanguard sessions), which is in 9/4. Somehow, the odd signature at that tempo produces a kind of hypnotic trance-like mood, very meditative. It was always one of the more attractive pieces for me from the *Vanguard Sessions* and I think it says a great deal about Scotty's sensibilities.

One more story. In 2007 I was involved in producing and playing bass on a tribute recording to Bill Evans. It's Eliane Elias' album on Blue Note records entitled *Something for You*. Eliane shares the same deep connection to the music as I do and it was a genuine work of love. We chose tunes that spanned Bill's repertoire throughout his career. Something really special happened. I was in Barrie Kolstein's string instrument shop about a month before the recording sessions. I knew Barrie owns the Prescott that belonged to Scotty. He had restored it in the late '80s[1] and I had seen and played a few notes on it, as Barrie sometimes had it out of the vault and let players play the bass if they wanted to when they visited. I told Barrie that I was about to make this tribute record to Bill and without missing a beat, he offered me the use of Scotty's bass for the sessions. I was at once excited at the prospect and yet, though a seasoned veteran of the road, not without a little performance anxiety. This is the first recording of the instrument since Scott's death in 1961. I can't say thanks enough to Barrie for the privilege. Even to have the instrument in the booth with me was inspiration enough, but to play "My Foolish Heart" with it was beyond anything I can tell you. The tune is a ballad so the performance is not about the instrument's ease in playing flurries of notes or executing daring leaps and turns. It was that ballad that informed so much of my emotional being in those formative years when I was first listening to this music. Ballad playing requires a certain patience and is a balancing act between implying a little motion here and there and then being more still, letting the notes ring. Scott seemed to reach the perfect proportion between activity and repose. And that Prescott bass has a sustain you can't believe. I remember Bill telling me once that Scott could strum the open strings, set it down, go out of the room and when he came back, it was still ringing. It felt like that. The instrument also has nicely tapered shoulders making it easier to get in and out of the upper register. It has that rich full sound with wonderful clarity and sustain. To have Scotty's bass in my hands was something beautiful and quite humbling. After hearing the playbacks from the session, I was reminded again that no two players will make exactly the same sound, even when playing the same instrument. And that's how it should be. However, on this recording, I couldn't resist the temptation to recreate a couple of Scott's phrases, motifs, and rhythmic devices and those who know the music intimately might smile at the recognition should they happen to hear this recording.

Scotty's sound, sense of time and melodic invention blazed a trail for modern bassists. Bill once described Scott's playing to me: "He was really discovering something every night on the bandstand. He had all these ideas that were just bubbling up out of him. And he had a way of finding notes that were more fundamental than the fundamental." To use this metaphor in my life as a jazz bassist, Scott's playing is at and beneath the root of all I am.

Both Eddie and Marc discussed a rehearsal tape of Scott and Bill made in the fall of 1960. It is a home recording of Scott and Bill rehearsing and discussing approaches to the tune "My Foolish Heart." Eddie noted:

> Scott would play different notes in a chord, like a third or seventh. Again, unique, and the way Bill voiced on the piano just made it work. I asked Herbie Hancock once about voicings and he said some of that came from Bill and Scott's way of approaching harmony. Interacting is one thing and the way they played through harmonic motion with different chord signs, really contemporary music. They really brought jazz up to a whole other center—really looking forward. Scott really had a very wide influence. I mean on pianists, drummers, and on horn players too.

Of this tape, Marc noted, "They decide on a key, and Scott is singing the melody and supplying bass notes, helping Bill to make the harmonic choices that will eventually become the basis for the rendition on the Vanguard sessions."

Joe LaBarbera, the drummer with the Bill Evans Trio from 1979 through 1980, when Marc was the bassist, told me that when he was with Bill, Bill wanted it to be the trio that it was with Scott. Joe said that Bill's trio was the "role model for me … not the drummers, but actually Scott." He continued:

> One thing Bill told me regarding the music: how important Scott was in the development of what the trio became. You know, a lot of people—and rightfully so—look at Bill Evans as a pioneer or a giant or a trendsetter in jazz and it's all true—but he points directly to Scott in terms of how the trio evolved musically. "My Foolish Heart" was input from them both.
>
> Bill said regarding Scott and the music—that Scott hated it when it remained the same. So they were constantly trying for fresh approaches and fresh improvisations … they would keep specific arrangements but wanted the improvs to change. And Bill told me—I remember it exactly—he said, "if I played the same lick on a tune two nights in a row—the next time I played it Scott would play it with me as if to say 'okay I've heard this enough' and if I played it again he would play it with me in harmony—he would actually harmonize it so at that point it was time for me to get rid of that lick and move on to something else." Scott was an instigator in terms of keeping people on their toes with the music.
>
> The other thing I remember specifically—this is a little more personal but he said that when Scotty was killed, Scotty's girlfriend, Gloria, gave him Scott's overcoat and Bill told me that he wore that overcoat until it was rags. He was just trying to stay connected with Scott and it literally was falling off his back before he was willing to give it up.
>
> Bill recognized in Marc Johnson a connection with Scott and not stylistically—he recognized this purity of spirit—that's exactly the way Bill put it. Marc's got

this purity of spirit that Scott had and that's, I think, what he, Bill, really sensed when he was auditioning bass players and chose Marc. He liked that quality.

Speaking to seminal changes—by Blanton and Scott—had as much to do with the technique they used on the bass as it does with how they changed the role of the bass player because, you know, Blanton because of his prodigious technique made the bass player a feature member of the band and Duke actually wrote around that technique. With Scott it was the whole idea of the bass player being more conversational as opposed to just walking four to the bar. Pianist Mike Wofford pointed out to me, although I was fully aware of this—Scott was ridiculous as a 4/4 walker—he could swing you right out of the room playing four to the bar. But what he did—that whole idea of the trio playing what they call broken time or "open time feel" that's such a huge contribution to the music—so it goes beyond just playing the bass, it goes to how they incorporate their abilities into a group and how it changes the feel of the music. That's a huge thing in my estimation anyway.

The thing about Scotty being able to play such strong 4/4 time in the traditional manner is what a lot of bass players and a lot of musicians aren't aware of. So that's kind of a gap in his recorded history that people don't really know about because when you think of Scott you think of him "doin' it his way."

Rufus Reid also mentioned Scott's metamorphosis. He wrote me: "My [*sic*] first time I was made aware of Scott was a Victor Feldman recording called *The Arrival of Victor Feldman*. It came out in 1958 when I was still in high school, but I didn't actually hear it until around 1962. I was in the Air Force Band as a trumpet player, just beginning to play the bass. Then I heard him play on the *Village Vanguard* recording with Bill Evans. It was amazing to me that it was the same person because his playing and approach was totally different on just those two recordings. It is hard to believe that there were not that many years for Scott LaFaro to make such a huge impact on playing the bass. I hadn't heard of anyone at that time, or even now, who truly understood what each playing concept meant. Scotty really knew what to do. As I get older, I do understand you play what you hear. Scott heard exactly what he wanted to play before he played it."

Critic Harvey Pekar in *Down Beat* magazine (October 11, 1962), wrote, "Even when accompanying, LaFaro didn't limit himself to one particular pattern: he might play two quarter-notes in one bar and superimpose a rhythmic figure containing 16th, dotted-8th, and quarter notes over the beat in the next one. LaFaro's improvising is reminiscent of John Coltrane's because he was seemingly more concerned with harmonic and rhythmic exploration that with overall construction … At times his playing suggests the human voice, and the passion with which he played is almost overpowering."

Bassist Don Payne told me, "Scotty connected all the notes. Nobody played broken time like the Evans Trio. Scott could really play a groove. Could really walk—had intense swing. He had this upper register thing. Everyone loved him. He had great time and expanded vision—rhythmic, harmonic, melodic, thematic."

When I talked to Brian Bromberg, who is recognized as a bassist of great virtuosity and musicality, he told me that "some of the things he [Scotty] did as a player and the voice he tried to have made more sense" when I told him that Scotty was first a sax player. Brian continued:

> I could not, not listen to Bill Evans and Scott. To me he was just so far ahead of his time, technically and inventively. Maybe he was the first guy to really actually play the bass as a musical instrument in a melodic sense and he was blessed enough to have the facility to do

it. He and Bill were complete, confident improvisers. There it is—the Holy Grail—the *Vanguard Albums*. He had a big influence on me and everybody else.

I met John Patitucci in the mid-1980s when he was playing with Victor Feldman at a club in Los Angeles. As I was working on this book in 2007 I spoke with John and he later wrote me: "Scott was a true innovator, trailblazer, and he changed the way people played and thought about the bass forever. I can't help but mention the powerful and emotional playing he did with Bill Evans, particularly the harmonic and rhythmic virtuosity that stunned the world. I am also reminded of the recording with Victor Feldman called *The Arrival* where he is swinging so hard that it shook the world. His work with Ornette Coleman and others show another side of creative playing in a then very new style of freer music."

Bassist Bob Magnusson also wrote me expressing what he feels about Scotty's musical contribution:

> Jazz bassists today are very deeply indebted to Scott LaFaro, a young visionary who changed the course of the bass by radically evolving its role in the jazz context. Bassists prior to Scott, (Jimmy Blanton, Oscar Pettiford, Charles Mingus, Ray Brown and Red Mitchell and his contemporary, Paul Chambers), had also been pushing the known limits of the instrument by soloing in a horn-like manner. However, Scott LaFaro's concepts took this horn-like soloing technique to a much higher plane with his virtuosic technique on the bass, and second, his ability to consistently play in the higher registers (the thumb positions) of the bass, unlike anyone prior to him, which were innovative developments.
>
> During his tenure with the Bill Evans Trio (1959–1961) Scott developed his greatest musical innovation.

When not soloing, the traditional bass role was walking or playing consecutive quarter notes to accompany the piano. Scott, however, developed the function of playing as if a dialogue or conversation with the piano and drums was taking place. While keeping the integrity of the basic function of the bass, this moved the bass to a completely new level. This revolutionary concept is now a standard approach to jazz bass playing. The concepts that he developed and his virtuosic technique continue to be a great influence and a mainstay of jazz bass playing today.

Gene Lees best states the lasting influence of this first trio in his book *Meet Me at Jim & Andy's: Jazz Musicians and their World*: "Bill formed a standing trio, with bassist Scott LaFaro and drummer Paul Motian, with which group Orrin Keepnews produced a series of Riverside albums that continue to be one of the most significant bodies of work in the history of jazz. Bill wanted it to be a three-way colloquy, rather than piano-accompanied-by-rhythm-section. And it was LaFaro, still in his early twenties, who had developed bass playing to a new level of facility. He had a gorgeous tone and unflagging melodicism. Motian, Armenian by background, had since childhood been steeped in a music of complex time figures and was able to feed his companions patterns of polyrhythm that delighted them both. Pianists waited for their albums to come out almost the way people gather at streetcorners in New York on Saturday night to get the Sunday *Times: Portrait in Jazz, Explorations,* and the last two, *Waltz For Debby* and *Sunday at the Village Vanguard,* derived from afternoon and evening sessions recorded live on June 25, 1961. These albums alone (which are best heard in the compact-disc reissue from Fantasy, which have superb sound), if Bill had never recorded anything else, would have secured his position in jazz."

• CHAPTER 14 •

HIS MUSIC II

Scott LaFaro
The Complete Musician

Jeff Campbell

Associate Professor of Jazz Studies
and Contemporary Media

Eastman School of Music, Rochester, New York

I NEVER MET SCOTT LAFARO. I never had the chance to hear him play live. In fact, he died some twenty months before I was born. The only tangible connection I have with him is through his relatively small, but significant recorded output. From circa 1956–1961 LaFaro was involved with an interesting and contrasting array of recording projects that document both his highly developed musical personality and extraordinary bass playing skills. As a jazz bassist, I am very tempted to be solely attracted to LaFaro's facility as an instrumentalist. But ultimately, it is the *soul* of the individual that breathes life into music and LaFaro understood how to combine his instrumental abilities with musicality to create a complete *musical* approach.

175

Scott LaFaro is perhaps best known for his work with the Bill Evans Trio's innovative concept of spontaneous/conversational improvisation. And while I (like many bassists) came to know La-Faro's playing with the Evans trio, I have also become fascinated with his work with other bandleaders and musicians. Despite the importance of his unique and forward-thinking concept as a soloist, perhaps most interesting to me is the way LaFaro functioned as an accompanist. After all, for much of his recorded work LaFaro's primary function was to support the musical concepts of his many and varied employers, including leaders such as Chet Baker, Ornette Coleman, Buddy DeFranco, Bill Evans, Victor Feldman, Herb Geller, Stan Getz, Benny Goodman, Hampton Hawes, Stan Kenton, Harold Land, John Lewis, Pat Moran, Buddy Morrow, and Marty Paich. Most of LaFaro's employers did not necessarily push the cutting edge, but rather used the constructs of swing and bebop to suit their individual musical personalities and to express their respective artistic voices.

These recordings represent a variety of musical styles within the jazz idiom and LaFaro designed bass parts that best fit each distinct musical situation. For every recording, his unique voice as a musician is clearly expressed but he in no way calls undue attention to himself. When appropriate, LaFaro uses his amazing technical facility across a musical spectrum from restraint and temperament to almost reckless abandonment depending upon the given situation. Perhaps the most compelling accolade is that he made all this great music in the space of about six years before his untimely death.

Because I was first introduced to Scott LaFaro's playing through the musical concept of Bill Evans (and LaFaro's gymnastic bass abilities), I foolishly assumed that Scott was disinterested in fulfilling the traditional role of the bass. It seemed his intent was to abandon the well-established practices of bassists such as

Ray Brown, Paul Chambers, Milt Hinton, or Red Mitchell. But as I studied the music more closely, I learned that LaFaro was, indeed, a disciple of the conventions of modern jazz bass playing current in mid- to late-1950s. He could walk harmonically savvy bass lines, play interesting two-beat accompaniment, choose the right notes with great sensitivity on a ballad, and provide a strong, propulsive time feel. Bill Evans commented on LaFaro's knowledge and experience with the conventional role of the bass: "He didn't overlook traditional playing, realizing it could contribute a great deal to his ultimate product."

Consider the opening sixteen bars of his solo walking bass line from Hampton Hawes' composition "For Real" (from the 1958 recording of the same name). If I didn't know that LaFaro was the bass player, it would be tempting to assume that this line was played by Ray Brown. Notice the accented/anticipated low E in bar 3 and the decorative triplets in bars 11 and 12, as well as the "walkup" in bar 9 into 10. In addition to note choices and rhythmic devices, LaFaro's sound is full, robust, and propulsive.

EXAMPLE # 1

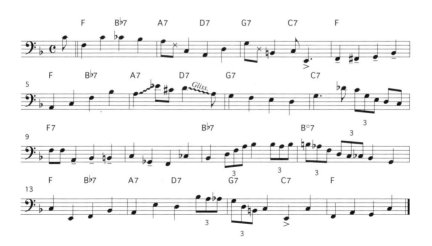

One of the most endearing qualities of LaFaro's bass playing is his innovative concept of sound. Remembering that he was professionally active before amplification and steel strings were commonly used, LaFaro's tone was very forward thinking for the time. Though he used gut strings, his sound possessed an unusual sustaining quality not typically heard in the late 1950s/early 1960s. In almost every case, his sound is well recorded and his tone is both deep and clear. An interesting example is heard in the John Lewis recording "Jazz Abstractions" (1960) where both LaFaro and George Duvivier share the bass chair duties. On Gunther Schuller's adaptation of John Lewis' piece "Django," Duvivier walks a bass line while LaFaro solos. Because the two bassists are playing simultaneously, the difference in their respective tone is quite noticeable. Duvivier's tone is warm and full with a percussive attack while LaFaro's, in contrast, is more agile and has a great deal of length and sustain to each note. (It is interesting to note that Duvivier also played on a record supporting another young and up-and-coming bassist named Ron Carter. The record *Where* [Prestige PRST 7843] was released in 1961.)

Another great example of LaFaro's sound is heard on the above mentioned Hampton Hawes recording "For Real!" This is a happy, straight ahead 4/4 record date, and LaFaro fits right into the spirit of the music. He is well recorded and the sound of the bass is exceptionally clear. While the sustaining quality mentioned before is easily heard during LaFaro's solos, it is the sound of LaFaro's walking bass lines that has the most impact on the group, with each quarter note almost crescendoing into the next. The sustaining quality adds both buoyancy and drive to the pulse. And combined with the energy of Frank Butler's ride cymbal, the feeling of the music is as swinging as any of the great rhythm sections in jazz.

Of course any fan of LaFaro's playing knows how beautiful his sound is on any of the ballads recorded with Bill Evans. On pieces such as "My Foolish Heart," "Detour Ahead," and "Spring Is Here," one can clearly hear the amazingly sustained note values played by LaFaro that support each harmony. In addition, the warmth and full spectrum of tone are important elements of his sound throughout the entire range of the instrument.

A great testament to LaFaro's musical respect and professionalism is found in two recordings he did with pianist Pat Moran. Both recordings were made in one session and yet LaFaro plays quite differently for each. The first, *This is Pat Moran* from December of 1957 features Moran on piano, Gene Gammage on drums, and LaFaro on bass where he takes an active, yet supportive role. His bass lines are well defined, his time feel is solid and supportive, and his solos are inventive and spontaneous. On the fast-paced tune "Onilosor" (Rosolino spelled backwards), LaFaro plays the bebop melody like a horn player with fluid articulation and agility. Example 2 shows the introduction to the tune played by LaFaro in the upper register of the instrument. Here, his bass melody functions as lead voice supported by Moran's piano accompaniment.

EXAMPLE #2

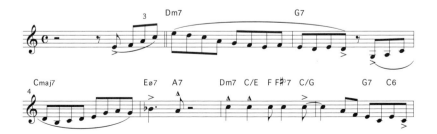

During the piece his solo vocabulary and articulation are closely aligned with that used by Paul Chambers. As an accompanist, he uses the entire range of the bass effectively without detracting from the direction or orchestration of the arrangements.

Throughout this record, Pat Moran finds different ways to feature LaFaro as she creates interesting arrangements with introductions and interludes that capitalize on his unique abilities. Example 3 shows the intro/outro played by LaFaro on the arrangement of "In Your Own Sweet Way."

EXAMPLE #3

He plays these tricky sets of tri-tone figures with very accurate intonation—which as any bassist will attest, is very difficult to execute on the instrument. For this date, LaFaro's musical energy seems boundless and he leaps into every solo opportunity with gusto and enthusiasm—but never at the expense of the music and never with a sense of inflated ego or showing off. And yet, despite his energy as a soloist, LaFaro never compromises his role as an accompanist as he supports the improvised solos of his leader, Pat Moran.

As a side note, LaFaro's solos on this record are highly recommended to the serious jazz bass student for careful study and assimilation. They also illustrate Paul Chambers' influence on LaFaro and serve as examples of both his technical facility and command of bebop jazz vocabulary.

In contrast, the second Moran trio recording *Beverly Kelly Sings with the Pat Moran Trio,* utilizes the same musicians, but this

time in a supportive role behind singer Beverly Kelly. Here, La-
Faro takes on a *completely* different character with a much more
subdued style of bass support. Since these two recordings were
made at the same session, it seems possible that LaFaro might
continue playing as he did for the first session. Instead, he makes
a conscious choice to rein in his technical prowess and creates
bass accompaniment that focuses on the lyrical message and the
stylistic traits presented by the vocalist. By showing such restraint,
LaFaro again illustrates that his sense of musicianship was greater
than his desire to display his amazing technical facility.

Another less well-known dimension of LaFaro's playing is his
work with big bands. There are only a few recordings that document his activity in this genre. During his short career he toured
or recorded with the bands of Buddy Morrow, Stan Kenton, and
Marty Paich. All three bands had their distinct style and repertoire, and LaFaro played to suit each band's sound and concept.
The 1956 recordings with Morrow are important because they
are the very first LaFaro made in his career. He was twenty at the
time. The other two big band records with Kenton and Paich
were made in 1959, during the same period that LaFaro was beginning his association with Bill Evans. The fact that he was well
qualified to play in both large and small groups simultaneously is
a tribute to his versatility.

As mentioned, the projects with trombonist Buddy Morrow
were recorded in 1956 and titled *The Golden Trombone of Buddy
Morrow* and *Let's Have a Dance Party*. Both feature popular repertoire of the era with pieces such as "Stairway to the Stars," "I
Can't Get Started," and "That Old Black Magic," orchestrated and
arranged in sweet, big band style. LaFaro fulfills his role perfectly
but his signature sound is not clearly expressed. This may be because of recording technology of the time or because he chose to
alter his tone to match the stylistic traits of the music or because

these recordings were made at the early stage of his career and his concept of tone was not fully matured. Whatever the case, these are the only recordings where Scott LaFaro's musical personality is not readily apparent.

With Morrow, there was little room for personal expression or musical commentary and LaFaro does not push the issue. This was LaFaro's first professional gig and it is logical to speculate that he was anxious to play according to Morrow's expectations. He takes the role required of him with dignity, showing respect to Morrow. Throughout, the bass function is almost exclusively in a two-beat texture supporting the orchestration of the arrangements and Morrow's Tommy Dorsey-like trombone style.

During LaFaro's time as a member of the Stan Kenton Orchestra he made one record in March of 1959. The recording, *The Stan Kenton Orchestra in Concert,* features Kenton hits such as "My Old Flame," "Intermission Riff," and "Out of This World." LaFaro shows command of various styles of big band bass playing including traditional walking bass, two-beat, and even a 6/8 bass pattern on the Latin piece "La Suerte de Los Tontos." Two other Latin arrangements, "Out of this World" and "I Concentrate on You," require LaFaro to play specific Latin bass patterns, which he does with rhythmic skill and accuracy. He is also heard playing arco within the ensemble on pieces such as "My Old Flame" and "La Suerte de Los Tontos" and is featured as a soloist on "Bernie's Tune." His musical personality is clearly present while he successfully fulfills the bass responsibilities of the repertoire and concept of Stan Kenton's music.

As an example, consider the notated segment below. Here we see twelve bars of Scott's bass line from Kenton's familiar hit "Intermission Riff." The tune is based on a simple harmonic rhythm that centers around the tonality of Db major.

EXAMPLE #4

As is typical, LaFaro's line is harmonically clear and rhythmically interesting. Also, in the first few bars of this excerpt, LaFaro can be heard pulling the time back as the drummer, Jerry Lestock, starts to slightly push ahead. Throughout the piece, LaFaro's bass lines are similar in their construction and even with his highly developed technical skill; he never overplays.

Another less well-known but fabulous big band record LaFaro made is with the arranger and pianist Marty Paich. The record from 1959, *The Broadway Bit*, features the playing of well-known jazz musicians such as Art Pepper, Jimmy Giuffre, Victor Feldman, Bill Perkins, and Mel Lewis. The arrangements show a balance of wonderful ensemble work combined with solo space for the musicians mentioned above. LaFaro is featured several times and plays fabulous solos in the texture of the big band. As usual, just as musically significant is the way he functions as an accompanist and he plays beautifully with drummer Mel Lewis. As a team, their time feel is strong and insistent and yet there is never a sense of force or pushing. In the well-written article by John Bany in *Bass World* (Vol. 14, no. 3, Spring 1988), Mel Lewis talks about LaFaro's participation on the Paich recording. He discusses the particulars about LaFaro's musical contribution and his high level of professionalism, particularly in his sight reading abilities. Says Lewis, "Paich was worried about whether or not Scott could read. [Victor] Feldman recommended Scott very highly and Scott played his ass off on this record. He played very well, swung good, nice sound, nice solos, and read the parts beautifully."

As an illustration of LaFaro's reading skills, consider the following passage from Paich's arrangement of "It's All Right With Me" where the entire ensemble plays a three-beat cross rhythm that *almost* feels like quarter note triplets. In response, the bass part provides a rhythmic counterpart that fits exactly between the second and third beat of each implied triplet. As the rhythmic figure continues to spin, the feeling of a strong downbeat dissolves but LaFaro's well-placed bass parts brings the sense of arrival and cohesiveness at the end of each eight-bar phrase.

EXAMPLE #5

In a more intimate setting on the Paich recording, LaFaro shows his keen sense of harmonic motion as he designs a bass line behind Art Pepper's solo on the ballad "I've Grown Accustomed to Her Face" as seen in Example 6. The rhythmic content is based on a double-time feel, which LaFaro and Mel Lewis perform with great taste and subtlety.

EXAMPLE #6

LaFaro uses guide tones in the upper register in bar 10 to help guide the harmonic movement. Also notice his use of tri-tone melodic leaps in bars 5, 11, and 14 providing smooth, stepwise motion to the arrival point following each leap. Throughout this excerpt LaFaro shows great craft as he improvises a line that is both melodically interesting and harmonically specific. This type of dual-purpose design was one of his most significant musical traits regardless of stylistic setting.

Almost all of the recorded examples of Scott LaFaro's bass playing are confined to the time limits imposed by commercial record's formatting and procedure. The majority of the pieces in LaFaro's recorded output are typically between three and seven minutes long. In contrast, there is a wonderful illustration of La-Faro's playing in a more informal setting where the length of the pieces is much more typical of a jam session or live date. The 1958 recording is with legendary saxophonist Harold Land made at a club called The Cellar in Vancouver, Washington. The group performs typical jam session tunes such as "Cherokee" and "Just

Friends" as well as a Charlie Parker blues entitled "Big Foot" and a walking ballad version of "Come Rain or Come Shine."

The first piece, "Cherokee," is played at a remarkably fast tempo with Harold Land and pianist Elmo Hope taking very long improvised solos. After fourteen minutes of supportive rhythm section playing, LaFaro takes a walking bass line solo where he shows absolutely no sign of fatigue. The entire piece is almost twenty minutes in length and LaFaro is a constant source of rock-solid time and inventive bass line construction. And to play at such a rapid tempo for so long clearly shows his strength as an instrumentalist. It is very rare to hear recordings of LaFaro in this type of setting and once again, he demonstrates another facet of his musicianship that makes him such a well-rounded musician.

The other pieces on the recording, while not played at such a fast tempo, are also quite lengthy, with "Just Friends" lasting twenty-one minutes, "Come Rain or Come Shine" at twelve minutes, and "Big Foot" lasting half an hour. For each piece Scott consistently plays inventive bass accompaniment as well as won-derfully creative solos. This document serves as a reminder that LaFaro undoubtedly spent most of his professional career in the trenches playing live dates and gigs that required long hours of physical and mental exertion. It was in these settings that he was able to work through his musical concepts and ideas with his col-leagues and friends.

Another important record made on the West Coast was with the British pianist and vibes player, Victor Feldman. Feldman was a champion of LaFaro's and promoted him with enthusiasm to fellow musicians and potential bandleaders. In January of 1958, Feldman recorded his first American release called *The Arrival of Victor Feld-man* featuring LaFaro and drummer Stan Levey. The repertoire and vocabulary is drawn directly from the bebop language and LaFaro once again demonstrates how well informed he was by this music.

All his solos on the date serve as defining models of bebop melodic construction and his right hand articulation sounds much like that used a saxophonist or trumpet player. In this setting, LaFaro is easily heard, especially because the stereo recording isolates Feldman on the left channel and LaFaro on the right. When Feldman plays vibes, there is no comping and LaFaro's bass lines are well designed to give clarity to the harmonic content in the absence of chords. Example 7 shows LaFaro's accompanying bass line on the Miles Davis composition "Serpent's Tooth."

EXAMPLE #7

As discussed earlier regarding his accompaniment behind Art Pepper, LaFaro designs a bass line that is both melodically interesting and harmonically complete. For the most part he uses small segments of rhythmic decoration that supply the line with forward motion. He also uses occasional accents on the "and of one" that breaks up the steady stream of walking quarters. Notice his use of glissandi in bars 9 and 10. This was a device that he was using more and more in his playing and typically not used by other bassists at this time. He chooses notes in bars 27–30 that are not harmonically correct but melodically savvy, but when the line finally comes to rest in bar 30 on the tonic Bb, the melodic logic and the harmonic tension come together in a most dramatic fashion.

As mentioned earlier, most of LaFaro's employers worked within the established constructs of swing and bebop. However, there was one leader whose musical outlook was anything but conventional. Ornette Coleman was very much an innovator in the lexicon of jazz music and pioneered the Free Jazz movement. His search for new musical landscapes led him to find unique musicians who were willing to experiment with the elements of music. The fact that LaFaro played on at least five Ornette Coleman recordings speaks to the bass player's open and searching musical mind.

Perhaps the most cited of LaFaro's work with Coleman is *Free Jazz,* recorded in December of 1960. For this recording, Coleman used two quartets in a simultaneous improvisational dialog. Using the relatively-new-at-the-time technology of stereo, each quartet was recorded on one of the two stereo tracks. The left channel quartet consists of Ornette Coleman (saxophone), Don Cherry (trumpet), Scott LaFaro (bass), and Billy Higgins (drums). On the right channel are Eric Dolphy (bass clarinet), Freddie Hubbard (trumpet), Charlie Haden (bass), and Ed Blackwell (drums). For the most part, Charlie Haden plays in the mid to lower range of the bass while LaFaro plays in the mid to upper register. Haden takes on the 4/4 walking duties while LaFaro plays a bubbly and textural "bass obligato." There are also two fascinating duets between Haden and LaFaro that clearly illustrate two great musical minds at work plus new and innovative methods of double bass playing. The significance of the advancement of extended techniques demonstrated by Haden and LaFaro on this recorded document cannot be overestimated.

A very significant aspect of Scott LaFaro's playing that is often overlooked is his sense of feel for time coupled with his ability to create deep, swinging grooves. Throughout all of his recordings, he demonstrates a strong pulse and beat. In every instance, he found a way to hook up with each drummer that he played with. It should be pointed out that in his short career, he performed with some very influential and important drummers including Ed Blackwell, Frank Butler, Roy Haynes, Billy Higgins, Elvin Jones, Pete LaRoca, Stan Levey, Mel Lewis, and Paul Motian.

Regardless of the complexity, texture, style, or tempo of the music, LaFaro always played with a great time feel. It is difficult to choose just one track or recording that best exemplifies LaFaro's gift—they are all good. But if pushed, I would have to recommend LaFaro's performance on the Stan Getz/Cal Tjader Sextet recording from February of 1958 titled *Stan Getz/Cal Tjader Sextet,* particularly on the tune "Ginza" by Pete Jolly. On this tune, LaFaro and drummer Billy Higgins create one of the most deep and infectious grooves captured in recorded jazz; it is truly inspirational!

Of interest are the liner notes from the Getz/Tjader recording by Ralph J. Gleason where he states: "But mark down the names of [Billy] Higgins and [Scott] LaFaro. They are youngsters in a young man's art. Higgins is from Los Angeles, only 21 and a

student of Bill Douglass and Lennie McBrowne. He's been playing only since 1954. LaFaro is from Geneva, N.Y., has worked
with Buddy Morrow and Buddy DeFranco and has been playing for four years. Higgins is a painter as well as a musician and
LaFaro says he's too busy for hobbies. He's catching up on Bird
recordings, he adds. Both these men will make their mark in jazz
history. Their technique and their ability to blow with the veterans on this date is almost frightening in light of their youth. It is
also a tribute to the intelligence and talent of the younger generation of jazz musicians."

In November of 1960, LaFaro joined pianist Steve Kuhn
and drummer Pete LaRoca to make an interesting trio recording simply titled *1960*. Kuhn leads the group through a mixture
of standards and jazz compositions including "Little Old Lady,"
"Bohemia After Dark," "What's New," and two versions of "So
What." Kuhn's trio combines elements of traditional, straight-
ahead playing with a searching, open approach, at times hinting at
the conversational style associated with the Bill Evans Trio. Again,
LaFaro maintains his unique musical personality without over-
shadowing the musical concept of Steve Kuhn.

There are two interesting examples of LaFaro's expanding
musical concepts heard on the Kuhn recording. The first is found
in the performance of "So What" where LaFaro and Kuhn engage
in a brief musical dialogue just prior to the return of the theme.
In this case both musicians improvise melodic ideas that are in-
tertwined in a conversational manner. While brief in duration
(sixteen bars), this short passage is akin to the way LaFaro was
beginning to play with Bill Evans.

The other example is found on the ballad "What's New"
where LaFaro combines the traditional conventions of ballad
playing with a much more active role to accompany Kuhn's rendition of the theme, as seen in Example 8.

EXAMPLE #8

The bass line combines open half notes with motion-filled commentary that fits between Kuhn's melodic statements. This was a new method of ballad bass accompaniment for the period and an innovation pioneered by LaFaro. Most of the activity is found on the tonic Eb major chord with the use of repeated notes—an identifiable trait that emerged during this time in LaFaro's playing. As usual, the long notes dramatically exemplify LaFaro's full-valued, sustained tone. This is one of the earliest examples of his concept of conversational bass accompaniment in a ballad setting.

An interesting point to remember is that the Kuhn trio date was made in November of 1960 almost a year *after* LaFaro's first recording with Bill Evans, *Portrait in Jazz* from December 1959. This was also during a time that the Evans trio was actively performing live dates and developing its concept of simultaneous or conversational improvisation. In the early stages of his tenure with the Evans trio, LaFaro's approach to ballad playing was more conventional than seen with Kuhn. Example 9 shows LaFaro's accompaniment from the opening sixteen bars of "When I Fall In Love" from the *Portrait* album.

EXAMPLE #9

Here we see a simple, direct approach using only root notes in conjunction with each chord change. LaFaro uses very little if any rhythmic commentary and designs a line that stays in a limited register of the bass.

It is an interesting fact that the earliest recorded example of LaFaro's active, conversational ballad accompaniment was with Steve Kuhn and not with Bill Evans. It wasn't until the final recordings with Evans, *Waltz for Debby* and *Sunday at the Village Vanguard,* that LaFaro's conversational ballad playing is seen in a much more developed stage, as exemplified on pieces such as "Detour Ahead," "My Foolish Heart," and "Jade Visions."

As stated earlier, I first became aware of Scott LaFaro through the music of the Bill Evans Trio. And after having spent time studying LaFaro's playing with other leaders, I have gained a much greater appreciation for the manner in which he played with Evans. As with other bandleaders, his musical choices with Evans demonstrate La-Faro's ability to show musical sympathy specific to the range and scope of Evan's pioneering concept of jazz improvisation.

Much has been written about the musical innovations of the Bill Evans Trio with Scott LaFaro and Paul Motian and its conversational and spontaneous improvisational style. And while the topic is important to the development of the syntax of the jazz language, I will focus on LaFaro's accompanimental role within the trio. I have chosen five pieces that document specific attributes of LaFaro's bass playing with the trio: "Autumn Leaves," "Peri's Scope," "Someday My Prince Will Come," "Sweet and Lovely," and "Detour Ahead."

"Autumn Leaves" (*Portrait in Jazz,* December 28, 1959)

LaFaro's performance on this well-known standard serves as a prime example of both his innovative and conventional musical support. To accompany Bill Evans' opening melodic statement, LaFaro creates a non-traditional bass line that musically bobs and weaves its way around the theme. He does anything but play simple half notes but the very active line does not detract in any way from the harmonic or melodic agenda of the tune. Almost as a surprise, LaFaro's busy line gives way to standard 4/4 walking on the bridge but the contrast between the two textures is absolutely seamless. LaFaro's line is notated in Example 10. Notice the use of quarter-note triplets in bars 7 and 8 and the repeated eighth-note triplets in bar 10.

EXAMPLE #10

The improvising section features a truly conversational duet between LaFaro and Evans that eventually morphs into a more conventional piano solo with walking bass support.

"Peri's Scope" (*Portrait in Jazz*, December 28, 1959)

For this piece, LaFaro plays bass lines that are traditional in design and scope. To support the melody, LaFaro plays a conventional "two-beat" texture clearly illustrating his knowledge of the customary function and expectations of the bass player. This piece was recorded early in the trio's brief life and it is logical to assume that they were comfortable with the traditional conventions of the piano trio. To support Bill Evans' solo, LaFaro plays a conventional walking bass line that clearly defines the harmonic content of the piece. It is interesting to point out that he uses very little rhythmic decoration and for the majority of the solo section, he almost exclusively chooses strict quarter notes. Given his highly developed technique, it would seem logical that he could choose much more flamboyant rhythmic decoration, but instead, his highly developed sense of musicianship calls upon his best musical senses. Of note is his use of the full range of the bass and as mentioned earlier, his sound influences the time feel and forward motion of the music.

"Someday My Prince Will Come" (*Portrait in Jazz*, December 28, 1959)

For this piece, LaFaro provides an interesting array of types of bass support. For the theme, he plays a mixture of simple dotted half notes and syncopated bass lines. See Example 11.

EXAMPLE #11

For the solo section, LaFaro does not engage in a conversational dialog with Evans. Instead he designs a 3/4 walking bass line with musically placed rhythmic decoration. Given the spontaneous improvisational style of the group, LaFaro's use of a walking bass line was a surprise to me, especially given the rhythmic freedom associated with a jazz waltz.

There is one very interesting point in the tune where the trio adds one beat to the 3/4 meter. At the beginning of the second improvised chorus, one extra count somehow finds its way into the music. It comes at a point where Evans is playing a "cross rhythm" against LaFaro's walking bass line. And what's so amazing is that the trio "corrects" itself without any hint of interruption or recalculation.

"Sweet and Lovely" (*Explorations*, February 2, 1961)

LaFaro's playing on this piece truly exemplifies his abilities in the context of the trio's spontaneous improvisational style. While he uses walking bass lines from time to time, most of his accompanimental support is realized in an open dialogue as he creates lines that cross fade from bass line function to contrapuntal commentary to melodic statements. LaFaro also provides stabilizing half-note and whole-note support behind Paul Motian's drum solo. And his use of the entire range of the bass helps give the texture of the music a light and mobile feeling.

"Detour Ahead" (*Waltz for Debby*, June 25 1961)

LaFaro's accompaniment on this less well-known standard serves as a prime example of both his conventional and innovative concepts of jazz bass accompaniment. The piece opens in a very slow ballad tempo with LaFaro using simple half notes and whole notes to articulate the bass motion of the tune. And while this was a typical approach for bass players at the time, LaFaro's innovative concept of sound allows each of these bass notes to realize its full metric value. The fact that these bass notes have so much sustain gives the very slow tempo of the music a feeling of forward motion.

As the piece unfolds, LaFaro's bass support gradually becomes more and more interactive. But he increases his level of activity in such a subtle way that he comfortably "invites" the listener into this more lively way of providing bass support. And while his approach was unconventional for the time, LaFaro's concept is absolutely loyal to the functional bass motion of the tune. This is evident by the way he designs a contrapuntal bass lines that include bass notes, chord tones, and their respective resolutions. To illustrate LaFaro's contrasting bass support, consider Example 12, where LaFaro's accompaniment on the first and second A sections of the tune are set in score format for easy comparison.

EXAMPLE #12

Notice that (with one exception) the bass note of each chord is embedded in the linear texture throughout the eight-bar example. LaFaro frequently uses ascending linear shapes to arrive at defining chord tones as seen in bars 1 and 2. At the end of bar 3, LaFaro's line ends on a D# (clarifying the B7alt. chord). The D# logically leads to E at the beginning of bar 4 which is the 7th of the Fmaj7 chord.

Each of these five pieces illustrates LaFaro's unique approach to bass playing. For each piece he found different ways to support the direction of the music. At times he was very active, using his highly developed technique in conversation with Evans and Motian. Other times he chose to take on a more supportive role, allowing the music to breathe. Throughout, his musical personality is clearly expressed but never dominates. And his passion for *the moment* is vital to the intangible magic associated with this remarkable and highly influential musical unit.

For his tragically short career, Scott LaFaro was a consummate professional. He approached every musical situation with the attitude and respect necessary to create music at the highest level regardless of stylistic or aesthetic outlook. To employ a cliché, Scott truly was a team player of the highest caliber whose individual contributions to jazz improvisation and bass playing are still having a major impact some forty-five years after his death. I never met Scott LaFaro, but through his recorded musical performance, I better know the soul of this great musician who injected life and passion into the *music* every time he picked up his bass.

· CHAPTER 15 ·

His Music III

Phil Palombi

I REMEMBER THE DAY THAT I bought the two Bill Evans albums *Waltz for Debby* and *Sunday at the Village Vanguard*. It was the summer before I started college at Youngstown State University, and I had just begun to play acoustic bass four months previously. At the time I was an electric bassist still largely into playing and listening to rock music, but I was heavily drawn to extended improvisation, which was mostly lacking in pop music.

I was hanging out in Cleveland with a bass player from the college who was showing me the ropes. We dropped into the Record Exchange, where I met a senior from YSU who was sifting through the stacks of vinyl. As we spoke, I told him I was learning upright and I was hoping to learn more about jazz. He told me "as a jazz bass player, these are two of the most important records that you need to own," and pulled those two Bill Evans albums out of the stack. In retrospect, I find it funny that a proverbial "piece of the puzzle" was dropped into place for me by a lead trumpet player.

When I heard Scott, it didn't occur to me that it was virtuosic or challenging for a bassist to play in such a manner. His playing simply struck me as melodic. I didn't notice that he wasn't laying the time down in a traditional sense because the trio as a whole was swinging. He approached the bass in such an effortless way that I figured all bass players could (and *should*) get around the instrument like that. I skipped over the awe of his technical prowess and identified with his soulfulness and passion. That is a lesson that has always stayed with me.

Fast forward to 2002. I was living in New York City, married, with a baby on the way. I was sitting around one day when I thought, "It's been a while since I've transcribed anything." I got the sudden urge to start a transcription right then and there. Then I thought "Who??" Scott LaFaro! I've probably listened to those two records more than any others in the world, but I had only transcribed one solo ("All of You"), which I did while I was in college. I figured now would be the perfect time to transcribe a little since the baby wasn't coming for a few months, so I sat down and transcribed "Gloria's Step." You have to keep in mind that ever since that fateful day in the Record Exchange, I've been obsessed with learning more about Scott as a person as well as Scott as a player. I spent a year with Buddy Morrow's band and I used to bug him constantly for stories about Scott, and he was happy to share them. When I was done transcribing "Gloria's Step," I felt like I was holding a piece of Scott in my hands. I felt like I was getting to know him personally. I wanted to do another one, so I did. This time I transcribed "All of You" (take 3) and I heard something I'd never heard in all my years of listening to the recordings—I heard Scott laugh after somebody knocked over a beer bottle (which, like a geek, I notated in the book). I was so excited that I even called my wife in the room to hear. That's when I thought, "Why not transcribe them all?" So I did. Transcribing just a few of the solos felt wrong. I loved the music so much that the solos became living entities to me and it felt wrong to leave even one solo behind. It may sound a little strange, but I couldn't even choose which solo to transcribe next until I decided to transcribe all of them.

It took me about three months to get all fifteen solos (which I bought on CDs) transcribed. By the end of it all, not only did I get a lesson from Scott, I learned a lot about what the trio was doing and how they achieved their sound.

I figured that somebody had already published the solos, so I thought it would be nice to buy the book and compare my work to his or hers. That's when I discovered that with a few exceptions, nobody had published these solos before. I couldn't believe it. Most bassists consider Scott one of the biggest influences in modern jazz bass playing, yet nobody had published these solos, which are the prime examples of Scott's developing style. I felt that I needed to put a book together. I searched the internet and came across Chuck Ralston's great LaFaro tribute site and decided to drop him a line and tell him what I did. He was nice enough to introduce me (via the internet) to Scott's sister Helene. Every day I'm thankful that Helene and the LaFaro family allowed me to be the person to publish the book.[1] To show my gratitude, I went the extra mile and looked over each solo with a fine-tooth comb. I spent about a year and a half proof-reading the solos (between diaper changes, by that time) to make sure I represented them accurately.

When asked to write about the technical prowess of Scott LaFaro for this book, still all I can think about is his musicality. To the casual listener, or even the erudite bassist, the technical aspect of Scott's playing is transparent. His solos don't necessarily sound like they would be difficult to play, though in fact it does take a lot of practice to make a bass sound like Scott does. In the last few years, I have been obsessed with the notion of what makes a great musician sound great. In the search, I've created a filter to quantify elements of a player's approach to the instrument and music.

I try to forget about sounding exactly like the person under the microscope, and instead focus on why players play the way they do. What brought them to their musical conclusions, why did they choose those notes, how do they get their sound? I like to break things down into four categories: Sound, Rhythm, Phrasing, and Tonality.

In writing this chapter, I would like to be a bit myopic. My LaFaro education began with the famous record date that created the two Bill Evans records, *Waltz for Debby,* and *Sunday at the Village Vanguard*. These were the first examples of Scott's playing that I encountered, and they made a lasting impression on my playing. I have always felt that Scott was just beginning to make his breakthrough (in terms of soloing) on that record date. It seems to me that his playing was constantly changing, evolving, improving, until one day all of this music came pouring out of him. It seems to me that his technique caught up with what his ear was telling him, and lucky for us someone was recording!

Sound

That is the sound of the recordings, the sound of Scott's bass, and the sound and blend of the trio. Sound is always the first thing that catches my attention on these recordings. The sound of LaFaro's bass is earthy and warm. No amp, just gut strings on a good old Prescott bass. Some speculate that he lowered the string height so that he could fly up and down the neck. That's not really necessary, and judging by the big sound he gets, I would say that his string action was medium-high.

He was playing a lot, practicing a lot, and as a result his chops were strong. You can hear it in the way the notes pop out of the bass when playing his fast eighth-note runs up and down the fingerboard. He played hard and clean—you can hear every eighth note, eighth-note triplet, and sixteenth note in his playing. He achieved this by having great coordination between his two hands. The sheer speed comes from this coordination and the way in which he used his plucking fingers, alternating the index and middle fingers of his right hand much as an electric bassist would.

Focusing on just his hands, I began to notice all of the little articulations LaFaro would interject into his playing: staccato, legato, pull-offs, hammer-ons, slides, appoggiatura. I love to listen to these two recordings in a quiet room with headphones on and soak in the different ways he could play one note.

Example 1

In Example 1, towards the end of bar 5, Scott begins the slide (notated above the bar with the letter S) on Db, which ultimately resolves to the B in bar 6. He plays the E's in bar 6 staccato, but legato on beat one of bar 7 followed by another slide to the b9 of the B7, which resolves by way of yet another slide to the 5 of the E minor chord. He pays attention to these small details in every solo he plays.

Rhythm

Coordination is nothing without control, and LaFaro maintained tight control of his rhythm. I was amazed at how easy it was to notate the rhythm of his solos. His transition, for instance, from quarter-note triplet to eighth notes, back to quarter note triplets then onto eighth notes within the quarter note triplets would be metronomic.

In Example 2, taken from "Detour Ahead" (take 1), you can see how often Scott would vary his rhythms.

Example 2

Scott often used his control over rhythm as an added decoration. For instance, in a swing tune, he would sometimes play the end of a solo phrase straight (without the swing eighth-note feel). Other times he may purposely drag or delay the start of the phrase, then snap right into perfect time.

Other times he would use a repetitive rhythmic device, like taking a three-note arpeggio and displacing it over eighth-note triplets repeatedly for three or more bars of music, then finally releasing the tension into a long flowing melodic line. Scott seemed to use this kind of rhythmic "tension and release" quite a bit in his playing.

Of course, no discussion of Scott LaFaro's rhythm would be complete without mentioning the quarter-note triplet. If there is one thing that truly defines Scott, it would be this rhythm. Just listen to his solo over "Gloria's Step." LaFaro often plays long, fast running lines into the upper register of the bass, then gracefully falls back down in quarter-note triplets, or eighth notes within the quarter-note triplets.

Phrasing

LaFaro rarely began a phrase on the downbeat of a bar. He seemed to start phrases anywhere in the bar, and generally mixed it up during a solo. In addition to start points, the end points tend to break up the traditional four- and eight-bar phrases of the songs. I thought this was a noteworthy observation since it seems that Scott's affinity for stretching the bar line is evident in his writing as well. Both "Jade Visions" and "Gloria's Step" have odd-numbered phrases.

As I alluded to in the section on rhythm, LaFaro used the full range of his instrument. Most of his phrases take you from one end of the instrument to the other in a kind of rollercoaster ride.

Example 3

In the first eight bars of his solo from "All of You" take 2, (Example 3), it is plain to see just how loose LaFaro was with his phrases, as well as the "rollercoaster" comparison.

Tonality

Now we arrive at tonality: what kind of note choices was Scott making? I have discovered that Scott's choice of what to play was very unbass-like. It seems that most bassists of the day tended to view soloing in terms of the individual chord changes they were playing over. LaFaro glided right over the top of the changes, much like a horn player (or Bill Evans, for that matter).

If you listen to Scott's opening solo line in his song "Gloria's Step," for instance, you can hear how he takes a group of changes and plays one beautiful descending line over all of them.

Example 4

In Example 4, Scott starts on a high A and tumbles down in a whole tone scale resolving to the C7(#9). The beauty of this line is how the whole tone scale produces color notes (9's, Maj 7's, #5's) on its way down. Listen to any of the songs that are based on the progression iii–vi–ii–V7 and you'll notice that he usually gravitates towards melodies based off of the tonic key center.

These are but a few examples of how LaFaro takes something complicated and makes music out of it. He will play very fast chromatic (or near chromatic) runs up into thumb position, then find all of the beautiful color notes (major 7's, 9's, #11's) to sit on when he gets up there. He has one of the strongest melodic senses of any bassist who has ever played, which I feel has been one of his strongest contributions to bass history.

Finally, all great paintings need an appropriate frame. Scott's frame was Bill Evans and Paul Motian. Without the support of these two great players, Scott would have had a much harder time expressing himself the way he did on these recordings.

Paul Motian's solid playing allowed Scott the freedom to break up his rhythm and take on the role of counterpoint to Bill, rather that simply laying down four-to-the-floor bass lines. If you listen closely, Paul is swinging along as if Scott is playing a walking bass line, which filled in the trio's bottom end and allowed Scott to dance around more than other bassists were doing at that time. Without Paul's understated elegance, Scott wouldn't have been able to have the interplay with Bill that helped to set this trio apart.

Bill Evans was the perfect accompanist for a bassist. Scott took many chances when soloing, and Bill was always right there to support him. There are a few instances where Scott strayed away from the changes, but Bill was always right there to voice the chord differently and support him. Actually, Scott was free to play anything because Bill would simply voice it and make it fit!

I think it is also noteworthy to discuss Bill's impact on Scott's development. As you have probably already learned in this book, Bill and Scott were close friends and they spent many many hours playing together. You can imagine how well your playing would improve if you were playing with Bill Evans every day. That said, I often go back and listen to these recordings and try to hear Bill's influence on Scott. Not surprisingly, I sometimes hear Scott's influence on Bill as well.

• CHAPTER 16 •

HIS LEGACY

THE PIANIST WALTER NORRIS ONCE observed, "The question in art is not who is best or better, but to be able to realize and appreciate the unique qualities of all whose playing is magical. Scotty had that quality and the power to go with it all."

A constant in my life since Scotty's death has been the many musicians who have asked about all aspects of Scotty's life and have expressed how he touched their lives and the impact he made on them. He does seem to have been the beacon for many, directly influencing bass playing and helping to steer the jazz trio in new directions. They remark that Scotty played swift melody lines, as if playing a horn or guitar. He mixed traditional timekeeping between lines with far-ranging countermelodies in free rhythm. With Evans, he played complex, interlocked lines. He helped develop what is called the "conversational" element to jazz ensemble playing, setting the standard for a new generation of players. Over the years Scotty's legacy has also been noted in many publications. The bibliography herein gives a listing of those that evaluate his work. Further, Chuck Ralston's excellent website dedicated to Scotty—scottlafaro.com—has not only a regularly updated listing but includes, in many cases, the text of the article, review, et al. More touching to me than the accolades noting his musical ability, however, is the more personal influence he had on so many over the years. Bass players—classical, jazz, contemporary rock—young

211

and old—from near and far—some well known, some everyday working musicians, and students. Drummers and other musicians as well. In talking to so many, I found that there was often some pleasing common ground.

Many were surprised to learn that tenor sax not the bass was Scotty's first instrument of choice. Some I talked to told me they also came to the bass in an off-beat manner. Stanley Clarke was introduced to the bass when, in high school, he arrived late on the day instruments were being distributed and acoustic bass was one of the few remaining. Brian Bromberg began on cello and his teacher wanted him to play bass. John Gianelli also began on the cello. Eddie Gomez told me that the bass "sort of picked me." He started playing at age twelve when a teacher looked at his hands and proclaimed him a bass player.

Many vividly remember when they first heard Scotty. Many felt that Scotty opened doors to the bass' possibilities.

Eddie Gomez recalls:

> Around fifteen I heard Bill's trio and then I heard Scott for the first time and the musical world they created was so free for the bass and Scott was—he was an in-novator and his vision was right there with Bill's, as was Paul Motian's. They were on the same page with the vision and it was very emotional, beautiful music and it really resonated with me in so many different ways. The way Scott played—he made a huge impact on me and the trio did for a lot of reasons. Of course the way he was very supportive in that context, he was so open and melodic and interactive with Bill. And Paul. Scott was so melodic and just had a whole new world that he opened up. I mean a whole new planet, a way of different colors, the way he played.

Marc Johnson first heard Scotty's playing on the Riverside recording *Explorations* when he was in his first year at the University of North Texas and said that discovering the Bill Evans Trio with Scott and Paul began his lifelong musical relationship with that trio.

Stanley Clarke, bassist and composer, is known, as was Scotty, for his chops, acumen, and virtuosity. Scotty and Charlie Mingus were his idols.

> I remember both Charlie and Scotty struck me very specifically. I was just amazed at Mingus'—that a bass player had his own records because my understanding of the bass before that was basically like Bill Wyman in the Rolling Stones—the guy that was just there in the back smiling. The bass player was just the guy holding down the beat, not doing anything special. And Scott. I was just amazed at his virtuosity on the bass—that was the first thing I was struck with. That and his melodic sense—that I could actually hear melody coming from what I thought was a crude instrument. I was struggling. Then I realized—I thought, gosh, he must have a better instrument than I do or something—something's got to be wrong here. Wait a minute, how can this guy get that sound?
>
> There were a lot of ways Scotty inspired me: to really inspect the bass and research the bass world, check out other basses. I realized that basses were made in different countries, that there were lots of different strings and different ways of playing. It was a really cool thing. Scotty lowered his bridge. He obviously researched the bass. His approach to the bass was very avant-garde, one of the first real revolutionary bass players. He had such a sense of melody and rhythm. I love the way he played bass, his inventiveness, lyricism, musicality, his virtuosity. Scotty was definitely amazing … that's all I can say.

The immensely talented bassist, John Clayton, a former artistic director of jazz for the Los Angeles Philharmonic Orchestra, as well as a seven-time Grammy nominee, wrote that he was a huge fan of Scott. He said, "In fact, he [Scott] is a pivotal figure for bassists and I even have my students study his work. They go so far as to transcribe his bass lines and play his music, note-by-note with his recordings. It's one of the best ways to really get inside what Scott did so beautifully."

Richard Davis, bassist and now a professor, states simply: "I feel that Scotty was a major influence on bassists generationally. Listening to him on recordings was a mind blower."

I met Nathan East years ago when he was playing with Victor Feldman. He is an original member of the jazz group Fourplay, and appears and records with folks as diverse as Herbie Hancock and Eric Clapton among many other well-known musicians. He told me, "Very few players have ever been able to make an upright bass sing like the great Scott LaFaro. I first heard him with Bill Evans and later with Vic Feldman. His lyrical style, taste, tone, and melodic contribution to the music captured my ear and immediately set a new standard for how the instrument should be approached. When someone comes along and revolutionizes the sound of an instrument like Scott did, it changes everything. As a young player myself, his melodic sensibility gave me something to strive for in my playing. While the primary role of the bass is support, Scott managed to create a more meaningful relationship between a support and the lead instrument impacting the role of the bass in jazz forever."

When first attending a concert in 2007 at jazz venue Gianelli Square in the San Fernando Valley near my home, I had no idea that Los Angeles bassist, John Gianelli, was someone also influenced by Scotty. In ensuing conversations John went into more detail:

> I first heard Scotty, around 1964. I heard the Bill
> Evans *Village Vanguard* album … that just knocked
> me out. To this day I still have that in my vehicle. The
> way Scotty harmonically dealt with the changes, like
> a soloist instead of just playing roots and fifths of the
> chords. Just harmonically. I listened to him so much.
> It got me listening to the harmonies both he and Bill
> did and it affects the way I play and I hear changes and
> everything. Scott definitely opened up the doors for
> bass players to add more to the harmony and melodic
> sense rather than just be time keepers and playing the
> bottom of the changes for soloists to play on top of.
> He was the guy that I think was the link in bass playing
> being the time keeper and becoming an actual integral
> harmonic voice … which made the trio more of a
> group rather than three people just playing together.

David Wong was playing with Roy Haynes in Los Angeles when I met him. He wrote me later about Scott's influence on him. "His playing has always kind of scared me because it is so prodigious and even sounds modern today. Scott's playing was shocking. My favorite record of his is Bill Evans' *Portrait in Jazz*. Scott's playing is so swinging and the sound he gets is so beautiful and in tune."

Craig Snazelle, a freelance bassist in Portland, Oregon, who notes that he is now fifty-six, wrote me in an email: "Scott continues to be a source of inspiration to the young rock 'n' roll bass player who heard the *Waltz for Debby* album at sixteen and realized what he wanted to do with his life in music and as a bass player."

In 1967, six years after Scotty's death, Gary Karr founded the International Society of Bassists. The Society has grown to nearly 3,000 members in forty countries. From the beginning, Scott has always been a touchstone and musical hero for the performers, teachers, students, makers, and hobbyists who make up the Society, and his memory has lived on in the pages of its journal, *Bass*

World. At their convention in 2001, I was fortunate to hear Gary Karr in concert and meet him.

Recognized as the world's leading classical solo bassist, Gary Karr made his debut with Leonard Bernstein and the New York Philharmonic Orchestra in 1962. During his forty-year career, he has performed as soloist throughout the world and holds many distinguished awards. He was born five years after Scotty, and was just beginning his own professional career as Scotty's was catching fire. Regarding Scott, Gary said,

> When I had my debut with the New York Philhar-monic in 1962, people were surprised that the double bass, which had been relegated as a kind of percus-sion instrument in the orchestra which kept the beat and produced the harmonic foundation, was suddenly thrust into the spotlight as a solo instrument much like the cello or violin. Until then, double bass players were never "stars" in the classical scene, but in jazz, even dur-ing the bop era, there were always players that achieved international recognition. When Scott LaFaro came on the scene and changed the role of the bassist as a "beat purveyor" to that of a soloist who could create musi-cal dialogues with the piano (Bill Evans), not only did I feel a strong connection with LaFaro because of the parallels of our anti-traditional approach to playing, but his pursuit of his vision of how the instrument can be elevated to new heights instilled within me great confidence and inspired me to step out on that precar-ious limb. I thought at the time, "If Scott LaFaro can turn the double bass into a soloist instrument in jazz, why couldn't I do the same in classical??" Without the conviction and artistic fortitude of Scott LaFaro, my life might have taken a different path. I am eternally grateful to him for his courage in stepping outside the box which had an enormous influence on my career and pursuit of that in which I believed.

At its fortieth anniversary convention in 2001, the ISB brought together three of Bill Evans' post-LaFaro bassists—Chuck Israels, Eddie Gomez, and Marc Johnson—in a gala concert tribute to Scott. At that time my sisters and I approached the ISB about creating and funding a living memorial to our brother, and so the first prize in the Society's biennial jazz competition became the Scott LaFaro Prize. The 2007 winner, Jorge Roeder, was born and raised in Peru and even there, was influenced by Scott's playing.

Jorge felt very honored to receive the prize since his admiration for Scott was long-standing. He began playing classical music, then rock before getting into jazz. He wrote me:

> What really let me understand that there was something special about jazz and opened a door whose frame I am still glancing at, was my first encounter with a Bill Evans Trio recording of "Autumn Leaves." The way they were improvising from the very beginning of the tune, and the counterpoint within the trio throughout the whole song, allowed me to understand that there was more to this music than just "swinging" and playing the chords correctly. Scott's influence goes even beyond music. I am fortunate to play regularly with great musicians, and I have found that with some of them a great musical connection is achieved. This, I think, is due to a certain level of compassion and detachment from one's self that allows this connection to be established. This allows the players to really achieve pure joy, thus hopefully conveying it to the audience, and showing the world that there's a kind of beauty we can enjoy only if we live in the present. This is what I feel Scott's real influence has been on me and on the musicians I play with.

As mentioned, over the years I have met and talked to a lot of bass players, and while doing this book, interviewed many more. They come from many places. Email made locating the family and communicating easier and so I learned of even more musicians from many places who admired Scotty.

Dave Swift is a bassist with Jools Holland and His Rhythm and Blues Orchestra, in the UK. We have had some email correspondence over the past three years and in 2007 when visiting the States, he visited the family. Dave told me about his first impressions upon hearing Scotty.

> The first time I heard of Scott was not through other bassists or teachers. Being self-taught, I was buying as many books on the bass that I could find, and one of them was *The Improviser's Bass Method* by Chuck Sher. There were transcriptions of Scott's bass line on *Alice in Wonderland* and his bass line and solo on "Gloria's Step." I was sixteen and I'd only just started playing the double bass, and his transcribed solo scared the life out of me. I'd never seen so many notes on a page! Fascinated by these transcriptions, I immediately went out and bought the two-record set *Bill Evans: The Village Vanguard Sessions*. As soon as I put the album on, I honestly couldn't believe what I was hearing. My jaw immediately hit the floor and stayed there for quite some time afterwards! Admittedly, I hadn't heard many other bass players at that time, and it took me many years to go back and study the full history of the instrument, its players and pioneers; but for me, the one that has always stood out head and shoulders amongst them, is Scotty.

Brazilian electric bassist Alex Malheiros of Azymuth, and Banda Utopia, is from a family of bass players. His grandfather, father, and uncle all played bass. His father crafted the first electric bass used in Brazil, carving the body out of jacaranda wood and using a magazine ad for his guideline. Alex wrote me, "I think it was around 1961 when I first heard Scott (I got totally crazy, I was only a fifteen-year-old boy) with the Bill Evans Trio. That became my musical compass."

Dave Green, regarded as one of the UK's finest bassists, turned professional at the age of twenty-one in 1963. He has since accompanied many of the world's greatest jazz musicians and has been a regular member of the Scott Hamilton quartet for the past fifteen years. He wrote me:

> My first exposure to Scott's playing was around 1962 or '63. I had bought the LP *Portraits in Jazz* by the Bill Evans' Trio. I was interested in hearing Bill in a trio context after listening to Miles Davis' *Kind of Blue*. I remember playing *Portraits* for the first time and on hearing the first few bars of "Come Rain or Come Shine," being captivated immediately by Scott's sound and facility. The whole concept of that first trio album knocked me out and straight away I wanted to hear more. Within a week I had got hold of *Sunday at the Village Vanguard* and *Waltz for Debby*. Listening to these albums had a very profound effect on me. Scott has been a great inspiration to me not only from the perspective of the music, but also for something else which is intangible: a feeling that somehow transcends the music itself.

Dieter Speck, who had a radio jazz show in Germany for twelve years and produced eight TV shows for the series of *Jazz Night Rider*, recalls first hearing Scotty in 1963 on a jazz program on British Forces Network (BFN) called *Music for Moderns*, moderated by Ian Fenner.

One night Ian played some music from the Village Vanguard Sessions. I was thrilled! Never before had I heard some one playing the bass like that. I wrote a letter to Ian trying to find out who that guy was on the bass and he wrote back that it was a certain Scott LaFaro, who had died in an accident two years earlier. It was a deep shock for me. I was deeply moved and I started following Scotty's short career. I was brought up with the music of Oscar Peterson and Ray Brown, but the music of Bill and Scotty was something that deeply touched my heart.

One of the first programs I ever did was in the memory of Scott LaFaro. Scotty to me has been THE greatest bass player ever! Scotty is unforgettable! He will remain my #1 on bass for all time! What's his secret? It is his sound, his tone, his kind of playing the bass, like a guitar almost, very fast, using the upper registers, using the bass as an emancipated instrument, equal to all others ... freed the bass from being a rhythm instrument. He, Bill Evans and Paul Motian wrote jazz history. You can hear Scotty's fire, his energy, his fresh sound. REALLY NEW at that time ... and today his spirit is still there ... he lives on in his music and in the music of others."

Another well-respected British jazz bassist, Jeff Clyne, first heard about Scott through Victor Feldman. "Vic, on one of his trips back here, was raving about a wonderful bass player he was working with: Scott LaFaro. Vic said Scott had an amazing two finger pizzicato technique which to me at that time was quite remarkable and most unusual. *The Arrival of Victor Feldman* was my first introduction to Scott's playing and from then on, I followed his every move. I am still thrilled by his wonderfully imaginative solos, and his beautiful time playing. Even now, listening to the Vanguard recordings, his empathy with the late Bill Evans is still unbelievable and remains a source of inspiration to me. Scott has made a lasting impression on my own musicality and bass playing."

Bronislaw "Bronek" Suchanek was studying at the Music Academy in Katowice, Poland, in 1967 and torn between classical and jazz music until a fellow bassist played Bill Evans' *Explorations* album for him. He said that at the time he was not experienced enough to understand the complexity of the music, but from hearing Scott's first solo, he knew what direction he wanted to go. He relates:

> I was mesmerized by the sound, his notes were like star showers and Scott a magician weaving rhythms, harmony and melody in sacred ceremony Music which blessed egoless masters with her presence. It was my greatest lesson, inspiration and vision for a life in music. I believe that profound and lasting changes can be ignited in a moment's notice. In 1975 I moved to Sweden where I was fortunate to work with Don Cherry and became friends with my neighbor, Red Mitchell. Red told me that "Scott would get up in the morning and after a few stretches would go practice. If you dropped in for a visit, he would greet you with music, saying 'check it out' and if you were there for the hang only, you were alone, Scott had no time for it."
>
> I moved to the USA and joined the Artie Shaw Orchestra under the direction of Dick Johnson. Dick had played with Scott during his Buddy Morrow Band stint and told me that on occasion Scott would confide to him his frustration with the process of mastering his concept of time … he was so much in a hurry. Jimmy Blanton and Scott LaFaro have been my inspiration. They set up everlasting standards for comping, soloing, pizzicato and arco as well as communication and passion in music.

Scott's influence extends beyond bass players. Drummer Dick Berk had mentioned Scotty told him, "not so loud on that," indicating the bass drum. When I spoke with Roy Haynes in May of 2007, and he remarked: "I remember him doing something different with Getz during that period (1961) because something different was starting to happen with the rhythm section between the bass and the drums. Scotty brought something different to the bass, a way of playing so I was a part of that, I was learning something about that as well. He never liked drummers to play loud … that I know … that's when I started getting away from that (playing the bass drum loudly), it affected other players later. That's when I started getting familiar with that … not too heavy on the bass drum … you feather it … that comes from the Scotty period. He was very fussy. He was definitely friendly with me. Of course there definitely is a relationship, a serious relationship between the drummer and the bassist … I can't even put it into words … the music we try to create … that speaks for us … you know … don't have lyrics for it, even though I consider myself a lyricist."

To the present day in the oddest of places, Scott's name will come up and instill a sense of awe. An old band mate from high school, Al Davids, tells of his 2006 Alaskan Cruise celebrating his 50th wedding anniversary. Al, a trumpet player and tremendous Louis Armstrong fan, was chatting with some of the musicians playing on the ship.

They were pretty young guys and he was relating having met Pete Fountain and Al Hirt a while back. "They didn't know who I was talking about. When I told them that I knew and played with Scotty in high school, their faces lit up and they wanted to know all that I knew of his history."

Josh Feldman, Victor's oldest son, relates the same kind of excitement when he was at a church coffee house talking with the musicians, and told them Vic was his dad and that we (Scotty's family) and he and his brothers were still very close.

Scotty's first and only bass teacher, Nick D'Angelo, recounts that in 1983 he was playing at a festival with his group in Scotland. Word got out that he had taught Scott LaFaro. "At the next concert, in walked ten guys and gals in black tie, orchestra players from the Scottish National Symphony, and they came to hear us because they heard that the conductor was Scott LaFaro's tutor … they came because of Scott."

It continuously amazes me to learn how known Scotty is. And Scotty would be utterly amazed as well that he would be so honored by so many.

In Okinawa City, Japan, there is a club named Jazz & Café Scott LaFaro. And just recently I became aware of a group in Belfast, Ireland. A four-piece heavy rock/alternative band, members Jonny Black (guitar/vocals), Dave Magee (guitar), Herb Magee (bass), and Alan Lynn (drums) chose to name the group "LaFaro" as a nod to Scott since his playing influenced each of them and encouraged them to explore what they could do with their instruments within the confines of a song. Their first release (Field Records, 2006) was the song "Scott."

Jeroen de Valk, Chet Baker biographer and a former double bass player himself, notes that, "Many of my colleagues in Europe are still under Scotty's spell. As they should!"

In the spring of 2007, Roy Haynes introduced me to the marvelous Christian McBride, and what he said not only had an impact on me, but seemed to sum up much of what I had been hearing as I talked to many musicians in writing about my brother. Christian said "Scotty's playing was the bible for bass players … Jimmy Blanton the old testament, Scotty, the new." A few months later, Woody Allen in his piece eulogizing Ingmar Bergman (*New York Times,* August 12, 2007) said, "But I did absorb one thing from him, a thing not dependent on genius or even talent but something that can actually be learned and developed. I am talking about what is often very loosely called a work ethic but is really plain discipline." And discipline is Scott's legacy as well.

From the very beginning Scotty was impatient with the limitations of the bass and he felt compelled to always explore, push boundaries. Scotty and the bass had just seven years together. We may all wonder what might have happened if he'd had more time.

Dave Swift expressed the melancholy that so many feel: "Every time I read the story of that fatal night, I so desperately want the text to miraculously change in front of my eyes. I want to read a different ending, a happy, joyous and fitting one for such an exceptional, inspiring and gifted human being."

REMEMBERING SCOTT LAFARO

by Robert Wooley

SCOTT LAFARO AND I WENT to school in Geneva, New York, a small city of about 15,000 in the heart of the Finger Lakes. Although small, the school had a very strong music program. The high school band director, Godfrey Brown, had worked hard, particularly in the elementary levels, to build his program. The lead trombonist when Scott was a sophomore went directly from high school to the Tommy Dorsey Band. It was possible to graduate from Geneva High School well prepared to go to music school, and many did.

Scott and I first met in 1950, and because of our musical interests became friends. The band director, who was Scotty's private teacher for clarinet and saxophone, recognized Scott's talent and made him a student band director. This meant Scott conducted rehearsals for the concert and jazz bands, and directed certain numbers in concerts. His rehearsals were very intense. Scotty was a perfectionist with perfect pitch. He was also a stickler on rhythm—I accused him of having a metronome built into his head. Whenever I listen to Scott's recordings, I'm certain of it.

Scotty was headstrong when it came to music. On more than one occasion, he argued so vehemently with the band director over the interpretation of a particular number that he was kicked out of the band for a couple of weeks. I'd say, "Why don't you apologize to Brownie (our director's nickname), what difference does it make?" Then I'd get the lecture of how you had to be true to your music, etc. It was interesting that before the annual band competition Scott was always "allowed" to return. Despite these disagreements, Brownie was Scott's, and all the other music majors', mentor. If someone asked me which teacher had the greatest impact on Scott (and me), I'd say without hesitation Godfrey Brown, and I know Scott would agree.

An advanced theory course was available for those going on to music school. During dictation, the instructor played a melody on the piano once to familiarize us with it, and then she played the individual parts for us to transcribe. While most of us were trying to decipher a particular interval, Scott was writing as fast as he could and finished long before the bass line had been played.

Scott practiced several hours every day. He earned an A in grade six clarinet and sax solos in competition, and played in the All State Band. He bought reeds by the box and used a device to shave the reeds, but usually threw away about half because he would only use the best. The only times Scott played bass during our high school years, however, was in breaks during practice with the jazz band. Brownie's attractive daughter was the bassist and I always thought he was more interested in her than in her bass. He would have her show him various finger positions, and sometimes he would do the positions and have me play rhythms on the strings. He told her he hoped someday to have the time to learn how to play the instrument. It looks like he found the time.

We formed a dance band—the Rhythm Aires—and played everything from the Elks Club to YMCA dances. Many of our arrangements were written by Scott. He transcribed the parts from a record, and then made his own modifications. Because I lived in the country, we often practiced at my home. My elderly aunt, who was a classical pianist, lived with my family and let us use her Steinway grand piano for band practice. It drove her crazy when Scott would improvise one of his jazz solos on either his sax or clarinet. She'd say, "He can play so well when he wants to, but I don't know where he gets those other notes!"

Scott's father was a very accomplished classical violinist who was a child prodigy. Scott's sister, Helene, had a beautiful voice and sang with several of the vocal groups and with the jazz band in high school. She told me she took piano lessons, but Scott wouldn't even stay in the house when she practiced. I understand he also continually told her what he thought of her piano playing talent as only a brother might do for a little sister. Helene's children are involved in the music business, supporting the theory of a musical gene pool.

In addition to his musical experiences in high school, Geneva also had two other musical organizations that had an impact on Scott. One group, the Seneca County Symphony Orchestra, was directed by a music professor from Hobart College. It was composed primarily of area music teachers and other adults who played for enjoyment. Nearby was a large Air Force base and some of the Air Force musicians volunteered to play with the county orchestra to give strength to various sections. Scott played clarinet, and each rehearsal was a tremendous learning experience.

The other organization was a nationally ranked Senior American Legion Drum and Bugle Corps specializing in numbers by arrangers from the major big bands, much like the current Phantom Regiment and other major corps of today but without the percussion pit areas. The bugle Scott played with them was a regulation single valve. The Corps, while a volunteer organization, was staffed by paid professionals in key positions. Each position was coveted, and we all knew that there was a waiting list of people ready to take our place if we didn't perform. Once Scotty gave some unsolicited advice to the arranger, and was told to mind his own business. About a week later, we received a revised score incorporating Scott's suggestions. After that, it was not unusual for the arranger to collaborate with Scott.

In the winter of 1953, we heard that Stan Kenton was coming to nearby Syracuse. Scotty, my brother, and I went. Kenton had Maynard Ferguson, with fake notes that you couldn't believe even when you heard them, the artistry of Stan Getz, and Shelly Manne, with the most melodic cymbals and difficult rhythm patterns I'd ever heard. This was probably the greatest collection of jazz artists ever assembled in one band.

After sitting there in awe for the entire concert, we were walking in the snow back to the car and Scott said to me, "I'm going to play with those guys some day." I replied, "Sure, Scott, and I'm going to cut Shelly Manne," but I could tell Scotty was serious.

Then a basketball game at the Geneva YMCA had a major impact on the role of the bass in modern jazz. Scott was playing and suffered a severely cut lip. The injury required stitches, and Scott, the perfectionist, never felt that his embouchure was the same afterward. Scott's sister told me that this was one of the impetuses for Scott to start playing the bass while at Ithaca. She also said that Scott regretted that his father had not pushed him into playing the violin. Scott felt that the violin was an instrument that must be started very early in life to become a virtuoso. When you consider Scott took a supporting instrument and earned a respected solo status, it is interesting to speculate what he could have accomplished with a violin. The question also remains whether he would have followed a jazz or classical track had the violin been his instrument. I personally believe that, because of his love of jazz, he would have broken ground in the violin's role.

After college, I received a commission and entered the Army. Scott was pretty hard to keep up with as he was playing with a number of groups on both coasts. Billeted next to my company was the U.S. Army band. Their commander and I became friends, and I'd go over and sit in on jam sessions. We talked about Scott on several occasions. One evening in July 1961, I received a phone call from my mother telling me of the tragic accident. I couldn't believe it. The next day I told the members of the Army band the bad news. They, and musicians the world over, were stunned.

Scott had attended a party while he was in his hometown on a visit, and fell asleep driving home. The tree that he hit was in the front yard of Joan Martin, who was the pianist with our dance band. She still lives there; and speaking with her recently, she said she thinks of Scott every time she looks at that tree. Incidentally, she teaches piano, and with her husband runs a music store in Geneva. She said a number of out-of-town bassists playing gigs in the area stop at the store to discuss Scott with her. Although Scott's sister Helene lives in California, they are still best of friends.

While I was talking with Helene recently, she told me that Joan had been in a regional hospital about twenty miles from Geneva. When her condition worsened she had to be rushed to a larger hospital in Rochester, New York. The young ambulance driver was making conversation and asked Joan where she lived. She told him she lived in a little area outside Geneva that he had probably never heard of—Flint, New York. The ambulance driver said he had most certainly heard of it, because he had been a bassist with the U.S. Air Force Jazz Band and that his idol, Scott LaFaro, was killed in Flint many years ago. While in music school he said he had written a thesis about Scotty, and wanted to know if Joan had ever heard of him. Helene told me that she remembered being contacted by the ambulance driver when he was research-ing his college thesis. She had no idea that her friend's life 3,500 miles away would be touched by this same man years later.

I am certain that the corridors of heaven are resounding with Scotty's unmistakable melodies and polyrhythms. I am also sure that there is a group of classical, winged harpists sitting with my aunt and asking each other, "I wonder where he gets those other notes?" The world lost a great musician, and those of us who knew him lost a good, dear friend.

This article first appeared in *Bass World,* The Journal of the Inter-national Society of Bassists, Volume 21, no. 2, Fall 1996, page 20.

WHEN SAM MET SCOTTY

A Remembrance of Scott LaFaro

by Barrie Kolstein

SCOTT LAFARO CAME INTO THE Kolstein "shop family" in the early years of my life. I was about nine years of age when the wonderful George Duvivier brought Scotty to my father's house/ shop in Merrick, New York. George had been involved in a project with Scott connected to Gunther Schuller. Scott had acquired his small Prescott bass through the efforts of his close friend and great bassist, Red Mitchell. Red had found both his Lowendahl bass, with the famous cutaway in the shoulder, and the ¾-sized Prescott while in California. Red felt the Lowendahl was perfect for his own needs and the Prescott was ideal for what Scotty was looking for. He immediately contacted Scotty about the smaller Prescott. Scotty consequently purchased the Prescott, bringing it back to New York.

Scott became aware that the problem with the Prescott was that dimensionally the bass was ideal, but tonally it was not. While in collaboration with George Duvivier, this problem surfaced. George was a lifelong client and, more importantly, a virtual member of my family. He suggested to Scott a trip to Sam Kolstein to evaluate the bass and see what could be done to improve the tonal and playing qualities of Scotty's bass.

George arrived with Scotty at the shop, walked into the shop area, and George, in his deep robust voice said, "Sam, I have a young man I want you to meet." Even before Sam could walk out to greet Scott for the first time, he heard playing from the showroom area that he never had heard before. Sam looked at George and simply said, "Who is that and what is that?" You have to understand that even by today's standards, Scotty's playing would turn heads. But back in those years, this style of playing was unheard of and completely unique in every aspect. George, basically, looked at my father and said, "Let's go meet this young man." As I was told many times by Sam, Scotty was literally a kid in a candy store, playing on every bass he could lay his hands on. There was an immediate mutual admiration between my dad and Scott. My dad basically told Scotty that whatever work it would take to make his Prescott bass right tonally, it would happen and that Scott should not even worry about the cost.

The work went on for several months and the bass was fully restored, structurally, as well as tonally. When Scott got his Prescott back, it was what he hoped for and the bass literally became an extension of him. The end results of the Prescott's playing qualities in the hands of Scott LaFaro were historic performances and recordings that are still revered by jazz aficionados and bassists internationally.

With Scotty's untimely passing the bass was literally destroyed and was offered to Sam by Mrs. LaFaro, Scotty's mother. My father wanted the bass and did purchase it in total disarray, promising Mrs. LaFaro that the bass would be resurrected back to playing condition. The ironic fact is that in my growing up with this bass as part of our family, Sam never had the heart to restore the bass. Sam looked upon Scotty as one of the great talents that touched his life, but perhaps more so in a fatherly sense. Without question, he could not approach the restoration due to his emotional connection with Scotty and his deep, profound loss that stayed with him after Scotty's passing.

In 1986, the International Society of Bassists announced its next convention was to be held at UCLA in Southern California and that the convention was to be dedicated to the memory of Scotty. I went to my father and asked his permission to accomplish the restoration on the LaFaro Prescott that had sat on shelves unrestored for twenty-five years. Sam responded that he would be very pleased to see the bass restored and brought back to playing condition in time for the convention in the summer of 1988. The restoration was quite arduous, as the damages sustained by the Prescott were so extensive, but over a year and a half period, I accomplished the work. I know that the work pleased my father, and I can only assume that the work would have pleased Scotty as well.

This article first appeared in *The Bass Line*, Spring 2004, Page 4. © Barrie Kolstein.

(Note: In 2003, Barrie announced that he would make a limited number of copies of Scott LaFaro's Prescott, and donate a significant percentage of each sale to the ISB's Scott LaFaro Prize, awarded every two years to the winner of its jazz competition.)

PRESCOTT RESTORATION: THE LaFARO LEGACY

by Barrie Kolstein

On the tragic early morning hours of July 6, 1961, the bass world lost a true jazz innovator and legend. Rocco Scott La Faro was the victim of a senseless automobile accident, depriving the jazz world of unforeseen musical accomplishments, but leaving an unprecedented style of playing, setting the standards that all bassists have strived to attain since Scott's untimely passing.

In the automobile was Scott's most prized possession: his bass. The instrument, the work of Abraham Prescott in Concord, New Hampshire, circa 1825, was obtained by Scotty through the efforts of the legendary Red Mitchell, a close friend and colleague. Red found both his cutaway Lowendahl bass and the Prescott in Stein on the Vine, in Los Angeles, California. Red immediately contacted Scotty, who came out to see the Prescott and subsequently purchased the bass. The bass was perfect in design for Scott. Not only was this bass a rare example of the work of Abraham Prescott, but it is of a most unique, smaller Busetto-cornered design, unlike most larger examples by Abraham Prescott. This design drew Scotty to this bass immediately.

In mid-1959, the late George Duvivier met Scott LaFaro at a joint musical project involving Gunter Schuller. George immediately recognized and was amazed by Scotty's talent. George, who was a lifelong friend and client of my father, Sam Kolstein, insisted that Scott meet him. George brought Scott to Sam's establishment, then located in Merrick, New York. Sam and Scott developed an immediate mutual admiration, respect, and friendship. Two decisions were reached between them in their discussions.

First, the Prescott bass was to be fully restored, enabling LaFaro to play it at its full potential. The second decision was the meeting of Scott with the revered Frederick Zimmermann, whereby a formalized approach to the bass would be introduced to Scott in order to embellish his phenomenal natural talents. Unfortunately, only one of the two decisions were fully accomplished, that being the restoration of the Prescott bass.

The original restoration accomplished by Samuel Kolstein included completely replacing all cross bars on the back table of the bass, repairing all damage to the ribs of the bass, fully restoring the top table including the installation of a new seasoned bass bar, and the full cosmetic restoration of the bass and of the instrument's varnish. Samuel Kolstein was further challenged with a new concept in setup for this bass, thus allowing Scott to accurately play the Prescott with his gut string setup of Golden Spiral gut bass strings at an unprecedentedly low string height. The success of this restoration can be attested to by the quality of sound produced on Scott's last and perhaps most acclaimed recording, *Live at the Village Vanguard*, with Bill Evans on piano and Paul Motian on drums, recorded at the famed Village Vanguard in New York City, June 25, 1961. A few days later, the creative genius of Scott La Faro abruptly ended.

After the reality of the tragedy of Scott's death was accepted, Scotty's mother, Mrs. Helen LaFaro, had to consider the only remnant of Scott's shattered career: the Prescott bass. Since it was her desire to have the instrument resurrected as she felt Scott would have wished, she offered the Prescott to Sam at an equitable price comfortable in the knowledge that he would be the best caretaker of the instrument in the future. The bass had suffered terrible damage to both the body chamber and scroll. The damage was primarily caused by the impact of the collision and the ensuing fire. Both the neck and the scroll were completely charred and shattered, as was the upper left bout of the top table and the upper left rib bout (photos A, B, and C).

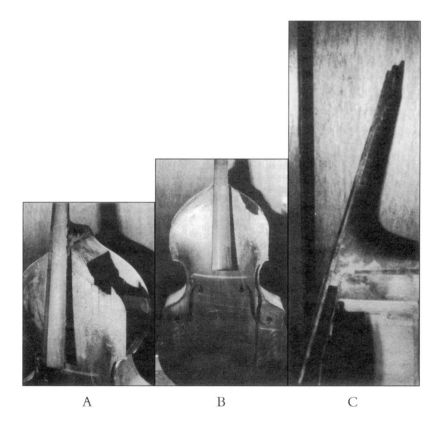

A   B   C

In addition, the top table of the bass sustained extensive damage in the left F-Hole area. Internally, all cross bars were loosened from the top table, as was the bass bar. Extensive damages were incurred to four of the six rib sections of the bass, with the most extensive damages sustained by the upper left rib bout, which endured the brunt of the exposure to the intense heat of the fire following the auto crash.

Dismayed by the tragic loss of his dear young friend, Samuel Kolstein chose to keep this remnant of the creative genius of Scott LaFaro in a stable condition that would not allow the bass to deteriorate any further, until Sam could bring himself to the point of emotionally facing the arduous task of restoring this instrument or delegating the responsibilities of the restoration to one who would approach this instrument, an extension of Scott LaFaro's life, with the same reverence and respect that existed in the relationship between Scott and Samuel.

I consider myself to be most fortunate to have been delegated this responsibility. Although I was too young to have known Scott well, I grew up aware of his creativity and listening to his creative genius in his recordings. Many hours were spent studying and contemplating the immense task of restoring the "LaFaro Prescott." This famed bass lay dormant for more than twenty-four years. Sam and I made a concerted decision that the restoration of the Prescott would be completed within the twenty-fifth anniversary year of the death of Scott LaFaro. With the International Society of Bassists dedicating the 1988 Convention at UCLA to Scott LaFaro and Fred Zimmermann, it was also decided that the bass would be displayed at the 1988 Convention. Although the restoration of the Prescott spanned a longer period of time than anticipated, it was to our immense satisfaction that the "LaFaro Prescott" was once again played within the twenty-fifth year and was fully restored in time for the ISB 1988 Convention. The following text will describe the actual restoration process that extended well over a two-year period.

In approaching the restoration of this fine instrument it was necessary to consider two important factors: the functional reconstruction of the bass and the protection of the integrity of a master instrument that has left a tonal legacy in Scotty's hands. In discussing the stage of development of the original restoration of the Prescott accomplished by my father in late 1950s, it was realized that, as great as this instrument was, the actual restorative work to the instrument was never given full opportunity to mature due to the circumstances. Thus, it was decided to leave as much of the original restoration work as possible, to not only restore the instrument to its full form, but to restore the sound as well to what it was when LaFaro played upon the bass.

My first task was the actual disassembling of the bass. There was extensive damage caused by all facets of this tragic accident (photo D).

D

It was necessary to first remove the top table, then to remove the severely charred upper left rib bout. Next the extensively damaged neck within the neck block was removed from the body of the bass. This procedure not only allowed access to damaged areas of the back table, but fully stabilized the instrument, eliminating the possibility of further damage.

At this point the actual restoration to the Prescott commenced.

All loosened cross bars to the flat back table were steamed and reglued. Total evaluation was made to ascertain whether the proper amount of spring still existed in these cross bars to protect the integrity of the back table. Naturally, quite a bit of the existing patchwork was dried out due to the nature of the accident as well as the considerable amount of time this instrument lay in storage. All repair patching was removed and replaced with highly seasoned patch wood. With the back table stable and restored, we next turned our efforts to the restoration of the ribs. Unfortunately, the damaged upper left rib bout was charred beyond restoration. Thus, we were faced with the task of matching a section of maple that would be in total accord with the highly distinctive character maple utilized by Abraham Prescott some 180-plus years ago. I chose to quarter and veneer a choice, highly seasoned maple section of cello back wood of substantial age with the most similar character to that of the remaining original ribs. Preparation of the rib material was accomplished, then the rib was carefully bent to the proper alignment with the top and back table. Next, wood for the outer adjoining moldings was chosen, prepared, bent, and glued into position on the new rib to match the traditional Prescott outer moldings on all original ribs. Finally, the internal lining of highly seasoned pine was bent and glued into position (photos E and F) to the remaining ribs

E   F

and cornerblocks and endblocks were fully checked and repaired where deemed necessary.

With full restoration accomplished on the ribs of the instrument, we elected to remove the remnants of the original neck from the already detached neck block. The neck block, being in usable condition, was repositioned and glued into proper position and alignment with the ribs and back table of the Prescott. It should be noted that the original design of the bass never had a conventional neck block. Rather, the instrument had an integrated crooked neck, which was glued to the back table with the upper ribs tucked and glued into the maple neck. The original conversion of this bass was accomplished in the original restoration by Samuel Kolstein.

The greatest challenge was faced next: the restoration of the top table of the bass. Unfortunately the top table, along with the neck and scroll areas of the bass, sustained the major impact and heat damage. The top table section, located at the upper left bout

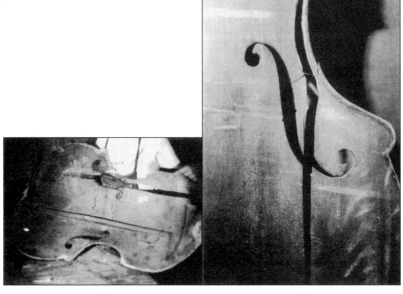

G   H

(photos G and H), was virtually nonexistent due to the extensive heat damage sustained.

My first task was to repair the major cracks and damage other than the area of fire damage in order to stabilize the top table. This procedure made the further extensive restoration to this charred area a more viable undertaking. The multiple cracks to the top table (photos I and J) clearly reveal the extensive damage sustained by the top table and the variety of repair techniques utilized to successfully accomplish these repairs.

With the top table stabilized, we now approached the difficult task of matching a section of pine to blend with the character of the existing woods utilized by Prescott. I most unexpectedly found a section of extremely aged pine with dimensions just large enough to be utilized. Because of the limited size of this section there was virtually no tolerance for error in the placement of this section into proper position. This matching section of pine was placed into the instrument by the process of a scarf joint, whereby the area of the existing plate was tapered on an angle, with the matching piece of pine receiving a reverse scarfed angle, allowing

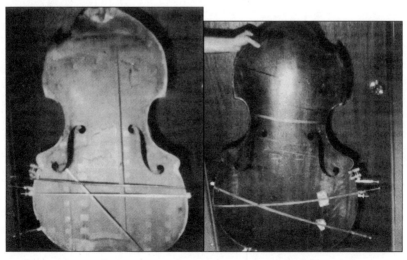

I   J

the newly positioned wood section to be grafted into the plate as if it were part of the top table (photos K, L, M and N).

K   L

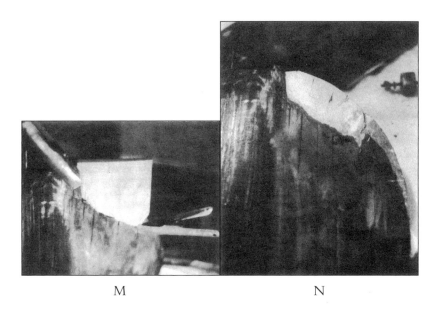

M   N

This technique also produced an exceptionally strong glue joint. With the new section of pine scarfed into position on the top table, this added section of wood could now be carved to match the original form of the top table, with the highest respect for the workmanship of Abraham Prescott. After accomplishing this work, normal restoration procedures were resumed: re-edging the top plate and reinforcing all repaired areas of the plate with highly seasoned spruce patching. At this point all wood added into the chamber of the bass was re-graduated to proper thickness so as not to affect the tonal quality of this fine instrument. A thorough re-check of the top and back tables and all ribs was accomplished to make certain all repairs were fully completed. Next, the top was reglued to the chamber of the instrument.

Our next task was the replacement of the existing scroll and neck. As mentioned earlier, the scroll and neck were subject to the brunt of the auto accident and, unfortunately, could not be restored to functional condition. The only alternative would be the copying of the Prescott scroll. The scroll model we chose was one of the traditional deep volutes with a convex channel at the rounded heel of the bass of the scroll. The installation of the gears involved the traditional inlaid Prescott brass plate tuning gears with Tyrolean knobs on the tuners. Upon the completion of the carving of the replacement neck and scroll, the neck was set into proper elevation and pitch in accord with the modern school of steel string playing.

The final stage of restoration was the cosmetic restoration of the instrument. Analysis of the Prescott varnish was exactingly accomplished, thus yielding the observation that a terpineol oil-base varnish must be made and utilized in order to match the original varnish and patina of this fine instrument. All damaged areas of the bass were meticulously restored to match the original varnish.

With the full restoration of the "La Faro Prescott" accomplished, the instrument completed its last stage of resurrection with the setup and tonal adjustment of the bass. We equipped the bass with a Kolstein Adjustable Bass Bridge and a conventional lower addle. Although Scotty played on gut strings, I decided to set the instrument up with Heritage Perlon Core strings, which emulate gut string quality but offer the responsiveness and true-ness of a fine steel string only at a reduced string tension. In our opinion, this setup offers the quality of sound that this instrument produced in the hands of Scott, but yet fulfills the modern re-quirements expected of an instrument of this caliber.

As stated earlier, I have considered it a great privilege and honor to have been delegated the responsibility of restoring Scott La Faro's Prescott. We are at the twenty-year anniversary of when this fine bass had its restoration completed. In this time, I have been honored to have the LaFaro Prescott displayed at numerous ISB Conventions and International Jazz Conferences, and pho-tographed in the famed Milt Hinton Scholarship Photo Session at the Manhattan Center in New York City. Most recently, it was recorded for the first time since Scotty recorded *Live at the Village Vanguard*, by jazz great Marc Johnson, last bassist with the Bill Evans Trio. The bass can be heard on the CD *Something for You*.

I have been most gratified to complete several copies of Scot-ty's Prescott as well.

Sam's and my sincere hopes were that this restoration would not only awaken a sleeping giant, but that it would continue the creativity that this instrument was so well known for in the hands of Scott LaFaro.

In the past twenty years, I am most pleased that these hopes have been fulfilled.

Descriptive information
on the LaFaro Bass Violin

THIS INSTRUMENT IS THE WORK of Abraham Prescott, made in Concord, New Hampshire, circa 1825.

The instrument is a three-quarter size, flatback model Bass Violin with gamba-shaped upper corners and traditional Busetto lower bout corners. The instrument is quite unusual in that it is one of the few Prescott designs that were made of smaller dimensions.

The top is a six-piece sectional plate of pine ranging in grain from medium at the outer flanks to slab cut at the center joint. The back table is a two-piece sectional plate of moderately flamed maple with flame ascending at the center joint. The back has an ebony strip inlaid at the center joint running the entire length of the back table. The ribs are of moderate slab-cut maple of highly irregular flame. The ribs have maple outer molding adjoining the back and top plates.

The color of the varnish is a deep brown amber.

Dimensions:	Inches	Centimeters
Upper bouts:	19-5/8	49.85
Center bouts:	14-1/2	36.83
Lower bouts:	28-1/4	71.76
Measure:	41-1/2	105.41
Overall body length:	43	109.22

This article first appeared in *Bass World: The Journal of the International Society of Bassists* 14:3 (Spring 1988): 56–63.

Scott LaFaro Discography

by Chuck Ralston

THIS DISCOGRAPHY PLACES IN CHRONOLOGICAL order public, commercially released recordings on which Scott LaFaro performed. For the most part, information has been compiled from "liner notes" printed on the container (the jacket or sleeve) accompanying long-play (LP) vinyl recordings, as well as from program booklets and inserts that accompany most compact disc (CD) digital recordings. I have included, however, information from other publications to make clearer a recording date, identities of performers, instrumentation, and related issues. Many recording companies, more focused on getting product to market, neglected to include details about recording session dates, performers, instrumentation, program content (compositions, tunes, alternate takes), initial release dates, re-issue dates, compilations, and so on.

The order herein is first by recording date, rather than by release or publication date, grouped by year recorded. Re-issued recordings are listed right after the bibliographic description of the original recording. If a recording was not released soon after the actual recording date, but much later (in some cases decades later) I have placed it in chronological order by actual date of the recording. For example, *West Coast Days,* recorded in 1958, is listed in year 1958 although it was first released in 1992 in CD format. One recording session that LaFaro worked with pianist Paul Bley in Los Angeles has never been released and therefore is not included. Some other recordings that LaFaro may have performed on (e.g., with Benny Goodman, Barney Kessel, or Frank Sinatra) have not yet been verified.

An Addendum at the end lists recordings that erroneously include LaFaro as bassist.

1. *Shorty-Tunes: Buddy Morrow and His Orchestra*
Chicago: Standard Radio Transcription Services, Inc. [No date, 1956?] ST-1039. 1 sound disc; analog, 33 1/3 rpm, monophonic; 12 in.

Performers:
Buddy Morrow, trombone and leader
Others are not identified

Program:
Side A (ST-1039-A)

   1. Day by Day (A. Stordahl-P. Weston-S. Kahn) 1:09

   2. Don't Worry About Me (Marty Robbins) 1:09

   3. They Didn't Believe Me (J. Kern-H. Reynolds) 1:28

   4. Little Girl Blue (Rodgers-Hart) 1:26

   5. If There's Someone Lovelier Than You (Dietz-Schwartz) 1:07

Side B (ST-1039-B)

   1. Somebody Somewhere (Frank Loesser) 1:45

   2. Blue Suede Shoes (Carl Perkins)1:02

   3. My Blue Heaven (Donaldson-Whiting) 1:07

   4. April in Paris (V. Duke-Y. Harburg) 1:25

   5. Main Title (Molly-O) (I. Berlin)1:34

Note: Helene LaFaro-Fernandez recalls her brother Scotty telling her that he performed with the Buddy Morrow Orchestra on this "air check" recording. This information is from her personal copy of this recording's circular "hole" label.

2. *Golden Trombone: Buddy Morrow and His Orchestra*
Featuring Buddy Morrow. Especially arranged by Walt Stewart [with] alto solos by Dick Johnson. Chicago: Mercury Record Corp., 1956? MG-20221. 1 sound disc; analog, 33 1/3 rpm, monophonic; 12 in. Container cover title: *Buddy Morrow and His Golden Trombone.*

Performers:
Buddy Morrow, trombone and leader

Dick Johnson, alto saxophone

Walt Stewart, trumpet

Others are not identified

Program:
Side A (MG-20221-A)

1. I'll Close My Eyes (Buddy Kaye-Billy Reid)

2. With a Song in My Heart (Rodgers-Hart)

3. There Will Never Be Another You (Harry Warren-Mack Gordon)

4. This Is Autumn (Walt Stuart)

5. My Foolish Heart (Victor Young-Ned Washington)

6. You'd Be So Nice to Come Home To (Cole Porter)

Side B (MG-20221-B)

1. With the Wind and the Rain in Your Hair (Jack Lawrence-Clara Edwards)

2. Portrait of Jennie (J. Russel Robinson-Gordon Burdge)

3. Symphony (Lawrence-Stone)

4. Cerise (Walt Stuart)

5. Laura (David Raksin-Johnny Mercer)

6. The Song Is You (Jerome Kern-Oscar Hammerstein II)

Note: Although this recording has not appeared in any previous listing of recordings on which Scott LaFaro has performed, it is included here because it is highly probable that LaFaro was a member of the Morrow band at the time. Moreover, Mark Carlsen, bassist, luthier, teacher, and a member of the Tommy Dorsey Orchestra (vintage 1981–1984), has shared with me his recollection of discussions about LaFaro with fellow band member, Linwood Blaisdell, trumpeter, and Morrow himself. Both Morrow and Blaisdell recalled LaFaro as the bassist on this recording. In addition, Carlsen recalled that Dick Johnson, alto saxophonist on *Golden Trombone*, and later leader of the Artie Shaw Orchestra, also confirmed LaFaro as the bassist.

3. *Let's Have a Dance Party! Buddy Morrow and His Orchestra*
[New York?] RCA Camden [1956?] CAL-381. 1 sound disc; analog, 33 1/3 rpm, monophonic; 12 in.

Performers:
> Buddy Morrow, trombone, vocals, and leader
> Frankie Lester, vocals
> Tommy Mercer, vocals
> Four Stars (music group)
> Others are not identified

Program:
Side A (H3PP-2439)
> 1. Heap Big Beat (Buddy Morrow)
> 2. Stairway to the Stars (from "Park Avenue Fantasy"; Parish-Malneck-Signorelli)
> 3. I Can't Give You Anything but Love (Dorothy Fields-Jimmy McHugh)
> 4. I Can't Get Started (Ira Gershwin-Vernon Duke)
> 5. I Wonder Why (Joe Thomas-Howard Biggs)
> 6. Memphis Drag (Buddy Morrow)

Side B (H3PP-2440)
> 1. Beale Street Mamma (Roy Turk-J. Russel Robinson)

2. Speak Low (K. Weill-Ogden Nash)

3. Rio Rita (Joseph McCarthy-Harry Tierney)

4. That Old Black Magic (H. Arlen-J. Mercer)

5. Confessin' the Blues (Jay McShann-Walter Brown)

6. I Ain't Got Nobody (And Nobody Cares For Me) (Roger Graham-Spencer Williams)

Note: Helene LaFaro-Fernandez recalls her brother Scotty giving her a copy of this recording and telling her he is in the band and performed on this recording. LaFaro was a member of the Buddy Morrow Orchestra from autumn 1955 to September 1956.

4. The 2 Trumpet Geniuses of the Fifties, Brownie & Chet: Clifford Brown [and] Chet Baker

Brownie's practice tapes (unaccompanied) [and] Chet's combos from the 50s (featuring Scott LaFaro). Produced by Paolo Piangiarelli. Macerata, Italia: Philology [Records] no date [1980s?]. Philology 214 W 13. 1 sound disc: analog, 33 1/3 rpm, monophonic; 12 in. At head of title on container: Black and White Serie [sic, in recté Series] Vol. 1.

Performers:

Clifford Brown (A-1 only)

Chet Baker, trumpet and leader

Phil Urso, tenor saxophone

Francy Boland, piano

Lawrence Marable, drums

Scott LaFaro, bass (B-4 and B-5 only)

Program:

Side A

1. Practice Tapes: Clifford Brown playing "Cherokee (Indian Love Song)" (Ray Noble) 13:10

2. Makin' Whoopee (Walter Donaldson-Gus Kahn) 3:15

3. Motel (Gerry Mulligan) 3:36

4. I'll Remember April (D. Raye-De Paul) 6:22

Side B

1. Just Friends (John Klenner-Sam Lewis) 4:33

2. Stella by Starlight (Ned Washington-Victor Young) 2:39

3. Sweet Georgia Brown (Ben Bernie-Maceo Pinkard-Kenneth Casey) 4:43

4. Intro [by Steve Allen] segué to "Extra Mild" (Phil Urso) [entitled "Lisa" by Baker] (4:37)

5. C. T. A.(Jimmy Heath) 2:58

6. Imagination (Burke-Van Heusen) 3:23

7. Jumpin' On A Cliff [?Jumping Off A Clef] (Al Haig) 2:36

Note: LaFaro performs on B-4 ('Intro' / 'Extra Mild') and B-5 ('C. T. A.') only.

5. *The Arrival of Victor Feldman*

Los Angeles: Contemporary Records, 1958. C-3549 / S-7549. 1 sound disc: 33 1/3 rpm, monophonic; 12 in. Recorded 21 and 22 January 1958, in Los Angeles. Sound by Roy DuNann and Howard Holzer. Produced by Lester Koenig. Program notes by Nat Hentoff, dated 30 March 1958. Container photograph by Stan Levey.

Re-issued: Berkeley: Fantasy Records, 1986. OJC 268–LP Los Angeles: Contemporary Records, 1998. OJCCC-268-2(S-7549)–CD

Performers:

Victor Feldman, vibraphone, piano, and leader

Scott LaFaro, bass

Stan Levey, drums

Program:

Side A (LKL 12-181)

1. Serpent's Tooth (Miles Davis) 3:24

2. Waltz [L'Adieu Valse, A-flat Major (Opus 69, No. 1)] Frederic
   Chopin; arr. by Feldman 5:00

3. Chasing Shadows (Feldman) 3:15

4. Flamingo (Theodore Grouya-Edmund Anderson) 3:15

5. S'posin (Paul Denniker-Andy Razaf) 4:25

Side B (LKL 12-182)

1. Bebop (Dizzy Gillespie) 2:43

2. There Is No Greater Love (Isham Jones-Marty Symes) 4:20

3. Too Blue (Feldman) 4:00

4. Minor Lament (Feldman) 3:55

5. Satin Doll (Duke Ellington-Billy Strayhorn-Johnny Mercer) 5:58

6. *Cal Tjader Stan Getz Sextet*

San Francisco: Fantasy Records. Fantasy LP-3266 / LPS-8005.
"Full Radial Stereo" 1 sound disc ; analog, 33 1/3 rpm, mono-
phonic ; 12 in. Red vinyl pressing. Recorded 8 February 1958.
Program notes by Ralph Gleason.

Re-issued: *Stan Getz [with] Cal Tjader, Billy Higgins, Scott Lo-
Faro [sic, in recté LaFaro], Vince Guaraldi, Eddie Duran.* [Berkeley,
CA:] Fantasy Records, 1963. "Fantasy 3348 High Fidelity"–LP
Berkeley: Fantasy, 1990. (Original Jazz Classics) OJCCD-275-2
(F-3266)–CD

Performers:

Cal Tjader, vibraphone and co-leader

Stan Getz, tenor sax and co-leader

Eddie Duran, guitar

Vince Guaraldi, piano

Billy Higgins, drums

Scott LaFaro, bass

Program:

Side A (F-1732)

1. I've Grown Accustomed to Her Face (Frederick Lowe–Alan Jay Lerner) 3:59

2. For All We Know (J. Fred Coots–Sam M. Lewis) 5:45

3. Ginza (Vince Guaraldi) 9:18

Side B (F-1733)

1. Crow's Nest (Cal Tjader) 8:22

2. Liz-Anne (Tjader) 3:47

3. Big Bear (Tjader) 4:33

4. My Buddy (Walter Donaldson–Gus Kahn) 5:18

7. *For Real!* [Hampton Hawes Quartet]
Los Angeles: Contemporary Records [1961?] S-7589. 1 sound disc: 33 1/3 rpm, stereo; 12 in. Recorded 17 March 1958. Sound by Roy DuNann. Produced by Lester Koenig. Program notes by Leonard Feather, dated 8 July 1961. Container cover photo of Hawes by Stan Levey. Photograph of LaFaro by Roger Marshutz.

Re-issued: Berkeley: Contemporary; distributed by Fantasy, 1992. OJCCD-713-2 (S-7589)

Hawes, Hampton. *Blues the Most*. Berkeley: Prestige, distributed by Fantasy, 1998. PRCD-11015-2. Includes two tracks, "Hip" and "For Real" from the 1958 recording.

Performers:

Hampton Hawes, piano and leader

Frank Butler, drums

Scott LaFaro, bass

Harold Land, tenor sax

Program:

Side A (LKS-199)

1. Hip (Hampton Hawes) 6:14

2. Wrap Your Troubles in Dreams (Harry Barris-Billy Moll-Ted Koehler) 9:20

3. Crazeology (Bennie Harris) 6:40

Side B (LKS-200)

1. Numbers Game (Hampton Hawes-Harold Land) 8:04

2. For Real (Hampton Hawes-Harold Land) 11:21

3. I Love You (Cole Porter) 3:50

8. *Live Date: Buddy DeFranco and His Septette*

[Los Angeles: Verve, 1958] MG-V-8383. 1 sound disc, analog; 33 1/3 rpm, monophonic; 12 in. Program notes by Benny Green, *The London Observer*. Recorded 4 April 1958 at Los Angeles (Ruppli discography, 243).

Re-issued: *Generalissimo + Live Date*. [Spain?] Lone Hill Jazz [2007] LHJ-10295. 1 sound disc; 4 and 3/4 in. Includes twelve-page program booklet with original program liner notes for both LP recordings and new commentary by Morton James. Re-issue includes the same, erroneous information: Bob Hardaway does not perform on *Live Date!*; Frank De Vito does. Also, "Tin Reed Blues" has been omitted due to "time constraints" but is included as a "bonus" track on the 2-CD recording, *I Hear Benny Goodman and Artie Shaw* (LHJ-10281).

Performers:

Buddy De Franco, clarinet and leader

[Frank De Vito, drums] per Ruppli discography (not listed on recording's container)

Victor Feldman, piano, vibraphone

Bob Hardaway, tenor saxophone (although listed did not perform on this recording)

Pete Jolly, piano, accordion

Barney Kessel, guitar

Scotty LeFaro [sic, in recté LaFaro] bass

Herbie Mann, flute, tenor saxophone, bass clarinet

Program:
Side A (51,008)

    1. Oh, Lady Be Good! (G. and I. Gershwin) [# 22200-4]

    2. Satin Doll (Duke Ellington-Billy Strayhorn-Johnny Mercer) [# 22201-3]

    3. My Funny Valentine (Rodgers-Hart) [# 22203-7]

    4. Blues for Space Travelers (Barney Kessel) [# 22204-7]

Side B (51,009)

    1. Tin Reed Blues (Barney Kessel) [# 22206-1]

    2. Crazy Rhythm (J. Meyer-R. W. Kahn-I. Caesar) [#22207-4]

    3. Ballad Medley: I'm Glad There Is You (DeFranco) / There's No You (Feldman) [# 22205-4]

Note: "Lullaby in Rhythm" [# 22202] was never issued. Matrix numbers [# nnnnn-n] are from Michel Ruppli, comp., *The Clef/Verve Labels: A Discography, Volume 1: The Norman Granz Era*. Westport, CT: Greenwood Press, 1986.

9. *Kamuca Feldman Tjader: Featuring Scott LaFaro*
Tokyo: Vantage Records, 1991. NLP 5007. (The Bob Andrews Collection) 1 sound disc, analog; 33 1/3 rpm, monophonic; 12 in. Recording by Bob Andrews, Re-mastering by S. O. S. Japan, Produced by Shuichi Iwama, Coordination by Toshiya Taenaka, Back Cover Illustration: Seiji Yamashita, Cover Design: Takeshi Msuda. Manufactured and Distributed by NORMA. Under License by Bob Andrews.

Program:
    (LaFaro performs on six tracks: A-4, A-5, and A-6; B-1, B-2, and B-3)

Side A

    1. Too Close for Comfort (J. Bock-G. D. Weiss-J. Holofcener) 3:16

    2. What's New? (Johnny Burke-Bob Haggart) 4:07

    3. Just Friends (J. Klenner-S. M. Lewis) 3:36

    4. Cherry (D. Redman-R. Gilbert) 2:50

5. Deep in a Dream (Eddie DeLange-Jimmy Van Heusen) 3:37

6. Chart of My Heart (R. Kamuca?) 3:17

Side B

1. There's No Greater Love (M. Symes-I. Jones) 3:15

2. Flamingo (T. Grouya-E. Anderson) 3:14

3. BeBop (Dizzy Gillespie) 2:47

4. Crow's Nest (Tjader) 3:47

5. Leazon (Tjader) 3:25

6. Tumbao (Tjader)

Performers:

Tracks A-1–A-3 (recorded 21 October 1957)

Richie Kamuca, tenor saxophone

Tony Bazley, drums

Carl Perkins, piano

Leroy Vinnegar, bass

Tracks A-4–A-6 (recorded 7 April 1958)

Richie Kamuca, tenor saxophone

Scott LaFaro, bass

Stan Levey, drums

Carl Perkins, piano

Frank Rosolino, trombone

Tracks B-1–B-3 (recorded 10 November 1958)

Victor Feldman, piano

Scott LaFaro, bass

Stan Levey, drums

Tracks B-4–B-6 (recorded 30 June 1958)

Cal Tjader, vibraphone

Vince Guaraldi, piano

Billy Higgins, drums

Scott LaFaro [sic, in recté Al McKibbon] bass

Bernard Verlardi, percussion (B-6 only)

Note: Bob Andrews during the 1950s recorded many West Coast jazz ensembles during live performances. Several of his recordings were issued on the Xanadu label. These sessions by NORMA and Vantage Records were never released previously. The 7 April 1958 session sounds identical to the same three tunes recorded as part of the Bobby Troup KABC-TV broadcast, "The Stars of Jazz." The 10 November 1958 session lists three tunes recorded in January 1958 by Contemporary Records and released as part of *The Arrival of Victor Feldman*. The 30 June 1958 session lists LaFaro as bassist, but the sound is not LaFaro's. Two of the three tunes, "Crow's Nest" (B-4) and "Leazon," the latter as "Liz-Anne" (B-5), however, are included on the February 1958 recording *Cal Tjader – Stan Getz Sextet*, which includes LaFaro as bassist.

10. *Jazz at A. N. A. [Army and Navy Academy]—2nd All Star Concert*
Produced by First Classmen of Army and Navy Academy [Los Angeles: 1958] 1 sound disc, analog; 33 1/3 rpm, monophonic; 12 in. Total time 44:10. Program notes by Mr. James F. Hannon, Sponsor, A. N. A. Class of 1958. On container's cover: "Jazz at ANA—Presented by Class of '58"

Performers:
None identified, however, a likely list would include:
Bob Cooper, tenor saxophone and oboe
Victor Feldman, piano and vibraphone
Scott LaFaro, bass (tracks A-2, A-3, and A-4)
Stan Levey, drums
Frank Rosolino, trombone
Howard Rumsey, bass (tracks A-1 and B-1, B-2, and B-3
Unidentified percussionist(s) on B-3

Program:
Side A
1. Dickie's Dream (Basie-Lester Young) 5:10
2. Pent Up House (Sonny Rollins) 6:30

3. [Blues] 10:20

4. Love Me or Levey (Bill Holman) 4:20

Side B

1. ["New Orleans" style "Happy Birthday"] 1:20

2. Angel Eyes (Matt Dennis-Earl Brent) 5:40

3. Mambo Las Vegas (Bill Holman) 10:50

Note: Helene LaFaro-Fernandez recalls her brother Scotty telling her that he performed with the Howard Rumsey Lighthouse All Stars for this recording at A. N. A. in 1958. Information about performers and program derives from conversations between Rumsey and LaFaro-Fernandez.

11. *Joe Gordon and Scott LaFaro: West Coast Days*

Featuring Ritchie Kamuca, Victor Feldman, [and] Russ Freeman. Switzerland: Fresh Sound Records, 1992. FSCD-1030. 1 sound disc: digital; 4 and 3/4 in. Total time 56:06. From previously un-released recordings made by Howard Rumsey at the [Hermosa Beach, CA] Lighthouse. Produced by Jordi Pujol, copyright 1992 by Camarillo Music, Ltd. Includes program booklet.

Performers:

Joe Gordon, trumpet and leader

Monty Budwig, bass

Russ Freeman, piano

Shelly Manne, drums

Ritchie Kamuca, tenor sax and leader

Victor Feldman, piano

Scott LaFaro, bass

Stan Levey, drums

Program:

1. Our Delight (Tadd Dameron) 5:29

2. Summertime (Gershwin-Heyward) 11:48

3. Poinciana (Simon-Lliso-Bernier) 11:42

4. It Could Happen to You (Burke–Van Heusen) 11.08

5. Bass Blues (John Coltrane) 15:12

Note: LaFaro performs on "It Could Happen to You" and "Bass Blues" only. The Joe Gordon session was recorded 31 July 1960; the Richie Kamuca session in September 1958.

12. *Harold Land Quartet: Jazz at The Cellar, 1958*
[Barcelona: Lone Hill Jazz [c2007] LHJ-10291; 1 sound disc; analog to digital; 4 and 3/4 in. Total time 79:37.

Recorded on location at The Cellar, Vancouver, Canada, November 1958. All tracks previously unissued in any format. Includes six-page program booklet by Morton James.

Performers:
Harold Land, tenor saxophone and leader

Elmo Hope, piano

Scott LaFaro, bass

Lenny McBrowne, drums

Program:
1. Cherokee (Ray Noble) 18:58

2. Just Friends (J. Klenner – S. M. Lewis) 19:39

3. The Scene Is Clean (Tadd Dameron) 1:17

4. Big Foot (Charlie Parker) 27:44

5. Come Rain or Come Shine (H. Arlen–J. Mercer) 11:57

Note: Announcer mentions performers by name during "The Scene is Clean" break theme.

13. *This Is Pat Moran: The Pat Moran Trio*
New York: Audio Fidelity [c1958] AFLP-1875 / AFSD-5875. 1 sound disc: analog, 33 1/3 rpm, monophonic / stereo; 12 in.

Re-issued: *Pat Moran: Complete Trio Sessions.* [Barcelona? Fresh Sound Records ca. 2007] FSR-CD-440; 1 sound disc; analog to digital; 4 and 3/4 in. TT: 76:00. Produced for CD re-release by Jorge Pujol. Compilation of most of two previously released Audio Fidelity long-play recordings: *This Is Pat Moran* (AFSD-5875) and *Beverly Kelly Sings with the Pat Moran Trio* (AFLP-1874). Includes two-page program booklet the cover of which reproduces the photograph of the LP *This Is Pat Moran*.

Performers:

Pat Moran, piano and leader

John Doling, bass [sic, in recté Scott LaFaro]

Johnny Whited, drums [sic, in recté Gene Gammage]

Program:

Side A (AFLP-A / AFSD-A)

1. Making Whoopee (Donaldson–Kahn) 5:25

2. In Your Own Sweet Way (Brubeck) 5:05

3. Onilisor (Rosilino) 4:10 [mirrored accurately this should be "Onilosor" for Rosolino]

4. Stella By Starlight (Young) 3:10

5. Someone to Watch over Me (G. and I. Gershwin) 2:48

6. Come Rain or Come Shine (Arlen–Mercer) 5:35

Side B (AFLP-B / AFSD-B)

1. Black-Eyed Peas (Glover) 3:25

2. When Your Lover Has Gone (Swan) 3:20

3. I Could Have Danced All Night (Lowe) 3:30

4. Farewells (Moran–Frey) 4:04

5. Yesterdays (Kern) 4:30

6. Blues (Moran–Frey) 4:05

Note: According to Patti Moran McCoy, this recording was made in New York in early December 1958 and Gene Gammage is the drummer and Scott LaFaro the bassist. McCoy believes that Audio Fidelity's producers inadvertently transferred the names of Doling and Whited from her 1956 and 1957 Bethlehem recordings.

14. *Beverly Kelly Sings with the Pat Moran Trio*
New York: Audio Fidelity [c1958] AFLP 1874. 1 sound disc: analog, 33 1/3 rpm, monophonic; 12 in.

Re-issued: *Pat Moran: Complete Trio Sessions.* [Barcelona? Fresh Sound Records ca. 2007] FSR-CD-440; 1 sound disc; analog to digital; 4 and 3/4 in. TT: 76:00. Produced for CD re-release by Jorge Pujol. Compilation of most of two previously released Audio Fidelity long-play recordings: *This Is Pat Moran* (AFSD-5875) and *Beverly Kelly Sings with the Pat Moran Trio* (AFLP-1874). Includes two-page program booklet the cover of which reproduces the photograph of the LP *This Is Pat Moran.*

Performers:

Pat Moran, piano and leader

John Doling, bass [sic, in recté Scott LaFaro]

Beverly Kelly, vocals

Johnny Whited, drums [sic, in recté Gene Gammage]

Program:
Side A (AFLP 1874-A)

1. Lover Come Back to Me (Romberg-Hammerstein) 2:45

2. The Man I Love (G. and I. Gershwin) 3:00

3. I Get a Kick out of You (Cole Porter) 3:22

4. I Wish I Knew (Harris-Young) 2:15

5. You Don't Know What Love Is (Raye-DePaul) 3:55

6. I'm Glad There Is You (Madeira-Dorsey) 4:50

Side B (AFLP 1874-B)

1. Sometimes I'm Happy (Youmans-Caesar-Gray) 3:15

2. You and the Night and the Music (Schartz-Dietz) 2:30

3. But Not for Me (G. and I. Gershwin) 3:32

4. This Love of Mine (Sanicola-Parker-Sinatra) 2:44

5. Embraceable You (G. and I. Gershwin) 4:50

6. Spring Is Here (Rodgers-Hart) 3:50

15. *The Broadway Bit: The Modern Touch of Marty Paich*
[Burbank, CA:] Warner Brothers, 1959. WB-1296 [and] WS-1296.
1 sound disc; analog, 33 1/3 rpm, stereophonic; 12 in. Recorded
on various dates during 1959 in Los Angeles.

Re-issued: Paich, Marty. *The New York Scene* (Warner Brothers
WS-1296)

Paich, Marty. *The New York Scene* (Discovery DS 844)

Paich, Marty. *Moanin'* (Discovery DSCD 962)

Performers:

Marty Paich, arranger, conductor, piano, and leader

Frank Beach, trumpet

Vince De Rosa, French horn

Bobby Enwoldsen, trombone

Victor Feldman, vibes [and] percussion

Jimmy Giuffre, baritone saxophone [and] clarinet

Scott Lefaro [sic, in recté LaFaro] bass

Mel Lewis, drums

Art Pepper, alto saxophone

Bill Perkins, tenor saxophone

George Roberts, trombone

Stu Williamson, trumpet

Program:
Side A (W-1296–8283)

1. It's All Right With Me—from *Can-Can* (Cole Porter)

2. I've Grown Accustomed to Her Face—from *My Fair Lady*
(Lowe-Lerner)

3. I've Never Been in Love Before—from *Guys and Dolls* (Frank
Loesser)

4. I Love Paris—from *Can-Can* (Cole Porter)

Side B (W-1296 – 8284)

1. Too Close For Comfort—from *Mr. Wonderful* (Bock-Holofcener-
Weiss)

2. Younger Than Springtime—from *South Pacific* / The Surrey with the Fringe on Top—from *Oklahoma* (Rodgers-Hammerstein II)

3. If I Were a Bell—from *Guys and Dolls* (F. Loesser)

4. Lazy Afternoon—from the Phoenix Theater musical *The Golden Apple* (Moross-LaTouche)

5. Just In Time—from *The Bells Are Ringing* (Styne-Comden-Green)

16. *The Stan Kenton Orchestra in Concert*

Burbank, CA: Hindsight Records, 1997. HCD-612. 1 sound disc: digital; 4 and 3/4 in. Produced and compiled by Bob Edmonson. Digital re-mastering and restoration [by] Joe Sidore. Liner notes [by] Dr. Herb Wong. Design [by] Mario Levesque. Executive producer, Tom Gramuglia. Original recording made in March 1959.

Performers:

Stan Kenton, piano and leader

Jim Amlotte, bass trombone

John Bonnie, tenor saxophone

Bud Brisbois, trumpet

Joe Burnett, trumpet

Rolf Ericson, trumpet

Frank Huggins, trumpet

Jimmy Knepper, trombone

Scott LaFaro, bass

Kent Larson, trombone

Archie Le Coque, trombone

Jerry Lestock, drums (the other Jerry McKenzie: Jerry Lestock McKenzie)

Roger Middleton, trumpet

Lennie Niehaus, alto saxophone

Mike Pacheco, Latin percussion

Billy Root, baritone saxophone

Bill Smiley, trombone

Sture Swenson, tenor saxophone

Bill Trujillo, tenor saxophone

Program:

1. Theme And Variations (Bill Holman) 3:43

2. Fearless Finlay (Bill Holman) 4:00

3. I Concentrate on You (Cole Porter) 3:40

4. My Old Flame (Sam Coslow and Arthur Johnston) 5:03

5. Intermission Riff (Ray Wetzel) 5:21

6. La Suerte De Los Tontos (from *Cuban Fire*—Johnny Richards) 3:58

7. Bernie's Tune (Bernie Miller) 3:39

8. Street Scene (Alfred Newman) 4:30

9. Out of This World (Cole Porter) 7:17

17. *Latinsville! Victor Feldman, An Unusual Meeting of Jazz Stars and Authentic Afro-Cuban Rhythms*

Los Angeles: Contemporary Records, [c1960] Contemporary M-5005. 1 sound disc: analog, 33 1/3 rpm, monophonic; 12 in. Recorded 2, 3, and 20 March and 4 May 1959. Sound by Roy DuNann. Produced by Lester Koenig. Program notes by Leonard Feather, dated 17 May 1960.

Re-issued: Feldman, Victor. *Latinsville!* Berkeley: Contemporary, 2003. CCD-9005-2. This CD re-release includes five additional tracks and program material not included in the original LP release.

Performers:

Victor Feldman, vibraphone and leader

Walter Benton, tenor saxophone

Willie Bobo, timbales

Conte Candoli, trumpet

Vince Guaraldi, piano

Scott LaFaro, bass

Stan Levey, drums

Armando Peraza, bongos

Frank Rosolino, trombone

Mongo Santamaria, congas

Program:

Side A (M-5005—LKL-12-277)

   1. South of the Border (M. Carr-J. Kennedy) 3:17 Mambo

   2. She's a Latin from Manhattan (H. Warren-A. Dubin) 3:20 Cha-cha-cha

   3. Flying Down to Rio (E. Eliscu-G. Kahn- V. Youmans) 2:56 Bolero

   4. Cuban Pete (J. Norman) 2:49 Cha-cha-cha

   5. The Gypsy (B. Reid) 3:05 Bolero

   6. Poinciana (Nat Simon-M. Lliso-B. Bernier) 3:35 Afro-jazz

Side B (M-5005—LKL-12-278)

   1. Lady of Spain (T. Evans-E. Reaves) 3:25 Guapa-cha

   2. Spain (G. Kahn-Isham Jones) 3:07 Bolero

   3. Cuban Love Song (H. Stothart-J. McHugh-D. Fields) 3:25 Cha-cha-cha

   4. In a Little Spanish Town (S. M. Lewis-J. Young-M. Wayne) 3:25 Afro-jazz

   5. Fiesta (Traditional) 3:05 Guapa-cha

   6. Woody' N You (D. Gillespie) 3:25 Afro-jazz

Notes: "Poinciana," "Spain," "Woody 'N You," and "Cuban Love Song" were recorded 2 March 1959, with Feldman, Candoli, Rosolino, Benton, Guaraldi, LaFaro, Levey, Bobo, Perazza, and Santamaria. "The Gypsy" and "In a Little Spanish Town" were recorded 3 March 1959 with same performers as on the 2 March 1959 session minus Rosolino and Levey. "South of the Border," "Flying Down to Rio," and "Lady of Spain" were recorded 20 March 1959 with the same performers as on 3 March 1959 except Al McKibbon, bass, replaced LaFaro. "She's a Latin from Manhattan," "Cuban Pete," and "Fiesta" were recorded 4

May 1959 with Feldman, vibes; Andy Thomas, piano; Tony Reyes, bass; Frank Guerrero, timbales; and Ramon Rivera, congas.

Additional program material is included on the 2003 re-release CD. The following five tracks were recorded 8 and 9 December 1958 with a quintet comprising Benton, Feldman, LaFaro, Rosolino, and Nick Martinis, drums, instead of Stan Levey. Feldman played both vibraphone and piano on tracks 15, 16, and 17.

> 13. Poinciana (Nat Simon-M. Lliso-B. Bernier) 5:34—8 December 1958 session
>
> 14. Pancho (Frank Rosolino) 5:34—ditto
>
> 15. The Breeze and I (E. Lecuona-A. Stillman) 3:19—9 December 1958 session
>
> 16. Bullues Bullose (Victor Feldman) 5:40—ditto
>
> 17. Lady of Spain (R. Hargreaves-T. Evans-R. Hargreaves-S.J. Damerell-H. Tilsley) 5:56—ditto

18. *Gypsy: Herb Geller and His All Stars*

New York: Atco Records, Division of Atlantic Recording Corp. [1960?] Atco High Fidelity 33-109. 1 sound disc: analog, 33 1/3 rpm, stereo; 12 in. Selections from the musical *Gypsy* with music by Jule Styne and lyrics by Stephen Sondheim. Recording engineers, Tom Dowd and Phil Lehle. Supervision by Nesuhi Ertegun. Program notes by Joe Muranyi. Recorded late 1959.

Performers:

Herb Geller, alto saxophone

Elvin Jones, drums

Hank Jones, piano

Thad Jones, trumpet

Scott LaFaro, bass

Barbara Long, vocals

Billy Taylor, piano (on "Cow Song" only)

Program:

Side A (SD 33-109—ST-C-59157)

   1. Everything's Coming Up Roses (Styne-Sondheim) 4:05

   2. You'll Never Get Away from Me (Styne-Sondheim) 5:11

   3. Together (Styne-Sondheim) 4:34

   4. Little Lamb (Styne-Sondheim) 3:54

Side B (SD 33-109—ST-C-59158)

   1. Some People (Styne-Sondheim) 4:52

   2. Mama's Talkin' Soft (Styne-Sondheim) 3:56

   3. Cow Song (Styne-Sondheim) 3:32

   4. Small World (Styne-Sondheim) 4:57

19. *Sung Heroes: Featuring Bill Evans, Scott LaFaro, Paul Motian*

[New York?] Sunnyside Communications, Inc., 1989. SSC-1015-D. 1 sound disc; analog to digital, 4 and 3/4 in. Produced by Tony Scott. Recorded in New York at Fine Studio, 28 and 29 October 1959. Master tape prepared by A. T. MacDonald, March 1986. Executive production by Ray Passmann and Francois Zalacain. Notes by Burt Korall.

   Re-issued: Scott, Tony. *Dedications: Featuring Bill Evans, Scott LaFaro, Paul Motian, Juan Sastre [and] Shinichi Yuize.* Hamburg, West Germany: Core Records (a Division of Line Music, GmbH) 1989. COCD 9.00803 O.

Performers:

   Tony Scott, clarinet, piano, guitar, baritone sax, composer, and
      leader

   Bill Evans, piano (tracks 1, 4, 5, 6, and 7)

   Scott LaFaro, bass (tracks 1, 3, 4, and 5)

   Paul Motian, drums (tracks 1, 3, 4, and 5)

   Juan Sastre, guitar

Program:

1. Misery (To Lady Day)

2. Portrait of Anne Frank

3. Remembrance of Art Tatum

4. Requiem For "Hot Lips" Page

5. Blues for an African Friend

6. For Stefan Wolpe

7. Israel

8. Memory of My Father

9. Lament to Manolete

Note: This recording was the first time Evans, LaFaro, and Motian recorded together.

20. *Dedications: Featuring Bill Evans, Scott LaFaro, Paul Motian, Juan Sastre [and] Shinichi Yuize*

Hamburg, Western Germany: Core Records (a Division of Line Music GmbH) 1989. COCD 9.00803 O. 1 sound disc; analog to digital, 4 and 3/4 in. Recorded 28 and 29 October 1959 at Great Northern Pine Studio, New York except: Track 4 recorded ca. 1958; Track 8 recorded live 9 June 1957 in Ljubjana, Yugoslavia; Tracks 10 and 11 recorded ca. 1960 in Japan. Compiled and coordinated by Arne Schumacher. Digitally re-mastered and prepared for compact disc by Ralf Linder. Cover and liner photos from Archive Tony Scott except [trademark HK] by Hannes Kalsov. Produced by Tony Scott. All compositions by Tony Scott. Published by Tonimo Music.

Re-issued: Scott, Tony. *Sung Heroes: Featuring Bill Evans, Scott LaFaro, Paul Motian.* [New York?] Sunnyside Communications, Inc., 1989. SSC-1015-D.

Performers:

Tony Scott, clarinet and piano, clarinet and baritone sax, guitar, and leader

Bill Evans, piano (tracks 1, 2, 3, 7, and 9)

Scott LaFaro, bass (tracks 1, 2, 5, and 7)

Paul Motian, drums (tracks 1, 2, 5, and 7)

Juan Sastre, Flamenco guitar

Shinichi Yuize, koto

Horst Jankowski Trio (track 8) comprising:

Horst Jankowski, piano

Horst Herman Mutschler, drums

Peter Witte, bass

Program:

1. Misery (To "Lady Day" Billie Holiday)

2. Blues for an African Friend

3. Atonal Ad Lib Blues (For Stephan Wolpe)

4. Lament to Manolete

5. Remembrance of Art Tatum

6. Portrait of Anne Frank

7. Requiem for "Hot Lips" Page

8. Blues for Charlie Parker

9. Israel

10. Cherry Blossoms Falling, Children Playing

11. The Cranes in Winter, Fly Away

12. Memory of My Father

21. *Portrait in Jazz: Bill Evans Trio*

New York: Riverside Records, Bill Grauer Productions, Inc., 1959. RLP 1162 [and RS 9315] 1 sound disc: analog, 33 1/3 rpm, stereo; 12 in. Recorded 28 December 1959 in New York. Produced, and program notes written by Orrin Keepnews; photograph (back of container) by Lawrence N. Shustak; Engineer, Jack Higgins [of] Reeves Sound Studios.

Re-issued: *Spring Leaves*. Bill Evans. Berkeley, CA: Milestone Records; distributed by Fantasy Records, 1976. Milestone M-47034. 2 sound discs: analog, 33 1/3 rpm, stereo: 12 in. Produced by Orrin Keepnews. Re-mastered 1976 by David Turner. Program notes by Conrad Silvert. Sides 1 and 2 are *Portrait in Jazz*. Sides 3 and 4 are *Explorations!* [LP] Berkeley, CA: Fantasy Studios, 1987. OJCCD-088-2 (RLP-1162) DIDX 010273 (Original Jazz Classics [series]) digitally re-mastered by David Luke [CD] Berkeley, CA: Fantasy, Inc., 2001. RCD-1162-2 (RLP-1162) DIDX 074038 Mastering engineer, Shigeo Miyamoto under supervision of Tamaki Beck for JVC Studios. Edition limited to 10,000 copies. [CD]

Performers:

Bill Evans, piano

Scott LaFaro, bass

Paul Motian, drums

Program:

Side A (RLP 1162-A)

1. Come Rain or Come Shine (Arlen-Mercer) 3:17

2. Autumn Leaves (Mercer-Kosmo-Prevert) 5:22

3. Witchcraft (Leigh-Coleman) 4:30

4. When I Fall in Love (V. Young-E. Heyman) 4:50

5. Peri's Scope (Bill Evans) 3:11

Side B (RLP 1162-B)

1. What Is This Thing Called Love? (Cole Porter) 4:33

2. Spring Is Here (Rodgers-Hart) 5:01

3. Some Day My Prince Will Come (Churchill-Morey) 4:48

4. Blue in Green (Miles Davis-Bill Evans) 5:18

22. *The 1960 Birdland Sessions: The Legendary Bill Evans Trio*. [Switzerland] Cool N' Blue Records, 1992. C&B-CD 106. 1 sound disc: digital; 4 and 3/4 in. Compilation of previously issued recordings of radio-broadcast "live" performances at the New York jazz club, Birdland. Master of ceremonies is "Symphony"

Sid Torin. Recorded 12 and 19 March, 30 April, and 7 May 1960. Author of program notes is not identified.

Performers:

Bill Evans, piano

Scott LaFaro, bass

Paul Motian, drums

Program:

Saturday 12 March 1960

    1. Autumn Leaves (Prevert-Kosma-Mercer) 4:56

    2. Our Delight (Tadd Dameron) 6:38

    3. Beautiful Love / Five (closing theme) (Young-Van Alstyne / B. Evans) 5:24

Saturday 19 March 1960

    4. Autumn Leaves (Prevert-Kosma-Mercer) 6:48

    5. Come Rain or Come Shine / Five (closing theme) (Arlen-Mercer / B. Evans) 6:48

Saturday 30 April 1960

    6. Come Rain or Come Shine (Arlen-Mercer) 4:55

    7. Nardis (Miles Davis) 7:26

    8. Blue in Green (Bill Evans-Miles Davis) 6:14

    9. Autumn Leaves (Prevert-Kosma-Mercer) 7:09

Saturday 7 May 1960

    10. All of You (Cole Porter) 6:58

    11. Come Rain or Come Shine (Arlen-Mercer) 4:39

    12. Speak Low (Kurt Weill-Ogden Nash) 6:48

23. *Booker Little*

[Los Angeles?] Time, [1960?] S-2011. (Series 2000) 1 sound disc: analog, 33 1/3 rpm, stereo; 12 in. Recorded 13 and 15 April 1960. Artist and repertoire, Bob Shad; produced by Irving Joseph; original recording engineers, Al Weintraub and Bill MacMeekin;

re-recording engineer, John Cue; mastering, Hal Diepold; liner notes, Nat Hentoff.

Re-issued: *Booker Little*.Van Nuys, CA: Bainbridge Entertainment Co., Inc. [c1980] BCD-1041; 1 sound disc : analog, 33 1/3 rpm, stereo; 12 in. *Booker Little*.Van Nuys, CA: Bainbridge Entertainment Co., Inc. [c1996] BCD-1041; 1 sound disc : analog to digital, stereo ; 4 and 3/4 in.

Performers:

Booker Little, trumpet and leader

Tommy Flanagan, piano

Roy Haynes, drums

Wynton Kelly, piano (on "Bee Tee's Minor Plea" and "Life's a Little Blue")

Scott LaFaro, bass

Program:

(all compositions by Booker Little, except "Who Can I Turn To" by Alec Wilder)

Side A

1. Opening Statement (Booker Little) 6:42

2. Minor Sweet (B. Little) 5:38

3. Bee Tee's Minor Plea (B. Little) 5:40

Side B

1. Life's a Little Blue (B. Little) 6:53

2. The Grand Valse (B. Little) 4:57

3. Who Can I Turn To? (Alec Wilder-Bill Engvick) 5:25

24. *1960: Steve Kuhn Scott LaFaro Pete LaRoca*

[Tokyo?] Polystar Co., Ltd, 2005 (Polystar Jazz Library) MTCJ-3024. 1 sound disc: digital; 4 and 3/4 in. in gate-fold, card stock "jewel case." Recorded 29 November 1960 at the Peter Ind Studio, New York, NY. Total time: 29:15. Includes six-page program booklet in Japanese. Program notes dated 22 August 2005. CD released or published 19 October 2005. Released under the legal license from Steve Kuhn. A& R: Takashi Tannaka (Polystar Jazz library); Mastering Engineer: Seiji Kaneko for Kingrecords Sekiguchidai Studios; Designer: Takafumi Kitsuda; Coordination: Yoko Yamabe. Alternate title: *Steve Kuhn Scott LaFaro Pete LaRoca: 1960.*

Performers:

Steve Kuhn, piano and leader

Scott LaFaro, bass

Pete LaRoca, drums

Program:

1. Little Old Lady (Hoagy Carmichael) 6:14

2. Bohemia after Dark (Oscar Pettiford) 5:48

3. What's New? (J. Burke-R. Haggart) 5:37

4. So What (Miles Davis) 5:37

5. So What (alternate take) 5:57

25. *Jazz Abstractions: Compositions by Gunther Schuller and Jim Hall*

New York: Atlantic Recording Corp. [1961] Atlantic 1365. 1 disc: analog, 33 1/3 rpm; 12 in. (Series: John Lewis Presents Contemporary Music, 1) Recorded 19 and 20 December 1960 in New York. Program notes by Gunther Schuller; engineer, Phil Ramone; supervision, John Lewis and Nesuhi Ertegun.

Re-issued: *Golden Striker /Jazz Abstractions* Narberth, PA: Collectables Records, 1999. COL-CD-6252 (Collectables Jazz Classics). Compilation of two John Lewis recordings: *Golden Striker* (Atlantic 1334) and *Jazz Abstractions* (Atlantic 1365).

Program and Performers:

Side A (1365—11799)

1. "Abstraction" (G. Schuller) 4:06

Alvin Brehm, bass

Ornette Coleman, alto saxophone

Sticks Evans, drums

Jim Hall, guitar

Scott LaFaro, bass

The Contemporary String Quartet: (Charles Libove, violin; Joseph Tekula, cello; Roland Vamos, violin; and Harry Zaratzian, viola)

2. "Piece for Guitar and Strings" (J. Hall) 6:22

Same performers as on "Abstraction" minus Brehm, Coleman, and Sticks Evans; plus Alfred Brown, viola

"Variants on a Theme of John Lewis (Django)" (G. Schuller)

3. a) Variant I—5:27

4. b) Variant II—1:38

5. c) Variant III—3:10

Eddie Costa, vibraphone

Robert DiDomenica, flute

Eric Dolphy, flute

George Duvivier, bass

Bill Evans, piano

Sticks Evans, drums

Jim Hall, guitar

Scott LaFaro, bass

The Contemporary String Quartet (Libove, Tekula, Vamos, and Zaratzian)

Side B (1365—11800)

"Variants on a Theme of Thelonious Monk (Criss-Cross)" (G. Schuller)

Same performers as on "Variants [...] (Django)" plus Coleman and Dolphy, bass clarinet, alto sax, and flute

1. a) Variant I—6:22

2. b) Variant II—1:49

3. c) Variant III—4:12

4. d) Variant IV—3:00

26. *Free Jazz: A Collective Improvisation by the Ornette Coleman Double Quartet*

[New York: Atlantic Recording Company, 1960] Atlantic 1364. 1 sound disc: analog, 33 1/3 rpm, stereo; 12 in. Recorded 21 December 1960. Program notes by Martin Williams; Recording Engineer, Tom Dowd; Supervision, Nesuhi Ertegun.

Re-issued: *Beauty Is a Rare Thing, Ornette Coleman: The Complete Atlantic Recordings*. Los Angeles: Rhino Records, 1993. Rhino R2-71410. 6 sound discs: digital; 4 and 3/4 in. Recorded 1959-1961. Program notes (sixty-eight-page booklet) inserted in container. (Atlantic Jazz Gallery [series]) Compilation by Yves Beauvais. Digitally re-mastered from the original stereo master tapes by Stephen Innocenzi, Atlantic Studios, New York, April and May 1993.

Free Jazz: A Collective Improvisation by the Ornette Coleman Double Quartet. [New York: Atlantic Recording Co., 1996?] Atlantic 1364-2. 1 sound disc: analog to digital; 4 and 3/4 in.

Performers:

    Ornette Coleman, alto saxophone and leader

    Ed Blackwell, drums

    Donald Cherry, pocket trumpet

    Eric Dolphy, bass clarinet

    Charlie Haden, bass

    Billy Higgins, drums

    Freddie Hubbard, trumpet

    Scott LaFaro, bass

Program:

Side A (ST-A-61343 PR)

    1. Free Jazz, part 1

Side B (ST-A-61344 PR)

    1. Free Jazz, part 2 [i.e., continued from Side A]

Note: *Free Jazz* was recorded in one uninterrupted "take" of 36 minutes 23 seconds. The LP release required that Side A end with a quick fade-out and resumption with minimum interruption on Side B. In stereo playback the left speaker will have Coleman, Cherry, LaFaro, and Higgins; the right speaker, Dolphy, Hubbard, Haden, and Blackwell. The CD re-issue, of course, provides the listener with the original uninterrupted studio version. At this recording session a first take of "Free Jazz" (Coleman) 17:00 was released a decade later on the LP *Twins*. New York: Atlantic Recording Corp., 1971. SD-1588.

27. *Ornette!*

London: Atlantic, London Records, Ltd., 1961. SAH-K 6235 [New York: Atlantic, SD 1378]. 1 sound disc; analog, 33 1/3 rpm, stereo; 12 in. Recorded 31 January 1961 in New York. Program notes by Gunther Schuller; recording engineer, Tom Dowd; supervision, Nesuhi Ertegun.

Re-issued: *Beauty Is a Rare Thing: Ornette Coleman, The Complete Atlantic Recordings.* Los Angeles CA: Rhino Records, 1993. Rhino R2-71410. 6 sound discs: digital; 4 and 3/4 in. Recorded 1959-1961. Program booklet (68-p) inserted in container. (Atlantic Jazz Gallery [series]) Compilation by Yves Beauvais. Digitally re-mastered from the original stereo master tapes by Stephen Innocenzi, Atlantic Studios, New York, April and May 1993.

A Meeting of the Times [and] *Ornette!* Narberth PA: Collectables Records, 1999. Col-CD-6266 (Collectables Jazz Classics) 1 sound disc: analog to digital; 4 and 3/4 in. Total time: 75:56. Produced under license from Atlantic Recording Corp. Manufactured by Rhino Entertainment Company, 1999. This CD is a compilation of two LP recordings: Rahsaan Roland Kirk, *A Meeting of the Times* (1972, Atlantic 1630) and Ornette Coleman, *Ornette!* (1961, Atlantic 1378).

Ornette! The Ornette Coleman Quartet. Burbank, CA: Warner Strategic Marketing Group (to include Atlantic Recording Corp. and Rhino [Records]), R2-73714 (Warner Bros. Jazz Masters [series]) CD reissue 2004; original LP January 1961. 1 sound disc: analog (monophonic)-to-digital; 4 and 3/4 in. Total time: 54:28. Includes 15-p. program booklet. Reissue supervision: Joel Dorn, Atlantic Jazz; Masters supervision: Patrick Milligan, Audio Supervision: Jeff Magid, Re-mastering: David Donnelly, DNA Mastering, Studio City, CA.

Performers:

Ornette Coleman, alto saxophone and leader

Ed Blackwell, drums

Donald Cherry, pocket trumpet

Scott LaFaro, bass

Program:

Side A

   1. W. R. U. (Coleman)

   2. T. & T. (Coleman)

Side B

   1. C. & D. (Coleman)

   2. R. P. D. D. (Coleman)

Note: This session included "The Alchemy of Scott LaFaro" (Coleman) 8:48 released as part of *The Art of the Improvisers*. New York. Atlantic Recording Corp., 1970. SD-1572.

28. *Explorations: The Bill Evans Trio*

New York: Riverside Records and Bill Grauer Productions, Inc., 1961. Riverside RLP-351 [Factory label "Stereo RLP 9351" superimposed on album jacket]. 1 sound disc: analog, 33 1/3 rpm, stereo; 12 in. Recorded 2 February 1961, New York, NY. Program notes by Orrin Keepnews. Produced by Orrin Keepnews. Recording Engineer, Bill Stoddard. Mastered by Jack Matthews. Container (jacket, sleeve) cover designed by Steve Schapiro. Photograph on back by Steve Schapiro.

   Re-issued: *Spring Leaves*. Bill Evans. Berkeley, CA: Milestone Records; distributed by Fantasy Records, 1976. Milestone M-47034. 2 sound discs: analog, 33 1/3 rpm, stereo: 12 in. Produced by Orrin Keepnews. Re-mastered 1976 by David Turner. Program notes by Conrad Silvert. Sides 1 and 2 are *Portrait in Jazz*. Sides 3 and 4 are *Explorations!* Berkeley, CA: Riverside Records; distributed by Fantasy, Inc., 1982. OJC-037 (RLP-9351) (Original Jazz Classics) 1 sound disc: analog, 33 1/3 rpm, stereo; 12 in. Berkeley, CA: Fantasy Studios, 1987. OJCCD-037 (RLP

9351) DIDX 010768; Digital re-mastering 1987 by David Luke. Berkeley, CA: Fantasy, 2002. RCD-9351-2 DIDX 082340; Mastering engineer, Shigeo Miyamoto under supervision of Tamaki Beck for JVC Studios; edition limited to 10,000 copies

Performers:

Bill Evans, piano and leader

Scott LaFaro, bass

Paul Motian, drums

Program:

Side A

1. Israel (John Carisi) 6:09

2. Haunted Heart (Deitz-Schwartz) 3:25

3. Beautiful Love (Gillespie-King-Van Alstyne-Young) 5:04

4. Elsa (Earl Zindars) 5:08

Side B

1. Nardis (Miles Davis) 5:49

2. How Deep Is the Ocean? (Berlin) 3:31

3. I Wish I Knew (Gordon-Warren) 5:51

4. Sweet and Lovely (Arnheim-Tobias-Lemare) 5:51

29. *Stan the Man*

New York: Verve [and Polygram Records] 1984. Verve 815 239-1. 2 sound discs: analog, 33 and 1/3 rpm, 12 in. Also issued as a magnetic tape "double play" cassette 815 239-4. Compilation of sessions produced by Norman Granz. Re-issue produced by Jim Fishel. Executive Producer, Barry Feldman; Re-issue Engineer, Steve Baldwin, Polygram Studios; Album Design and Art Direction, Tom Hughes, Hughes Group, New York; Cover Photo of Stan Getz by Chuck Stewart. Ensembles with Stan Getz as leader, recorded between 1952 and 1961. All but four selections have been previously released.

Performers:

Stan Getz, tenor saxophone and leader

Steve Kuhn, piano

Scott LaFaro, bass

Pete LaRoca, drums

Program:

"Airegin" (Rollins) 5:59

A Michel Ruppli discography provides the following matrix data for the Stan Getz quartet recording session in New York Tuesday 21 February 1961:

23486-3 Baubles, Bangles, and Beads—unissued

23487-1 Little Old Lady—unissued

23488-1 I Remember Clifford—unissued

23489-2 For You, For Me, For Evermore—unissued

23490-3 Airegin (issued, Verve 815239-1, *Stan the Man* LP)

23491-4 Speak Low—unissued

23492-4 Spring Can Really Hang You Up the Most—unissued

The previously unreleased "Evening in Paris" (Quincy Jones) was recorded in Chicago Monday 20 February 1961.

Performers:

Stan Getz, tenor saxophone and leader

Victor Feldman, piano

Louis Hayes, drums

Sam Jones, bass

Program:

23485-1 Evening in Paris (Quincy Jones) issued, Verve 815239-1, *Stan the Man* LP)

30. *Memories for Scotty: Don Friedman with Scott LaFaro*

Tokyo: Insights Records; Manufactured by Camerata Tokyo, Inc., 1988. Insights 32CJ-3. 1 sound disc: analog-to-digital; 4 and 3/4 in. Total time 65:36. Produced by Hiroshi Isaka. Recorded in 1961 (tracks 1-10) and 1985 (track 11). Collaborator: Georg Klabin; Digital re-mastering engineer, Iwao Kojima; Recording engineer (track 11) Iwao Kojima; Cover photography, Hiroshi Isaka; Cover design, Keijiro Kubota. Includes program booklet (in Japanese).

Performers:

Don Friedman, piano and leader (1–11)

Joe Hunt, drums (6–10)

Chuck Israels, bass (6–10)

Scott LaFaro, bass (1–5)

Pete LaRoca, drums (1–5)

Program:

1. I Hear A Rhapsody (G. Fragos -J. Baker)

2. Sacre Blue, take 1 (Don Friedman)

3. Sacre Blue, take 2

4. Woody 'N You (Dizzy Gillespie)

5. On Green Dolphin Street (B. Kaper-N. Washington)

6. The Bears of Bern, take 1 (D. Friedman)

7. Dawn (D. Friedman)

8. The Bears of Bern, take 2

9. How Deep Is the Ocean (I. Berlin)

10. Rush Hour (D. Friedman)

11. Memories for Scotty (D. Friedman)

Notes: Compilation of three separate recording sessions, the first two from 1961 with two different rhythm sections supporting Don Friedman. The third from 1985 is a solo piano tribute to LaFaro. Specific recording dates have not been determined. This 1961 session with LaFaro and LaRoca may have occurred soon after the Stan Getz *Stan the*

Man 21 February session because of the fact that LaFaro and LaRoca performed together on that session as well.

31. *Bill Evans Trio: Sunday at the Village Vanguard Featuring Scott LaFaro*

New York: Riverside Records and Orpheum Productions, Inc., 1961. RLP 376—sound disk: analog, 33 1/3 rpm, stereo; 12 in. Recorded live at the Village Vanguard, New York City, 25 June 1961. Program notes by Ira Gitler. Photograph of LaFaro, Evans, Motian by Steve Schapiro. Side bar "In Memoriam" by Orrin Keepnews.

Re-issued: *The Village Vanguard Sessions*. Berkeley, CA: Milestone Records; distributed by Fantasy Records, 1973. M-47002. 2 sound discs: analog, 33 1/3 rpm; 12 in.

More From The Vanguard. Berkeley, CA; Milestone Records, Distributed by Fantasy Records, 1984. M-9125. 1 sound disc: analog, 33 1/3 rpm; 12 in.

At the Village Vanguard. Berkeley, CA: Riverside Records, 1986. FCD-60-017, DIDX 000668; selections compiled by Ed Michel [CD]

Sunday at the Village Vanguard. Berkeley, CA: Fantasy, 1987. OJCCD-140-2 (RLP 9376) DIDX 010264. (Original Jazz Classics [series]) [CD]

Sunday at the Village Vanguard. [Tokyo] Fantasy, JVC, 2001. RCD-9376-2 DIDX 074040. Edition limited to 10,000 copies. [CD]

32. *Bill Evans: The Complete Live at the Village Vanguard 1961*

[Tokyo] Victor Entertainment, 2002. VICJ-60951-3 Boxed set of 3 sound discs each 4 and 3/4 in., in separate jewel cases with thirteen-page program booklet in English and Japanese. [CD]

Performers:

Bill Evans, piano and leader

Scott LaFaro, bass

Paul Motian, drums

Program:

Side A

   1. Gloria's Step (Scott LaFaro) 6:05

   2. My Man's Gone Now(G. and I. Gershwin) 6:21

   3. Solar (M. Davis) 8:51

Side B

   1. Alice in Wonderland (Fain-Hilliard) 8:32

   2. All of You (Cole Porter) 8:20

   3. Jade Visions (Scott LaFaro) 3:41

33. *Waltz for Debby: Bill Evans Trio, with Scott LaFaro [and] Paul Motian*

New York: Riverside Records and Orpheum Productions, Inc., 1961. RLP 9399. 1 sound disc: analog, 33 1/3 rpm, stereo; 12 in. Recorded live at the Village Vanguard, New York City, 25 June 1961. Program notes by Joe Goldberg.

   Re-issued: *The Village Vanguard Sessions*. Berkeley, CA: Milestone Records; distributed by Fantasy Records, 1973. M-47002. 2 sound discs: analog, 33 1/3 rpm; 12 in.

   More From The Vanguard. Berkeley, CA; Milestone Records, Distributed by Fantasy Records, 1984. M-9125. 1 sound disc: analog, 33 1/3 rpm; 12 in.

   At The Village Vanguard. Berkeley, CA: Riverside Records, 1986. FCD-60-017, DIDX 000668; selections compiled by Ed Michel [CD]

   Waltz for Debby. Berkeley CA, Fantasy, 1987. OJCCD-210-2 (RLP 9399) DIDX 010234. (Original Jazz Classics [series]) [CD]

   Waltz for Debby. Berkeley, CA: Fantasy, 2000. RCD-9399-2 (RLP 9399) DIDX 71924. Edition limited to 10,000 copies. [CD]

   Bill Evans: The Complete Live at the Village Vanguard 1961. [Tokyo] Victor Entertainment, 2002. VICJ-60951-3 Boxed set of 3 sound discs each 4 and 3/4 in., in separate jewel cases with thirteen-page program booklet in English and Japanese. [CD]

Performers:

   Bill Evans, piano and leader

Scott LaFaro, bass

Paul Motian, drums

Program:

Side A

   1. My Foolish Heart (Washington-Young) 4:56

   2. Waltz for Debby (Bill Evans) 6:54

   3. Detour Ahead (Lou Carter-Herb Ellis-John Frigo) 7:35

Side B

   1. My Romance (Rodgers-Hart) 7:11

   2. Some Other Time (L. Bernstein-B. Comden-A. Green) 5:02

   3. Milestones (Miles Davis) 6:37

34. *Miles Davis / Stan Getz: Tune Up*

Featuring John Lewis, Milt Jackson, Scott LaFaro and special guest Lester Young. Margaretville, NY: Natasha Imports, 1992. NI-4008. 1 sound disc: analog to digital, stereo; 4 and 3/4 in. Total time 48:50. Tracks 1–4 recorded 12 November 1956 in West Germany; tracks 5–7 recorded Sunday 2 July 1961 at the Newport [Rhode Island] Jazz Festival.

   Re-issued: *Rare Live: Stan Getz / Miles Davis*. Tokyo: Venus Records, Inc., 1994; License from Stash Records through Art Union Corp. TKCZ-79046. 1 sound disc: analog to digital, stereo; 4 and 3/4 in. Total time 48:50.

Performers:

Tracks 1 and 2:

   Miles Davis, trumpet

   Lester Young, tenor saxophone

   John Lewis, piano

   Milt Jackson, vibraphone

   Percy Heath, bass

   Connie Kay, drums

Kurt Edelhagen Big Band (track #2)

Tracks 3 and 4:

   Miles Davis, trumpet

   Rene Urtege [sic, in recté Utreger], piano

   Pierre Michelot, bass

   Christian Garros, drums

Tracks 5, 6, and 7:

   Stan Getz, tenor saxophone

   Roy Haynes, drums

   Steve Kuhn, piano

   Scott LaFaro, bass

Program:

1. How High the Moon (Morgan Lewis-Nancy Hamilton) 8:07

2. Lester Leaps In (L. Young) 9:10

3. Tune Up (M. Davis) 2:50

4. What's New? (J. Burke-B. Haggart) 3:36

5. Baubles, Bangles, and Beads (Robert Wright-George Forrest) 8:17

6. Where Do You Go? (Alec Wilder) 8:14

7. Airegin (Stan Getz [sic, in recté Sonny Rollins]) 8:26

ADDENDUM: Recordings that erroneously list Scott LaFaro as a performer.

   Assorted Flavors of Pacific Jazz: Hi-Fi Sampler. Hollywood, CA: Pacific Jazz Enterprises, 1956. HFS-1 1 sound disc: analog, 33 1/3 rpm, monophonic; 12 in. Richard Bock, Production; Narrative Copy, Woody Woodward; Packaging, William Claxton and Will MacFarland. Recording is narrated by Frank Evans.

Notes: Helene LaFaro-Fernandez recalls her brother Scotty telling her that he performed with Chet Baker on one of the selections on this Pacific Jazz compilation. Royston Edwards, bassist and LaFaro researcher, however, believes the following bassists—Jimmy Bond, Carson Smith, Monty Budwig, Red Mitchell and Joe Mondragon—played on the several individual albums that comprise this "sampler" but not LaFaro (e-mail, Edwards to Ralston, 1 September 2002). James Harrod, student of the Pacific Jazz recordings, has provided a list of the sixteen recordings comprising this sampler (e-mail, Harrod to Ralston, 3 August 2004):

1. JWC-501 *Jazz West Coast*, Vol. 2 ([…] Gerry Mulligan, Chet Baker, Chico Hamilton, Bud Shank, Bill Perkins, Hampton Hawes, Cy Touff, Richie Kamuca, Claude Williamson, Buddy Collette, John Lewis, Bob Brookmeyer, Carl Fontana, Russ Freeman, Shelly Manne, Kenny Drew, Jack Sheldon, Jim Hall, Percy Heath)

2. P-2001 *Pacifica: A Quiet Evening with the Mighty Wurlitzer in Hi Fi: The Wurlitzer Pipe Organ Played by Bill Thompson*

3. PJ-1202 *Chet Baker Sings and Plays with Bud Shank, Russ Freeman and Strings*

4. PJ-1203 *Chet Baker Quartet: Jazz at Ann Arbor*

5. PJ-1204 *Laurindo Almeida Quartet (featuring Bud Shank)*

6. PJ-1205 *Bud Shank, Shorty Rogers, Jimmy Rowles, Harry Babasin, Roy Harte*

7. PJ-1207 *Gerry Mulligan Quartet*

8. PJ-1208 *Jack Montrose Sextet (featuring Bob Gordon, Conte Candoli, Shelly Manne)*

9. PJ-1209 *Chico Hamilton Quintet (featuring Buddy Collette)*

10. PJ-1210 *Gerry Mulligan Quartet Paris Concert*

11. PJ-1211 *Cy Touff: His Octet & Quintet*

12. PJ-1212 *The Richard Twardzik Trio*

13. PJ-1213 *Bud Shank / Bob Brookmeyer: Strings & Trombones*

14. PJ-1214 *Arranged by Montrose: Bob Gordon, Clifford Brown, Zoot Sims, Russ Freeman, Shelly Manne Play the Arrangements of Jack Montrose*

15. PJ-1215 *The Bud Shank Quartet*

16. PJ-1216 *Chico Hamilton Quintet in Hi Fi*

Bird Song
Hampton Hawes Berkeley, CA: Contemporary Records, 1999. Contemporary OJCCD-1035-2 (Original Jazz Classics) 1 sound disc : analog to digital; 4 and 3/4 in. Total time 55:27. Produced

by Lester Koenig. CD production by Eric Miller. Recorded [March 1958] at Contemporary Studios, Los Angeles CA. Recording engineer: Roy DuNann. Digital editing and transfers: Angel Balestier and Steve Livingston (May–June 1999, ALB Studios ; Burbank, CA) Mastering, 1999: Kirk Felton (Fantasy Studios, Berkeley, CA). Program notes: Robert Gordon.

Performers on tracks 1 through 7, 9, and 11 (recorded 18 January 1956)

Hampton Hawes, piano

Paul Chambers, bass

Larance [sic, in recté: Lawrence] Marable, drums

Performers on tracks 8, 10, and 12 (recorded March 1958)

Hampton Hawes, piano

Scott LaFaro, bass [sic, in recté Red Mitchell]

Frank Butler, drums

Program:

1. Big Foot (C. Parker) 5:33
2. Ray's Idea (R. Brown-Fuller) 4:39
3. Stella by Starlight (Washington-Young) 4:35
4. Blues for Jacque (H. Hawes) 4:50
5. I Should Care (Cahn-Stordahl-Weston) 4:40
6. Bird Song (Thad Jones) 4:02
7. Yesterdays (Kern-Harbach) 5:27
8. What's New? (B. Haggart) 5:28
9. Just One of Those Things (Cole Porter) 3:12
10. I'll Remember April (Raye-DePaul-Johnston) 5:23
11. Cheryl (C. Parker) 3:42
12. Blue 'N' Boogie (Gillespie-Paparelli) 3:21

LaFaro is named on three program selections for which Red Mitchell is bassist: Track 8 "What's New?" has a solid 4-4 pulse but LaFaro might have played this more legato and even a bit behind the beat. The bass solo here is symmetrical and measured. LaFaro at the time was bubbling over (Bill Evans's critical observation), and not as balanced in his approach to soloing. Track 10, "I'll Remember April," has an arco bass solo that recalls bassist Paul Chambers' play on the Miles Davis recordings, *Workin', Relaxin', Steamin', and Cookin'*. Track 12 "Blue 'N Boogie" exhibits good, balanced foundation playing, but does not have LaFaro's tone. My own reservations coupled with those of Mike Davis and Roger Hunter, compilers of a Hampton Hawes discography (Manchester, UK: 1986) require withdrawal of this entry from this discography.

Stan Kenton and His Orchestra
[Biloxi, MS: 1958] Artistry Record 101.

Note: Steven D. Harris, author of *The Kenton Kronicles: A Biography of Modern America's Man of Music, Stan Kenton* (Pasadena, CA: Dynaflow Publications, 1999) has provided that this recording was made 11 November 1958 at Keesler Air Force Base near Biloxi, Mississippi. The bassist is Thomas "Red" Kelly (based upon Harris's interview with Kelly). LaFaro joined the Kenton band 6 March 1959 and left on or before 25 March 1959, a tenure of about three weeks, and was succeeded by bassist Carson Smith. This recording has been re-issued as *Stan Kenton: Keesler Air Force Base*.

At Ukiah
[England: Status Records; 1990] STCD-109. Total time 74:44. Recorded at Ukiah, CA, County Fair Building, 26 February 1959. 1 sound disc: digital; 4 and 3/4 in. Alternate titles: *Stan Kenton at Ukiah 1959* and *Kenton at Ukiah*.

Note: Steven D. Harris, author of *Kenton Kronicles*, is positive that the bassist on this recording is Red Kelly and not LaFaro.

ENDNOTES

Following is a list of author's personal and phone interviews and letters received. Unless otherwise noted, direct quotations are from the below interviews or correspondence.

Alkyer, Frank	New York, NY	letter	10/18/06
Anzalone, Valentine	Fairport, NY	letter	10/10/08
Bahn, Dr. Cordell	University Place, WA	letter	05/18/04
Barbe, John	Roswell, GA	phone	06/30/07
Bennett, Robert	Geneva, NY	letter	05/09/00
			07/30/00
		letter	07/12/04
			08/18/05
Berk, Dick	Henderson, NV	phone	03/28/06
Berzinsky, Dave	Los Angeles, CA	letter	05/26/03
			03/24/06
			04/27/06
			06/16/06
Bley, Paul	Florida	phone	03/18/07
Bromberg, Brian	Los Angeles, CA	phone	07/25/07
Bruce, Jack	Pasadena, CA	phone	04/22/06
Budimer, Dennis	Los Angeles, CA	phone	01/05/07
Campbell, Jeff	Rochester, NY	letter	04/11/07
Chinello, Bob	California	letter	11/23/06
		letter	09/14/07
Clarke, Stanley	Los Angeles, CA	phone	12/14/06
Claxton, William	Los Angeles, CA		11/12/07
Clayton, John	Los Angeles, CA	letter	10/31/08
Clyne, Jeff	UK	letter	07/27/08
		letter	08/23/08
Coleman, Ornette	New York, NY	phone	02/28/07
Crouch, Madeleine	Dallas, TX		01/15/06
		letter	06/19/07
		phone	10/10/07
Cunliffe, Bill	Culver City, CA		09/10/07
Davids, Al	Waterloo, NY	letter	07/27/04
			08/10/05
Davis, Richard	Madison, WI	letter	08/08/07
Dawson, Decosta	New Jersey	phone	07/20/06

D'Angelo, Nick	Ontario, NY	phone	09/12/05
		phone	01/19/06
		letter	06/26/07
deBenedictis, Dick	Thousand Oaks, CA	phone	09/06/06
DeFranco, Buddy	Panama City, FL	phone	10/12/05
Denver, Maggie Ryan	Saugerties, NY	letter	08/03/00
			06/15/01
		letter	05/25/04
		phone	01/11/07
East, Nathan	Tarzana, CA	letter	09/11/07
Falco, Gil	Sherman Oaks, CA	phone	07/06/07
Feldman, Josh	Henderson, NV	phone	07/07/06
Fischer, Clare	Studio City, CA	phone	02/11/06
Flores, Chuck	Los Angeles, CA	phone	03/10/06
Ford, Dick	Syracuse, NY	phone	09/19/06
		letter	10/03/06
			01/20/07
Fospero, Cosmo	Geneva, NY		07/14/05
Friedman, Don	New York, NY	phone	02/07/06
Gabriel, Gloria	Palm Springs, CA	phone	07/13/06
			06/08/07
		phone	11/28/07
		phone	02/05/09
Gaylor, Hal	Middleton, NY	phone	11/27/06
Geller, Herb	Germany		09/26/05
			10/02/05
		letter	12/11/06
Giacobbe, Maxine Baroody	Sarasota, FL	letter	09/26/04
Gianelli, John	Northridge, CA	phone	07/27/07
Gibbs, Terry	Los Angeles, CA	phone	03/04/06
Golding, Ann Pacuilli	Pacific Palisades, CA	letter	07/09/06
		phone	05/18/07
Gomez, Eddie	Yorktown, NY		06/15/01
		phone	08/17/07
Grauer, Joanne	Reno, NV	letter	05/14/07
Green, Dave	UK	phone	05/14/07
		letter	06/06/07
		letter	01/30/08
Gruber, Freddie	Los Angeles	phone	03/24/06
			05/25/07
Haden, Charlie	Westlake Village, CA	phone	07/21/06
		phone	01/20/08
		phone	03/01/08
Harris, Steve	Los Angeles, CA	letter	06/03/07
Hartsfield, Sandra Upson	Geneva, NY		08/10/05
Haynes, Roy	Los Angeles, CA		05/25/07
Henke, Karmy	Rochester, NY		08/20/05
Hoffman, Gordon	Englewood, CO	letter	06/20/95
		letter	07/16/95

Israels, Chuck	Bellingham, WA		06/15/01
		letter	08/04/04
		letter	03/23/06
		letter	11/03/07
Jeffrey, Paul	North Carolina	phone	03/29/06
Johnson, Dick	Brockton, MS	phone	06/13/07
Johnson, Marc	New York, NY		06/15/01
		letter	02/25/03
		letter	07/20/07
		letter	09/06/07
		letter	03/23/09
Johnston, Nancy	Winthrop, NY	letter	05/20/04
		letter	10/07/04
Karr, Gary	British Col, CAN	letter	08/18/07
Keepnews, Orrin	San Francisco, CA	phone	06/01/06
		letter	12/27/06
		letter	12/31/06
Kelly, Beverly	Long Beach, CA	letter	10/29/05
		letter	11/23/05
		letter	04/22/06
Kirk, Gail Brown	Waterloo, NY	letter	02/01/05
			08/14/05
		phone	03/22/06
		phone	10/14/07
Kirk, Tom	Waterloo, NY		08/14/05
		letter	05/16/06
Klein, Philip	Syracuse, NY	phone	09/25/06
		letter	09/27/06
Kloess, Joe	Colbert, WA	phone	06/14/06
		letter	07/04/06
Knight, Suzanne Stewart	Trumansburg, NY		08/15/05
		letter	03/09/06
		letter	07/20/06
		letter	10/06/06
Kolstein, Barrie	Baldwin, NY	letter	10/27/05
Kuhn, Steve	Tarrytown, NY	phone	02/12/06
			09/20/08
LaBarbera, Joe	Woodland Hills, CA		05/25/93
		phone	01/17/06
LaFaro, Linda	Lakeport, CA	phone	07/07/05
LaFaro, The	Belfast, Ireland	letter	11/10/08
(Jonny Black, Alan Lynn,		letter	01/03/09
Herb Magee, Dave Magee)			
Lees, Gene	Ojai, CA		09/26/05
Levey, Angela	Los Angeles, CA	phone	03/06/06
Levey, Chris	Rasdon, MD	letter	03/06/06
Levey, Robert	Texas	letter	03/06/06
Lloyd, Charles	Santa Barbara, CA	phone	05/18/07
		phone	08/09/07

Magnusson, Bob	San Diego, CA	letter	03/17/07
Malheiros, Alex	Niteroi, Brazil	letter	10/10/07
Mangione, Gap	Rochester, NY	letter	03/09/05
			08/17/05
Marable, Larance	Los Angeles, CA		04/27/06
Markewich, Maurice	Pleasantville, NY	phone	03/25/06
		letter	03/28/06
Martin, Joan	Geneva, NY		08/20/05
		phone	10/16/06
Massa, Nick	Rochester, NY		08/22/05
McBride, Christian	Los Angeles, CA		05/25/07
McCoy, Pat Moran	Central Point, OR	letter	02/09/98
		letter	03/05/98
			05/26/01
		letter	05/21/03
		letter	04/11/06
McKenzie, Jerry	Palm Springs, CA	phone	01/19/08
Mele, Anthony "Tony"	Lowell, MS	phone	09/18/06
Mickman, Herb	Van Nuys, CA	phone	05/05/08
Morrow, Buddy	Maitland, FL	phone	11/28/06
Motian, Paul	New York, NY	letter	08/15/05
		letter	09/24/05
		phone	03/25/06
		letter	07/22/07
		phone	03/15/09
Most, Sam	Los Angeles, CA		10/14/07
Muranyi, Joseph	New York, NY	letter	05/25/07
Newmark, Harvey	Los Angeles, CA		10/22/07
Norris, Walter	Berlin, Germany	letter	02/16/07
O'Brian, Hod	New York, NY	phone	07/23/07
Oleszkiewicz, Darek	Valencia, CA		11/16/08
Palombi, Phil	Bronx, NY	letter	01/29/06
Patitucci, John	Hastings on the	phone	04/18/07
	Hudson, NY	letter	05/26/07
Payne, Don	Plantation, FL	letter	05/06/06
		phone	12/10/06
Peacock, Gary	Claryville, NY	phone	07/07/06
		phone	01/19/07
			03/05/08
Peters, Elwood "Woody"	Syracuse, NY	phone	09/19/06
Poston, Ken	Long Beach, CA		06/16/06
Price, Ruth	Culver City, CA		09/10/07
Proto, Frank	Cincinnati, OH	letter	01/08/08
Reid, Rufus	Teaneck, NY	letter	10/10/07
Robinson, Paula	New York, NY	letter	12/15/07
Roeder, Jorge	Brooklyn, NY	letter	05/02/08
Rubin, Eddie	Los Angeles	phone	08/06/07
Rumsey, Howard	Los Angeles, CA		10/01/05
Schuller, Gunther	New York, NY	phone	11/01/06

Shank, Bud	Los Angeles, CA		10/10/05
	Tucson, AZ	letter	03/07/06
Smith, Putter	S. Pasadena, CA	letter	01/15/08
Snazelle, Craig	Portland, OR	letter	01/23/07
		letter	06/27/07
Speck, Dieter	Germany	letter	04/21/07
Starr, Nancy		letter	01/16/05
Stewart-Benedict, Edee	Trumansburg, NY		08/15/05
Strazzeri, Frank	Los Angeles, CA	phone	11/19/07
Suchanek, Bronek	Fulton, MA	phone	02/04/08
		letter	02/11/08
Sullivan, Ira	Florida	phone	09/08/07
Swift, Dave	UK	letter	02/17/07
	Los Angeles, CA		04/14/07
Thompson, Don	Toronto, Canada	letter	10/16/06
Trotter, Terry	Los Angeles, CA	phone	02/11/06
Umiker, Robert	Fayetteville, AK	letter	09/20/04
		letter	10/10/05
Urso, Joe	Monroe TWP, NJ	phone	05/08/07
		letter	05/18/07
		letter	07/07/07
Urso, Phil	Lakewood, CO	letter	10/18/06
		phone	04/28/07
		phone	08/08/07
Weislow, Judy	Geneva, NY	letter	03/24/00
			06/09/01
		phone	03/04/05
			08/12/05
Wofford, Mike	San Diego, CA	letter	03/26/06
Wong, David		letter	07/08/07
Wooley, Bob	Wilmington, NC	letter	10/20/05
		letter	11/15/07
Young, Eldee	Chicago, IL	phone	04/14/06
Zampino, Gerry	Syracuse, NY	phone	10/05/06

Chapter 1. La Famiglia

1. Czech violinist (March 22,1892–January 18, 1934). World renowned teacher and writer of many violin studies and methods.

Chapter 3. Early Influences

1. Godfrey D. Brown (June 6, 1911–March 3, 1987) Music Masters, Ithaca College, Ithaca, NY, Fred Waring School, Shawnee on the Delaware, PA.

2. Mary Baker Eddy (Born Mary Morse Baker, July 16, 1821–December 3, 1910). Founder of Christian Science movement.

Chapter 4. High School Days

1. Val Anzalone B.S MusEd, SUNY Fredonia, NY. Music Masters, Eastman School of Music, Rochester, NY. Published works include: *Breeze Easy Books I & II for Clarinet, Sax, Flute, Oboe & Bassoon, Six Early 20th Century Duets for Two Clarinets, Album of Classics Volumes I, II & III for Clarinet Quartet.*
2. See complete article in Appendix I.

Chapter 5. Beginning Bass to Buddy and Baker

1. Nicholas V. D'Angelo, Professor of Music at Hobart and William Smith Colleges. Recipient of numerous composition awards including a 1985 Pulitzer Prize nomination in music. His music is recorded and performed throughout the U.S., Canada, Mexico, and Europe.
2. Buddy Morrow Orchestra Itinerary. Scotty joined BMO fall of 1955 as they were completing the eastern portion of their tour. They spent September, October, and November touring the Midwest, Northwest, and Texas. InDecember they were back in the East and played on December 26 at the Frederick High School Gym for the Alumni Association.

The itinerary of the remainder of Scott's time with the BMO is as follows, giving major dates, though they were booked at other clubs and venues in the touring area as well:

1956

January 20	Ohio Northern University, Taft Gym, Inter-Fraternity Ball
February 5	Elms Ballroom, Youngstown, Ohio
March 13	Suzanne Stewart joins BMO as vocalist Kirkland Service Club, Kirkland Air Force Base, New Mexico
April	Tour continues through the Midwest
May 11	Aragon Ballroom, Chicago
May 17	Valencia Ballroom, Rochester, Minnesota

May 27	Crystal Beach Park, Vermillion, Ohio
June 3	Club Ballroom, Chicago, Illinois
June 4	Midway Ballroom, Cedar Lake, Indiana
June 11–24	The Peabody, Memphis, Tennessee
July 8	Idora Park, Youngstown, Ohio
July 9	Midway Ballroom, Cedar Lake, Indiana
July 20–26	Steel Pier, Atlantic City, New Jersey
July 27	Dance Pavilion, Braddock Heights, Maryland
July 28	Hershey Park Ballroom, Gettysburg, Pennsylvania
	BMO on KNX Radio 9:30 p.m. Los Angeles, California
August 10–16	Coney Island Park, Cincinnati, Ohio
August 22	Wellington Fairground, Lorain County Fair, Ohio, 2 Shows
August 28	Surf, Clear Lake, Iowa
September 5–23	Palladium, Hollywood, California Scott left BMO at the end of this engagement.

Chapter 8. Kenton, Goodman, and Monk (1959)

1. Stan Kenton Orchestra Itinerary, March 1959

6	Civic Auditorium, Santa Monica, CA
7	Claremont College, Claremont, CA
8	NCO Club, March Field Air Force Base, Riverside, CA
9	Riverside Ballroom, Phoenix, AZ
10	San Juan Country Club, Farmington, NM
12	Auditorium, Wichita Falls, TX
13	Cimarron Ballroom, Tulsa, OK
14	Blue Note Ballroom, Wichita KS
15	Meadow Acres Ballroom, Topeka, KS
16 ?	Millburn Country Club, Pittsburgh, PA
17	Electric Park, Waterloo, IA
18	Frog Hop Ballroom, St. Joseph, MO
19	Iowa State University, Iowa City, IA
20	Hub Ballroom, Bradley University, Edelstein, IL
21	Val Air Ballroom, Des Moines, IA
22	Million Dollar Ballroom, Milwaukee, WI

23   Jackson Co. Blvd Auditorium, Jackson, MI
2. Sidney Bechet May 14, 1897–May 14, 1959. African-American jazz clarinetist, soprano saxophonist.

Chapter 9. New York: Getz, Coleman, and Evans (1960)

1. See complete article in Appendix II.
2. Aaron Bell, Jimmy Blanton, Wellman Braud, Milt Hinton, Charlie Mingus, Oscar Pettiford, and Jimmy Woode all played with Ellington.

Chapter 10. Realization (1961)

1. Coleman did not tour Europe at this time.
2. Coleman was awarded the 2007 Pulitzer Prize in Music.
3. Paul Motian note regarding the 6/25/61 recording session for *Sunday at the Vanguard:* They were paid $136 for recording, $110 for the gig, and another $107 for the second session.

Chapter 16. His Legacy

1. See complete article in Appendix III

BIBLIOGRAPHY

A Select Annotated List of Books and Articles about Scott LaFaro

by Chuck Ralston

Amram, David. *Vibrations: The Adventures and Musical Times of David Amram*. New York: Macmillan, 1968. Reprint, New York: Viking Compass paperback edition, 1971. Describes a conversation (p. 375) between Amram and LaFaro about the latter's delight with Ornette Coleman's music.

Anon. "A Light Gone Out." *Down Beat* (August 17, 1961): 13. Obituary with remembrances by Marian McPartland and Ray Brown.

Anon. "La route qui tue." *Jazz Magazine* 7 (septembre 1961): 16. Obituary with a closing remark that like Clifford Brown before him, LaFaro suffered from that most terrible malady of the century: the killer highway accident.

Anon. "Scott LaFaro (1936–1961)" *Metronome* 78:9 (September 1961): 1. Obituary "in memoriam" with a photograph of LaFaro.

Anon. "2 Die in Fiery Crash at Flint: Geneva High Grads Killed; Car Hits Tree." *Geneva* [NY] *Times* (July 6, 1961): 1. Includes photographs of the automobile and of Frank P. Ottley and LaFaro.

Agonito, Chuck. "GHS Tribute to Scott LaFaro […]" in *Jump Start Your Weekend*, a publication of the *Finger Lakes Times* (Thursday, May 12, 2005): 16. The author, a Geneva High School alumnus, reports on the school's tribute to fellow alumnus, Scott LaFaro,

Class of 1954. Bassist Phil Flanagan, alumnus from the Class of 1975, and a musician inspired by his hometown hero, demonstrated LaFaro's bass technique by performing "Gloria's Step," a LaFaro composition.

Balliett, Whitney. *Goodbyes and Other Messages: A Journal of Jazz, 1981–1990*. New York: Oxford University Press, 1991. Includes a review of *Bill Evans: The Complete Riverside Recordings*, in which the author (p. 140) perceives LaFaro as having become the principal "voice" in the Bill Evans Trio.

Balliett, Whitney. *Collected Works: A Journal of Jazz, 1954–2001*. New York: St. Martin's Press, 2002. An account (p. 182) of the inner workings of the Bill Evans Trio (with Motian and LaFaro in 1959) which describes LaFaro's influence on Evans.

Bany, John. "The Legendary Scott LaFaro." *Bass World: The Journal of the International Society of Bassists* 14:3 (Spring 1988): 38–54. Includes photographs of LaFaro and transcriptions of LaFaro's composition "Gloria's Step," of his solo on "Nardis" from the Bill Evans Trio recording *Explorations,* and of "S'posin'," followed by a discography.

Berendt, Joachim Ernst. *The Jazz Book: From New Orleans to Rock and Free Jazz*. New York: Lawrence Hill, 1975. Translated by Dan Morgenstern and Helmut and Barbara Bredigkeit from the German fourth edition, 1973. Discusses the history of the development of the double bass in jazz and considers LaFaro along with Charlie Haden (p. 282) as principal contributors to the "second emancipation" of the bass from the confines of rhythm-only play, after Jimmy Blanton and Oscar Pettiford, bass's initial emancipators.

Berliner, Paul. *Thinking in Jazz: The Infinite Art of Improvisation*. Chicago: University of Chicago Press, 1994. Chicago Studies in Ethnomusicology, edited by Philip V. Bohlman and Bruno Nettle. LaFaro is mentioned four times in this marvelous, intriguing tome (800 pages!) about how jazz musicians think about their craft and how they learn from one another. Discusses (p. 131) the mutual discovery and fascination by LaFaro and bassist George Duvivier of their respective two-finger and one-finger approach to playing bass.

Binchet, Jean-Pierre. "Le Phare LaFaro." *Jazz Magazine* 153 (avril 1968): 20–23. Includes two photographs of LaFaro, one by himself; another with Don Cherry and Ed Blackwell. A thorough article discussing LaFaro's musical origins and development.

Carr, Ian, Digby Fairweather, and Brian Priestley. *Jazz, the Rough Guide: The Essential Companion to Artists and Albums.* 2nd ed. London: Rough Guides, Ltd., 2000. In addition to providing a concise summary of his contribution to jazz (p. 441), co-author Brian Priestley observes that LaFaro's rhythmic approaches, ranging between "straight-ahead" time playing and almost out-of-tempo, had considerable impact on the Miles Davis Quintet of 1963 (Davis along with George Coleman, tenor saxophone; Tony Williams, drums; Herbie Hancock, piano; and Ron Carter, bass).

Case, Brian, and Stan Britt. *The Illustrated Encyclopedia of Jazz.* New York: A Salamander book published by Harmony Books, a division of Crown Publishers, 1978. This coffee-table book gives surprising insight (pp. 26, 50–51, 72, 84, 90, and 127) into LaFaro's variety of musical contributions to the groups of Ornette Coleman, Hampton Hawes, Booker Little, and Bill Evans.

Crow, Bill. *From Birdland to Broadway: Scenes from a Jazz Life.* New York: Oxford University Press, 1992. Reprint, New York: Oxford paperback, 1993. A bass player's view (p. 154) of the interplay between Bill Evans and LaFaro performing at the Village Vanguard.

Dutilh, Alex. "Les basses de Bill [Evans]: Lex jeux amoureux de quatre bassistes et d'un pianiste." *Jazz Hot* 316 (mai 1975): 18–21. The author analyzes the contributions of four of the bassists who have contributed to the Bill Evans Trio: Scott LaFaro, Chuck Israels, Gary Peacock, and Eddie Gomez, giving each a unique quality, respectively: "La beauté," "La douceur," "La liberté," and "La rêve." In English respectively, beauty, softness, freedom, and (roughly) dream-like, perhaps more at "imagination."

Eichenhofer, Jim. "Geneva Musician Remembered in Article." *Finger Lakes Times* [Geneva, NY] (March 17, 1997): 3. This is a newspaper account of an article by Robert Wooley, "Remembering Scott LaFaro," in *Bass World: The Journal of the International Society of Bassists* 21:2 (Fall 1996): 21–23. Eichenhofer adds a recollection by Joan Martin, high-school friend and classmate of LaFaro's, about members of the Geneva High band, including LaFaro, sitting in with the Tommy Dorsey Orchestra in 1953 at a performance at De Sales High School in Geneva. (De Sales High was directly across the street from Geneva High.)

Feather, Leonard. *The Book of Jazz: From Then Till Now; A Guide to the Entire Field*. Rev. ed. New York: Horizon, 1965. Reprint, New York: Dell, 1976. Offers a snapshot (pp. 140–41) of the development of jazz double bass around 1960 and those players who chose to ignore the (then) current "laws" of timekeeping and tonality, with LaFaro as the unofficial founder of the "new" school of jazz bassists.

Gelly, Dave. *Stan Getz: Nobody Else But Me*. San Francisco: Backbeat Books, 2002. The author gives a positive, upbeat description (p. 112) of the energy and imagination LaFaro contributed to the Stan Getz Quartet vintage 1961, especially LaFaro's play on the studio version of Sonny Rollins's composition "Airegin," recorded in February 1961.

Giddins, Gary. *Visions of Jazz: The First Century*. New York: Oxford University Press, 1998. Discusses (pp. 470–71) Ornette Coleman's Atlantic recordings, in particular the four pieces that comprise the recording, *Ornette!*, and LaFaro's technical fluency that includes resonating "plucked" strings on "R.P.D.D," and his "vocal" timbre quality on "W.R.U."

Gilonis, Harry. "Remembering Scott LaFaro." *Oyster Boy Review* 11 (April 1999): unpaged. A diamond-cut poem capturing image and essence retrievable online at http://www.oysterboyreview.com/issue/11/GilonisH-Remembering.html.

Gioia, Ted. *The History of Jazz*. New York: Oxford University Press, 1997. Calls attention (pp. 300, 332) to the influence of the Bill Evans Trio (with LaFaro) and its innovative "internalized beat" (Evans's phrase) on subsequent jazz piano trios, in particular the interplay of Herbie Hancock, Ron Carter, and Tony Williams in the Miles Davis quintet of the mid-1960s.

Gioia, Ted. *West Coast Jazz: Modern Jazz in California, 1945–1960*. New York: Oxford University Press, 1992. Reprint, Berkeley: University of California Press, 1998. Draws an interesting comparison (p. 91) between the way pianists Dave Brubeck and Bill Evans utilized their respective bassists, with Brubeck insisting that his bassist stay close to a song's harmonic root, this in spite of the harmonic similarities between the pianists, and discusses LaFaro among other prominent musicians: Cal Tjader, Billy Higgins, Vince Guaraldi, Eddie Duran, Mongo Santamaria, Willie Bobo, Don Cherry, Charles Lloyd, Dick Whittington, to name a few, who performed at Howard Rumsey's Lighthouse Cafe at Hermosa Beach, California.

Gitler, Ira. [Bill Evans Trio 1961 Village Vanguard recording] *Swing Journal* 56:8 (July 2002): 203–10. Journal is published in Tokyo in Japanese. Cover of issue #7 (July 2002) is a photograph of Herbie Hancock. "Interview and Text by Ira Gitler" (p. 204). Photographs of Evans, LaFaro, Motian, and Orrin Keepnews by Steve Schapiro (pp. 205, 207, 209). Photograph of Helene LaFaro-Fernandez, LaFaro's sister, who wrote a remembrance paragraph about her brother for this issue. Gitler's article supports the remastered re-release of *Bill Evans: The Complete Live at the Village Vanguard 1961*. Tokyo: Victor Entertainment, Inc., 2002. Catalog code: VICJ-60951~3, which is a boxed set of 3 compact discs that place the five sessions recorded Sunday, June 25, 1961, in chronological order as follows: Disc 1 (afternoon set one, 6 tracks; afternoon set two, 3 tracks); Disc 2 (evening set one, 4 tracks; evening set two, 6 tracks); and Disc 3 (evening set three, 7 tracks).

Gleason, Ralph J. "Monterey: The Afternoons." *Down Beat* 27:23 (November 10, 1960): 18, 47. A review of two afternoon musical programs at the 1960 Monterey Jazz Festival, one by the Israel Baker String Quartet which played Gunther Schuller compositions and other by the Ornette Coleman Quartet, with LaFaro performing in both. Performers in the Baker ensemble included: Israel Baker, first violin; Ralph Schaefer, second cello; Alvin Dinken, viola; Armand Copra, cello; Red Mitchell and Scott LaFaro, basses; Jim Hall, guitar; Larry Bunker, drums, and Ornette Coleman as special soloist.

Goldsby, John. "Scott LaFaro." *Bass Player* (July/August 1992): 72–73. Includes a transcription by Bob Bauer of the composition "Detour Ahead" (Carter, Ellis, and Frigo). This article summarizes LaFaro's career and discusses his approach to improvisation with analysis of his solo during performance of "Detour Ahead" from the Bill Evans Trio recording *Waltz for Debby*.

Gopnik, Adam. "That Sunday: Jazz's Perfect Afternoon, Forty Years Later." *The New Yorker* (August 13, 2001): 30–33. This essay about New York at the beginning of the summer of 1961, particularly the quality of one special Sunday in New York in June at the Village Vanguard jazz club when the Bill Evans Trio (with Paul Motian, drums and Scott LaFaro, bass) was recorded live, the results of which may be heard on the recordings *Sunday at the Village Vanguard* and *Waltz For Debby*. Framed in a Proustian evocation of New York's disdain for remembrance of things past, Gopnik's essay attempts just that: an evocation of the meditative quality listeners still find in these recordings. Gopnik discusses these Vanguard sessions with Orrin Keepnews, their original producer; with Lorraine Gordon, owner of the Village Vanguard, and with the drummer that Sunday afternoon, Paul Motian.

Gourse, Leslie. *Straight, No Chaser: The Life and Genius of Thelonious Monk*. New York: Schirmer Books, 1997. Provides a glimpse (p. 178) of a 1960 Monk ensemble playing at Boston's Storyville jazz club that included "Pete Mondrian" (alias for drummer Paul Motian) and LaFaro.

Gridley, Mark C. *Concise Guide to Jazz*. Englewood Cliffs, NJ: Prentice-Hall, 1992. In his discussion of the styles and influence of Bill Evans (pp. 148–52), the author provides a "listening guide" to "Solar," which includes remarks about LaFaro's playing of this tune as captured on the *Sunday at the Village Vanguard* recording.

Harris, Steven D. *The Kenton Kronicles: A Biography of Modern America's Man of Music: Stan Kenton*. Pasadena, CA: Steven D. Harris [2000] Provides detailed information about LaFaro's brief, three-week tenure with the Stan Kenton Orchestra during March 1959. Also, provides details about two Kenton recordings that do *not* include LaFaro: *Stan Kenton and his Orchestra* (Artistry Record 101, 1958) and *At Ukiah* (Status Records, 1990). The one Kenton recording with LaFaro is *The Stan Kenton Orchestra in Concert* (Hindsight Records, 1997) which captures the March 6, 1959, performance at the Santa Monica Civic

Auditorium, which was the first time LaFaro performed with the Stan Kenton Orchestra.

Heckman, Don. "Jimmy Garrison: After Coltrane." *Down Beat* 34:05 (March 9, 1967): 18–19, 40. This is a most interesting essay on bassist Jimmy Garrison (1934–1976) who was the rhythmic underpinning of the John Coltrane Quartet at its epitome. I attended the Coltrane concert at the Olympia Theatre in Paris in March 1960 and got autographs of all the musicians except Elvin Jones on the container of my copy of *My Favorite Things* and a few years later listened to them again at the Half Note Café in New York. Garrison also performed with Ornette Coleman, Bill Evans, and Stan Getz, "crossing paths," as Garrison puts it, with Scott LaFaro many times according to Heckman.

Hunt, David C. "The Musician's Musician: Cases of Seven Underrated Jazzmen." *Jazz and Pop* 6 (July 1967): 19, 22–24. The author argues for a rejection of environmental, emotional and financial issues as a necessary prerequisite for artistic creativity by jazz artists, using as illustrations the successes of musicians Roy Haynes, Scott LaFaro, George Duvivier, Ed Shaughnessy, Harold Land, Eli "Lucky" Thompson, and Eddie Costa.

Keepnews, Orrin. *The View from Within: Jazz Writings, 1948–1987.* New York: Oxford University Press, 1988. Reprint, New York: Oxford University Press paperback, 1990. The author describes the inner workings of recording sessions involving several Riverside artists, Thelonious Monk, Julian "Cannonball" Adderley, and Bill Evans, among others. Provides details about each of the Bill Evans Trio recordings with Motian and LaFaro: *Portrait in Jazz*, *Explorations*, and the five sessions recorded "live" June 25, 1961, at the Village Vanguard that resulted in the two albums: *Sunday at the Village Vanguard* and *Waltz for Debby*.

Kleinzahler, August. "What It Takes." in his *Earthquake Weather*. Mount Kisco, NY: Moyer Bell Ltd, 1989, p. 34. This poem alludes to the performance of "My Foolish Heart" by the Bill Evans Trio from *Waltz for Debby*. It was translated into French by Alain Pailler with the title "Ce Qu'il en Coute" appearing in *Le Courrier de Centre Internationale d'Etudes poétiques* (No. 202–203, avril–juin 1994), p. 74.

Kopel, Guy. "Scott LaFaro." *Les Cahiers du Jazz* (1969): 40–45. This essay, like that by J.-P. Binchet (see above), covers the entire career of LaFaro, and exhibits critical insight into his musical and technical accomplishments.

Kolstein, Barrie. "The 'LaFaro-Prescott' Restoration." *Bass World: The Journal of the International Society of Bassists* 14:3 (Spring 1988): 56–63. Reprinted in this volume as Appendix III. This essay, with photographs, discusses the second restoration by the author of Scott LaFaro's instrument, which underwent severe fire and structural damage as result of LaFaro's fatal automobile accident on July 6, 1961. The instrument was made by Abraham Prescott of Concord, NH, around 1801. LaFaro obtained the instrument from fellow bassist, Red Mitchell. Bassist George Duvivier introduced LaFaro around 1960 to the author's father, Samuel Kolstein, who first restored the LaFaro-Prescott instrument.

LaFaro-Fernandez, Helene. "Scott LaFaro: A Chronological Discography." *Bass World: The Journal of the International Society of Bassists* 21:2 (Fall 1996): 23–24. A listing of recordings and transcriptions by LaFaro's oldest sister who accompanied him on many of his performances in Los Angeles and New York.

Lange, Art, and Nathaniel Mackey, eds. *Moment's Notice: Jazz in Poetry and Prose.* Minneapolis: Coffee House Press, 1993. Includes the poem "To the Pianist Bill Evans" by Bill Zavatsky (p. 285–287), with allusions to LaFaro and to the automobile accident which ended his life but not his music. Poem was published first in Bill Zavatsky, *Theories of Rain and Other Poems.* New York: Sun, 1975.

Lees, Gene. "Inside the New Bill Evans Trio." *Down Beat* (November 22, 1962): 24–26. Discusses the Evans trio with Chuck Israels as bassist and with reference to the (then) late Scott LaFaro.

Lees, Gene. *Cats of Any Color: Jazz Black and White.* New York: Oxford University Press, 1994. Reprint, Cambridge, MA: Da Capo Press, 2000. LaFaro is mentioned in several contexts: when Lees first met LaFaro; a discussion with bassist Red Mitchell who considered both Gary Peacock and LaFaro as protégés and who demonstrated a two-finger string-pulling technique to them; comments by drummer Jack DeJohnette on "colored" or "broken" versus "stated" time of Paul Motian and LaFaro and its effect on rhythm section in Chicago then; and a comment by Miles Davis about the departure of Bill Evans from his 1958 quintet.

Lees, Gene. *Meet Me at Jim and Andy's: Jazz Musicians and their World.* New York: Oxford University Press, 1988. Reprint, New York: Oxford University Press paperback edition, 1990. Provides a poignant remembrance of Bill Evans and the pianist's own feelings about LaFaro after his tragic death and the sense of guilt Evans felt. Lees captures a fundamental truth about Evans and LaFaro: the relationship was musical and spiritual and loving. It is there in the music.

Levitt, Al. "Du Temps de La Faro." *Jazz Magazine* 283 (fevrier 1980): unpaged. An informative memoir by American expatriate jazz drummer Al Levitt which includes comments regarding his meeting and playing with Scott LaFaro. In 1955, while working with pianist Paul Bley and bassist Jimmy Bond, Levitt recalled seeing LaFaro carrying his bass into the same hotel where Levitt was staying. It seems that LaFaro, for only one night, was playing with Dan Terry (and the Band with the Hi-Fi Sound). A year later in 1956, Levitt was in Paris (he stayed until 1958) and living in the midst of several other jazz musicians, Donald Byrd, Bobby Jaspar, Walter Davis Jr., Arthur Taylor, and Doug Watkins, all of whom performed frequently at the cellar club Le Chat Qui Pêche. Levitt and Watkins returned to New York in November 1958 on the last voyage of the luxurious ocean liner SS *Ile de France.* Levitt worked in and around New York, Boston, and Washington, DC, with many other musicians, including Toshiko Akiyoshi, Charles Mariano, J. R. Monterose, pianist Hod O'Brien, singer Shirley Horne. Levitt recalls the evening in New York in 1959 in front of Birdland when Herb Geller introduced him to LaFaro. Levitt asked LaFaro if they had not met before, and LaFaro reminded him of the time they met in the lobby of a hotel in Baltimore when he was with the Dan Terry band. Geller, who was on break, had to return to the bandstand, and LaFaro and Levitt went to the nearby Hickory House where the Pat Moran Trio was performing (with drummer Gene Gammage and bassist John Doling). LaFaro told

Jade Visions: The Life and Music of Scott LaFaro

Levitt it was possible that the two of them could sit in during the last set of the evening, and for Levitt this was the first time he had heard LaFaro play and the first time they played together. During the time in New York, Levitt recalls running into LaFaro often, in particular one evening at Birdland where they performed with Geller, Booker Little, and pianist Kenny Drew. Levitt recalls LaFaro listening to a recording of Béla Bartók's *Le Mandarin Merveilleux* and all of Bartók's string quartets, Charles Ives, and Zoltan Kodaly, especially his *Suite for Violoncello* recorded by Janos Starker. In jazz, Levitt remembered that LaFaro loved the music of Miles Davis, especially his collaboration with Gil Evans, and also the music of Stan Getz, Chet Baker, and Art Blakey's Jazz Messengers. Levitt thought that LaFaro was impressed with pianist Martial Solal, and also with Booker Little and George Coleman when both musicians were with Max Roach. LaFaro indicated his favorite bassists were Charles Mingus and Paul Chambers and he loved the work of drummer Elvin Jones with whom he hoped to play one day. LaFaro was particularly impressed with pianist Bill Evans, especially with the appearance of the recording, *Everybody Digs Bill Evans*. Levitt recalls LaFaro playing Evans' "Piece Peace" on the piano. LaFaro also praised the musicians he worked with in California, in particular pianist Don Friedman, drummer Nick Martinis, and fellow bassists Charlie Haden and Gary Peacock. LaFaro liked the David Allen recording *Sure Thing* with arrangements by Johnny Mandel, which included a marvelous version of "The Folks Who Lived on the Hill" and the compositions of Tommy Wolf and Fran Landesman, particularly "Spring Can Really Hang You Up the Most," which LaFaro sang one day in front of the Colony Music store on the corner of 52nd Street and Broadway according to Levitt.

Litweiler, John. *Ornette Coleman: A Harmolodic Life*. New York: W. Morrow, 1992. Reprint, New York: Da Capo Press, 1994. The author explores the interplay among Ornette Coleman and his "collaborators" as he says. He recognizes the forceful personalities of both Coleman and LaFaro and poses the question that many have asked, namely, what might have happened had these two inventive and original musicians worked more with each

other? Discusses the contrasting styles of LaFaro and Charlie
Haden on Coleman's *Free Jazz* and the multi-faceted play of
LaFaro on Coleman's *Ornette!*

McCarthy, Albert, et al. *Jazz on Record: A Critical Guide to the First 50
Years, 1917–1967.* New York: Oak Publications, 1968. Includes
remarks by British jazz critic Alun Morgan (p. 95) that LaFaro's
surging bass lines achieved unbelievable prominence and that
he was a strong individual voice in jazz and as revolutionary a
pioneer as was bassist Jimmy Blanton.

Maggin, Donald L. *Stan Getz: A Life in Jazz.* New York: W. Morrow, 1996. The author describes (p. 198) the February 21, 1961,
Stan Getz quartet recording session with Pete LaRoca, drums;
Steve Kuhn, piano; and LaFaro, and the rapport between Getz
and his bassist on "Airegin" which is comparable to that between Getz and guitarist Jimmy Raney a decade earlier. Maggin reports also (p. 199) that Getz gave LaFaro "time off" to
record with Bill Evans that Sunday, June 25, 1961, at the Village
Vanguard, and again after the Getz quartet performance at the
Newport Jazz Festival, Sunday, July 2, 1961. Interestingly, Getz
had planned to record later in July orchestral arrangements of
Eddie Sauter with his quartet that most certainly would have
included LaFaro, had he not died. The recording, *Focus,* was the
result and John Neves was the bassist.

Marmande, Francis. "Rocco et ses Freres." *Jazz Magazine* 232 (avril
1975): 26–29. Discussion of LaFaro's music in context with his
"brother" bassists: Charlie Haden, Charles Mingus, Monk Mont-
gomery, David Holland, Eberhard Weber, Stanley Clarke, Barre
Phillips, Harry Miller, and one Maarten Van Regteren Altenat.

Milkowski, Bill. *Jaco: The Extraordinary and Tragic Life of Jaco Pastorius,
"The World's Greatest Bass Player."* San Francisco: Miller Freeman
Books, 1995. This book is not indexed. At p. 76 is one (indirect)
reference to Scott LaFaro where Milkowski quotes from Mark
C. Gridley, *Jazz Styles: History and Analysis,* to wit: "He [Pastorius]
walks persuasively, as he proved on 'Crazy About Jazz' (contained
in [the recording *Weather Report*] Weather Report's eleventh album, which has the same title as their first [album]). He plays in
the non-repetitive, interactive way [identified by Scott LaFaro],
as evidenced on 'Dara Factor One' (also on [Weather Report's]

eleventh album) and 'Dream Clock' ([Weather Report's] *Night Passage*)." Although Jaco Pastorius, christened John Francis Pastorius III (December 1, 1951–September 21, 1987, aet. 35), had a meteoric rise to fame as musician and self-proclaimed "world's greatest bass player," no information is provided that Pastorius ever listened to LaFaro on record. These two musicians are linked, however, by way of their shared musical experience with pianist Paul Bley and trumpeter-saxophonist Ira Sullivan. Pastorius recorded with Bley in June 1974 on a recording entitled simply *Pastorius / Metheny / Ditmas / Bley* (Milkowski, p. 57). LaFaro played with Bley at the It Club in Los Angeles (1958) but the recording of this ensemble unfortunately was never released and the recording's tapes were lost in a warehouse fire. Pastorius recorded with Ira Sullivan on the latter's *Ira Sullivan* (Milkowski, p. 53) and LaFaro played but did not record with Sullivan in Chicago in late 1957.

Monti, Pierre-Andre. "Discographie de Scott LaFaro." *Jazz 360* [degrees] 21 (octobre 1979): 9–13. Provides detailed information about recording sessions LaFaro made with Buddy DeFranco, Pat Moran, Victor Feldman, Herb Geller, Stan Getz, Hampton Hawes, Booker Little, Pat Moran, Marty Paich, Gunther Schuller, as well as those with Bill Evans and Ornette Coleman.

Nelson, Don. "Bill Evans: Intellect, Emotion, and Communication." *Down Beat* 27:25 (December 8, 1960): 16–18. In this his inaugural article for *Down Beat*, Don Nelson portrays the pianist as a well-rounded, well-read, normal individual who happens to be a jazz pianist. Nelson lists the authors of books in Evans' book cases (Freud, Whitehead, Margaret Meade, Santayana, Mohammed) and describes his bourgeois Manhattan apartment as a "three-room piece of ordinary" with its single bed, a few chairs, a kitchen table, hi-fi set, television (for sports news), and a piano which takes up half the living room. Nelson captures Evans' thoughts about Zen being similar to jazz, the influence of Lennie Tristano, the art of William Blake, his time in the US Army, and his thoughts about fellow musicians Paul Motian and LaFaro.

Nelson, Don. "Don Friedman: A Pianist For All Seasons." *Down Beat* (October 22, 1964): 17–18. A discussion of the San Francisco-born jazz pianist who shared an apartment with Scott LaFaro in New York City and who made a (then unreleased) recording that included LaFaro on bass. Nelson reports that Friedman and LaFaro shared a common interest in the music of Arnold Schoenberg (1874–1951), Béla Bartok (1881–1945), Anton Webern (1883–1945), and Alban Berg (1885–1935).

Palombi, Phil. *Scott LaFaro: 15 Solo Transcriptions from the Bill Evans Trio Recordings* Sunday at the Village Vanguard *and* Waltz for Debby. Transcribed by Phil Palombi. [New York:] Palombi Music, 2003. A technical analysis by a bassist who has performed with the Village Vanguard Orchestra and recorded with many other jazz musicians, including Joe LaBarbera, drummer in Bill Evans' last trio. In the "Notation" section, the author discusses transcription methodology and other techniques known to bassists as "hammer-on, pull-off, and slide."

Pekar, Harvey. "The Development of Modern Bass." *Down Beat* (October 11, 1962): 19–21. The author compares and contrasts the performances of Charlie Haden and LaFaro with Ornette Coleman who considered his fellow musicians as partners in free group improvisation. Harvey also believes that LaFaro's approach to improvisation is similar to that of John Coltrane's in that both are concerned more with harmonic and rhythmic exploration than with over-all construction of a solo.

Pettinger, Peter. *Bill Evans: How My Heart Sings*. New Haven, CT: Yale University Press, 1998. The author, an accomplished concert pianist himself, who recorded the music of his countryman, Sir Edward Elgar (1857–1934), in addition to the works of other composers, examines Evans through his myriad recordings, in chronological sequence, examining themes, harmonies, even the quality (or lack thereof) of the pianos Evans played. Pettinger, who listened to Evans perform at Ronnie Scott's jazz club in London, but could not muster the courage to approach the jazz master to engage in conversation, died tragically just prior to the publication of this book. Pettinger provides insightful comments also about LaFaro's rapport with Evans, noting, for example, the work both contributed to Tony Scott's composition "Misery (to Lady Day)" on *Sung Heroes.*

Porter, Lewis. *John Coltrane: His Life and Music.* Ann Arbor: University of Michigan Press, 1998. The author discusses LaFaro in the context of Ornette Coleman's approach to musical structure and John Coltrane's interest in Coleman's "free" approach to jazz improvisation. Furthermore, according to the recollections of Los Angeles resident and jazz enthusiast David Berzinski, LaFaro and Roy Haynes sat in for Steve Davis and Elvin Jones, members of the John Coltrane quartet, in April 1961 at the Zebra Lounge in Los Angeles. Porter's "Chronology" places Coltrane there. LaFaro and Haynes (and Steve Kuhn) were playing with the new Stan Getz quartet at that time.

Roberts, Jim. "A Classic Revisited: *Bill Evans Trio/Sunday at the Village Vanguard*" in *Bass Player* (December 1995): 74. Reviews LaFaro's contribution to the double bass in jazz in the context of electric bassist, Jaco Pastorius, and also LaFaro's contemporaries of the 1950s, Charles Mingus, Paul Chambers, and Wilbur Ware. Emphasizes LaFaro's lyrical quality which may derive from his having played clarinet and tenor saxophone. Discusses LaFaro's promise as a composer and leader as exemplified in this recording and its sister album, *Waltz For Debby.*

Shadwick, Keith. *Bill Evans: Everything Happens to Me, a Musical Biography.* San Francisco: Backbeat Books, 2002. Includes a welter of commentary about LaFaro by fellow musicians, especially bassist Charlie Haden who shared an apartment with LaFaro in Los Angeles and performed with him on Ornette Coleman's *Free Jazz.* The author provides lucid commentary on each Evans recording and in many cases on each track thereof. The book includes color reproductions of the container covers of Evans' recordings.

Szwed, John. *So What: The Life of Miles Davis.* New York: Simon & Schuster, 2002. The author mentions LaFaro (p. 168) in the context of Miles Davis' hiring of Bill Evans. Professor Szwed, John M. Musser Professor of Anthropology, African-American Studies, Music, and American Studies at Yale University, provides an interesting comment on the possibility that Miles Davis might have recorded with the Bill Evans Trio at one time. The reference to Paul Motian's remark about Davis possibly recording with the Evans trio is from p. 137 of the program booklet accompanying *The Complete Bill Evans on Verve.*

Tudor, Dean and Nancy Tudor. *Jazz.* Littleton, CO: Libraries Unlimited, 1979. (American Popular Music on Elpee [series]) Includes several comments about LaFaro with Ornette Coleman, and discusses the selection "Check Up" from Coleman's *Twins* recording, as providing an excellent example of LaFaro's counterpoint play behind Coleman's solo.

Tynan, John. "The Monterey Festival." *Down Beat* 27:23 (November 10, 1960): 14–17. The author gives a description of the musical program of the third and final evening of this jazz festival. Most striking was the bizarre incident involving Ornette Coleman and trumpeter Don Cherry. Evidently just before the Ornette Coleman Quartet was to take the bandstand, Coleman struck Cherry while the latter was warming up his horn, injuring his lip. The "quartet" then became a trio with Coleman, drummer Ed Blackwell, and LaFaro. The trio performed Coleman's "Diminished Night," an ironic event by itself, and the ballad, "You'll Never Know," during which LaFaro played an extended bass solo that astounded all who heard it.

Walton, Ortiz. *Music: Black, White, and Blue; A Sociological Survey of the Use and Misuse of Afro-American Music.* New York: William Morrow, 1972. The author argues (p. 115) that LaFaro dismissed the roots and traditions of jazz for technical virtuosity and by so doing placed considerable pressure on African-American bassists to relinquish pulsation and rhythm for speed. An appendix displays in two columns, "Name of Black Source" and "Name of White [Imitators]," with James Blanton and Charles Mingus in the left column; LaFaro, Charlie Haden, and others in the right column. I mention this book as an example of the absurd and ridiculous.

Williams, Martin T. "Introducing Scott LaFaro." *Jazz Review* 3 (August 1960): 16–17. The one and only published interview of LaFaro. On page 17 is a full-page photograph of LaFaro by Gerry Schatzberg.

Williams, Martin T., ed. *Jazz Panorama: From the Pages of "The Jazz Review."* New York: Crowell Press, 1962. Reprint, New York:

Collier Books, 1964. The editor includes two articles, one his interview cited above, "Introducing Scott LaFaro," and the other "Two Reviews of 'Third Stream' Music," both of which are essential reading on LaFaro.

Williams, Martin T. *Jazz Changes*. New York: Oxford University Press, 1992. Provides interesting commentary about LaFaro's influence on other musicians, in particular bassists Steve Swallow and Gary Peacock and discusses pianist Steve Kuhn's experience with Stan Getz, again with mention of LaFaro.

Wilson, John S. "Music: A Third Stream Sound; Schuller Conducts at Circle in the Square." *The New York Times* (May 17, 1960): 44. A review of a recital of Gunther Schuller compositions, the season finale to the "Jazz Profiles" concerts, presented at the Circle in the Square, 357 Bleecker Street, New York City. LaFaro is not mentioned by name but the Bill Evans Trio, of which LaFaro was a member at the time, is noted.

Wooley, Robert. "Remembering Scott LaFaro." *Bass World: The Journal of the International Society of Bassists*, 21:2 (Fall 1996): 21–23. Reprinted in this volume as Appendix I. A fond remembrance by fellow musician and high school friend along with photographs of LaFaro.

Zavatsky, Bill. *Theories of Rain and Other Poems*. New York: Sun, 1975. Includes the poem "To the Pianist Bill Evans" (p. 285) with allusions to LaFaro and the automobile accident which ended his life, but not his music. The poem's opening stanzas are an epiphany:

> When I hear you
> play "My Foolish Heart"
> I am clouded
> remembering more than
> Scott LaFaro's charred bass
> as it rested
> against a Yonkers wall
> in its transit
> from accidental fire […]

INDEX

Page numbers for illustrations are in *italics*.

Chambers, Paul, xxii, xxiii, 68, 78, 112, 159, 172, 177, 180
Cherry, Don, 65, 66, 120, 123, 131, 133, 189, 221
Chinello, Bob, 121
Christian, Charlie, xxi
Circle in the Square, 117
Clarke, Stanley, 212–13
Claxton, William, 87
Clayton, John, 214
Cloister Inn, 75, 76, 99
Clyne, Jeff, 220
Cobb, Jimmy, xxii
Cole, Bobby, 125–26
Cole, Nat King, 14, 29, 34
Coleman, Ornette, xxvi, 66, 69, 100, *142*, 176, 189; Scott plays with, 85, 117, 118, 120–21, 124, 128–32, *160*, 172
Collier, Graham, 141
Coltrane, John, xi, 70, 90, 112, 115–16, 135, 171
Cooper, Bob, 81
Cosmo's Alley, 70, 73, 80
Crescendo, The, 70, 73
Crosby, Israel, xxii, 96
Crouch, Madeleine, xvii
Crow, Bill, xxii, xxiii, xxv, xxviii
Crupi-Henke, Karmy, 4

D

D'Angelo, Nick, 41, 48, 49, 223
Davids, Al, 30, 222
Davis, Richard, 118, 214
Davis, Miles, xxvii, 44, 70, 90, 101–2, 124, 127, 134, 141, *144*, 149, 188, 219
Dawson, Decosta, 42, 43
deBenedictis, Dick, 43, 44
Dedications, 101
DeFranco, Buddy, 67, 85, 91, 176, 191
DeJohnette, Jack, xxii, xxiii
Dennis, Kenny, xxvii, 102

Denver, Bob, 93
Denver, Maggie Ryan, 86–88, 93, *107*
DeSio, Ray, 48
Desmond, Paul, 36
DeVito, Frank, 85
Dietsche, Robert, 49
Diggers, 80
Dolphy, Eric, 117–19, 189
Down Beat, 42, 79, 81, 83, 85, 89, 105, 120–21, 127, 152, 154, 171
Drift In, 82
Duffy's Gaiety, 70
Duran, Eddie, 79
Duvivier, George, 76, 115, 118, 178, 231, 236

E

East, Nathan, 214
Ellington, Duke, xi, 34, 118, 140
Ertegun, Ahmet, 97
Evans, Bill, xi, xii, xxi, xxii, xxiii, xxvi, xxvii, 42, 46, 48, 68, 69, 87, 90, 101, 104, 111–13, 115, 117, 123–28, 133–34, 140, 149, 158, 160–61, 164–66, 169–72, 176, 179, 181, 191–95, 201, 204, 207–9, 213–21, 236, 245; and drug use, 16; falls ill, 120; meets Scott, xxviii, 95–96, 102; and Scott's death, 152–55. *See also individual albums.*
Explorations, xxiii, xxix, 173, 197, 221

F

Falco, Gil, 52
Feldman, Josh, 222
Feldman, Victor, 17, 42, 68, 70, 71, 77, 78, 81, 85, 94, *108–9*, 115, 170, 172, 176, 183–84, 187, 214, 220, 222. *See also individual albums.*
Ferguson, Maynard, 35, 70, 228
Fernández, Haiden, xx

Fernández, Helene LaFaro, 5, *23, 37, 109*; birth of, 5; childhood of, 7–16; closeness to brother, 6, 31; meets future husband, 88; piano lessons, 17–18
Fernández, Jesslyn, xx
Fernández, Kristen, xx
Fernández, Manny, 88, 94, *109*, 124, 135–36
Fischer, Clare, 64, 67
Five Spot, 128
Flanigan, Lon, 148
Flanigan, Tommy, 66
Flores, Chuck, 82
Ford, Dick, 43, 44
For Real!, 85, 177–78
Fospero, Cosmo, 148
Fournier, Vernel, 96
Free Jazz, 128–29, 160, 189
Friedman, Don, 64, 67, 98, 99, 137

G

Gabriel, Gloria, 100, 113, 116–17, 123, 126, 130, 133, *142–43*, 147, 151–52, 155, 169; and "Gloria's Step," 113; and Jerome Robbins, 133
Gammage, Gene, 71, 91, 108, *110*, 179
Garrison, Jimmy, xxvii, 102, 115
Gaylor, Hal, 69
Geller, Herb, 64, 65, 67, 70, 95–97, 115, 176
Geller, Lorraine, 64, 70
Geneva, New York, xvii, xix, xxiii, 3, 4, 6, 7, 9, 11, 12, 16, 19, 26, 27, 30, 34, 46, 48, 51, 60, 62, 86, 80, 94, 147–50, 152, 191, 225, 228–29
Getz, Stan, 32, 35, 43, 79, 80, 86, 94, 101, 134–35, 140–41, *143*, 152, 176, 190, 228
Giacobbe, Maxine Baroody, 14, 15
Gianelli, John, 212, 214
Gibbs, Terry, 60, 89, 99

Gillespie, Dizzy, xxv, 25, 34, 43, 89
Gioia, Ted, 138
Gleason, Ralph J., 78, 136, 190
"Gloria's Step," 100, 113, 138–39, 155, 157–58, 166, 202, 206–7, 218
Golden Trombone of Buddy Morrow, The, 50, 51, 181
Golding, Ann (Anna Marie) Pacuilli, 31, *38*
Goodman, Benny, xxvii, xxviii, 95–98, 176
Gopnic, Adam, 139
Gomez, Eddie, xxi, 157, 162–64, 168, 212, 217
Gordon, Max, xxviii
Grauer, Joanne, 65
Green, Dave, 219
Gruber, Freddie, 65
Guaraldi, Vince, 79
Gypsy, 96–98

H

Haden, Charlie, xxv, xxvi, 70, 83, 84, 101, 111, 189–90
Haig, The, 70
Harris, Steve, 94
Hartsfield, Sandra Upson, 71–74
Hawes, Hampton, 68, 70, 85, 86, 176–78
Haymes, Dick, 99, 100
Haynes, Roy, 114, 134, 140–41, *143*, 152, 190, 215, 222–23
Heath, Percy, 51, 52, 68, 76, 112
Hentoff, Nat, 64, 78
Hickory House, 102
Higgins, Billy, 66, 79, 80, 86, 87, 189–91
Hill, Marigold, 65
Hillcrest Club, The, 65, 70, 83, 85
Hinton, Milt, xxiii, 68, 98, 177, 245
Hoffman, Gordon, 35, 47
Holland, Dave, xxi
Holman, Bill, 83
Holt, Red, 76

W

Walkers, The, 128
"Waltz for Debby" (song), 139, 158
Waltz for Debby (album), xxix, 137, 164, 173, 201, 204–5, 219
Ware, Wilbur, 78, 89
Weislow, Judy, 148–49
West Coast Days, 89
Wilber, Bob, 96
Williams, Martin, 54, 90, 91, 111, 112
Williams, Tony, xxii
Willoughby, Bob, 87
Wilson, John S., 103, 124

Wofford, Mike, xxiii
Wong, David, 215
Wooley, Bob, xix, 35

Y

Young, Eldee, 75

Z

Zampino, Gerry, 44
Zebra Lounge, 115, 135
Zen, 127–28, 130, 135
Zimmermann, Fred, 126, 236, 238